POPE FRANCIS, THE FAMILY, AND DIVORCE

Pope Francis, the Family, and Divorce

In Defense of Truth and Mercy

STEPHEN WALFORD

PREFACE BY
Pope Francis

FOREWORD BY
Cardinal Óscar Andrés Rodríguez Maradiaga

Paulist Press
New York / Mahwah, NJ

Nihil obtat/Imprimatur:
His Eminence, Joseph William Cardinal Tobin
Archbishop of Newark
3rd July 2018

Cover image: background by ilolab/Shutterstock.com
Cover and book design by Lynn Else

Library of Congress Control Number: 2018945175

ISBN 978-0-8091-5429-6 (paperback)
ISBN 978-1-58768-823-2 (e-book)

Published by Paulist Press
997 Macarthur Boulevard
Mahwah, New Jersey 07430

www.paulistpress.com

Printed and bound in Great Britain by
Marston Book Services Ltd, Oxfordshire

I dedicate this book to our beloved Pope Francis in thanksgiving for his courageous witness to the divine mercy of the Lord.

CONTENTS

ACKNOWLEDGMENTS

I owe a debt of gratitude to many people for their most generous help in bringing this work to fruition. I thank His Eminence Cardinal Óscar Andrés Rodríguez Maradiaga, for kindly writing the foreword; and Their Eminences Cardinals Donald Wuerl, Kevin Farrell, and Joseph Tobin for their various contributions. I am deeply honored to have been the beneficiary of their support for this venture. To the late Cardinal Cormac Murphy-O'Connor who advised me on some historical research, I ask the Lord to grant the eternal peace of his heavenly Kingdom.

I am also grateful to various priests who have helped and encouraged me in a variety of ways: Fr. Thomas Rosica, CSB, Fr. Paul Keller, CMF, Fr. Manuel J. Rodriguez, Monsignor Cyril Murtagh, Fr. James Carling, Fr. Reginald Malicdem, Fr. Michael Najim, Fr. Daniele Rebeggiani, Fr. Tom Ryan, SM, Monsignor Philippe Bordeyne, Fr. Diego Fares, SJ, Fr. Sean Budden, Fr. John Chadwick, STD, and Fr. Mark-David Janus, CSP. I apologize to those others whom I have forgotten to mention! You are all in my prayers. Special thanks go to Fr. Mark Hogan, who translated a text from English to Spanish for me.

I am also indebted to the prayerful support of Sr. Dorcee Clarey and the Sisters of *The Servants of God's Love* in Ann Arbor, Michigan.

I thank Bill Barry, my agent, for his expert advice and help in navigating my way through the entire process, and to Trace Murphy and the staff at Paulist Press for their faith in me.

I am also deeply grateful to many lay brothers and sisters throughout the world. I thank my friend Mike Lewis, who has been there day in day out with me throughout the writing process, to Scott Smith, who really should have been writing this book not me—I am forever grateful for sending me some absolutely crucial historical documents, and for giving me so much of his time to find them—thank you! To Carmen Aguinaco who saved the day for me in translating at very short notice—I will never forget that act of kindness. To Austen Ivereigh, I am grateful for his help in several ways, but especially in speaking to Fr. Diego Fares, SJ, on my behalf in Rome. To Emmett O'Regan and Dawn Eden Goldstein, I thank them for their encouragement and prayers, and to Dr. Robert Fastiggi, I am very grateful for the benefit of his advice, encouragement, and prayers. To Andrea Tornielli, I am deeply grateful for his help in promoting my writings, and for some very useful suggestions along the way.

Special thanks go to Fr. Antonio Spadaro, SJ, who helped me in several very important ways.

Last but certainly not least, I thank with all my heart our beloved Holy Father, Pope Francis. The gift of his preface is something truly remarkable for me. I can only hope that the book serves to reinforce his beautiful teachings in *Amoris Laetitia* and brings some hope to suffering souls in need of the medicine of divine mercy. For me, that will be the best way I can express my great gratitude.

PREFACE*

The Post-Synodal Apostolic Exhortation *Amoris Laetitia* is the fruit of a long ecclesial journey which involved two Synods and a subsequent consultation with the local Churches through the bishops' conferences. Institutes of consecrated life and other institutions, such as Catholic universities and lay associations, also participated in this consultation. The entire Church prayed, reflected, and, with simplicity, offered various contributions. Both Synods presented their conclusions.

One of the things that most impressed me in this whole process was the desire to seek God's will in order to better serve the Church. Seeking in order to serve. This was done through reflection, the exchange of views, prayer, and discernment. There were of course temptations during this journey but the Good Spirit prevailed. Witnessing this brought spiritual joy.

The Exhortation *Amoris Laetitia* is a unified whole, which means that, in order to understand its message, it must be read in its entirety and from the beginning. This is because there is a development both of theological reflection and of the way in which problems are approached. It cannot be considered a *vademecum* on different issues. If the Exhortation is not read in its entirety and in the order it is written, it will either not be understood or it will be distorted.

Over the course of the Exhortation, current and concrete problems are dealt with: the family in today's world, the education of children, marriage preparation, families in difficulty, and so on; these are treated with a hermeneutic that comes from the whole document which is the magisterial hermeneutic of the Church, always in continuity (without ruptures), yet always maturing. In this regard, Stephen Walford mentions Saint Vincent of Lérins, in his *Commonitorium Primum*: *"ut annis scilicet consolidetur, dila-tetur tempore, sublimetur aetate."* With respect to the problems that involve ethical situations, the Exhortation follows the classical doctrine of Saint Thomas Aquinas.

I feel certain that this book will be helpful to families. I pray for this.

Pope Francis
From the Vatican, August 2017

---

*Please see the appendix at the end of the book for the complete text of the letter from His Holiness Pope Francis, from which this preface has been extracted.

FOREWORD

When I finished reading this book, I said to myself, "I hope it will be translated as soon as possible into many languages because it will accomplish much good."

We have all witnessed how the Apostolic Exhortation *Amoris Laetitia*, the fruit of two Synods of Bishops, has been received as an invaluable gift for a new stage of pastoral care of marriage.

At the same time we have seen with sadness that some Catholics and even bishops and cardinals have not read it completely and have focused solely on the eighth chapter.

As is often the case, many simply follow media commentaries, or read articles published by others, instead of going directly to the text. We have even seen the publication of some doubts, "dubia," signed by four cardinals of our Church.

This precious book does not respond merely with criticism but goes deeper into the subject with a positive explanation that, beginning with the current crisis of Marriage, seeks the response of a Church that is above all else a Mother.

He rightly affirms that a large part of the whirlwind around this current situation arises from the lack of love and devotion in the family. Many marriages fail in ecclesial communities across five continents. Separation and divorce are tearing families apart, while a second civil marriage is already common.

The issue has been often raised in recent papal teachings on the family.

The Post Synodal Exhortation shows a journey of families toward God whose love accompanies the human family by means of his grace toward eternal life. The Word of God is a traveling companion in which the road to Emmaus is continually repeated throughout history. All families, even those who are in complex situations, are not problems in the eyes of God, but opportunities for a spiritual growth that with time and God's grace and patience reveal the victory of divine love and mercy over sin and evil.

The famous chapter 8 shows us the perspective of the Pope as a merciful shepherd. It is concerned with the pastoral care of couples in irregular situations, like that of the divorced and remarried, challenging the reader to leave the comfort zone of general rules and discipline, in order to embrace the very heart of mercy.

It asks us to consider the total truth about each person and their specific situation. Individuals are not simply yet more examples of people who have fallen into mortal sin. It is about reaching those who need the medicine of mercy, helping them gradually to reintegrate themselves in the church community progressively.

The author analyzes in depth this chapter that must be considered in the light of one of the basic criteria of the New Testament: discernment (δοκιμαζειν). It is a true gift of the Holy Spirit that should accompany pastors in their ministry.

It is not about simply stopping at a footnote or arguing about whether Holy Communion can be allowed for the divorced and remarried.

The Pope reminds priests that the confessional should not be a torture chamber but rather an encounter with the Lord's mercy. He also points out that the Eucharist is not a prize for the perfect but a powerful medicine and sustenance for the weak.

Walford next gives a biblical reflection on grace and mercy, in which these topics that are so central to the revelation are illuminated.

How far can mercy stretch without reaching the breaking point?

Walford answers by examining and applying the biblical texts through the history of salvation, showing how they are revealed in the life and ministry of Jesus. Only then can it be said that this is truly the work of the Holy Spirit. This chapter can be thought of as a beautiful and profound *lectio divina* that enlightens us with the beauty of the mercy theme it reveals.

Where does it leave moral theology?

We are given a reflection on moral theology and the famous chapter 8 that is inspired by *"caritas in veritate."* Walford takes us on a solid journey through St. Thomas, St. Augustine, Vatican II, St. John Paul II, and Pope Benedict XVI. The author tells us that the Church of the twenty-first century is in the era of divine mercy, an era that has emerged as an antidote to the onslaught of evil. Many souls swim in the sea of ignorance of moral truths, or are crushed under the weight of the bondage of sin. The Holy Spirit has sent a Pope who understands these problems; who has spent his life in the trenches alongside his people. His teachings do not seek to undermine marriage or the great mystery of the Holy Eucharist.

On the contrary, he takes to heart the words of Jesus in the parable of the wedding banquet: "Go out into the roads and lanes, and compel people to come in, so that my house may be filled" (Luke 14:23). Of course, these words do not refer to forcing people against their will, but commands us to go out to look for sinners, lost sheep, those considered unworthy. Pope Francis does not abandon anyone; and as a faithful disciple of Jesus, he does not give a superficial service, but touches the wounded and administers to them mercy. Thanks to the inspiration of the Holy Spirit, some people now have the joy of embracing the Lord and Master and prostrating at the feet of his mercy. Instead of feeling bitter at that possibility, we should all ponder the joy of the Savior and the sinner in that encounter. In this way, the Communion of Saints exults and rejoices!

It is interesting to see how he approaches the correct concept of Tradition as something alive and active now, two thousand years after Christ. It is not simply a matter of repeating what we have received, but of a path of dialogue with the "newness" of the Spirit that continues to act in history. We find here a doctrinal development taking as starting point one of the principles formulated by Pope Francis in his Apostolic Exhortation *Evangelii Gaudium:* time is superior to space. Later he focuses on the magisterium of the Pope as "freedom in the Holy Spirit." There follows a profound development of the subject of the internal forum which he calls "heart speaking unto heart," showing how, in the course of its history, the Church has sometimes made use of the internal forum in particular cases. It is about the role of conscience and the role of Canon Law.

It concludes with a beautiful eschatological reflection based on the Book of Revelation entitled "A Marriage Made in Heaven" that can benefit those who have gone through the trauma of a broken marriage, a divorce, and another civil marriage. He ponders whether there is anything left of that marriage in eternity. It is about bringing hope to those who suffer complex relationships and those who have been affected by the "manufactured confusion" of those who dissent from the Pope's teaching. We live in times of great tribulation and the world has so many wounded people who need compassion and mercy.

I found the author's conclusion quite beautiful: "Many struggle for years with addictions or sins that they cannot fully control, but a trusting attitude, and a confidence in divine help, allied to the practice of the virtues wherever possible, can give us the moral security that God will eventually ensure his will and our salvation is fulfilled. That must be our hope and our prayer. Let us look then toward the new heaven and new earth with great joy knowing that one day the Lord's final victory over evil will also be ours. It will be a marriage made in heaven."

Cardinal Óscar Andrés Rodríguez Maradiaga, SDB
Archbishop of Tegucigalpa, Honduras
Chairman of the "C9" Council of Cardinals

INTRODUCTION

Pope Francis often reminds us that we are the children of a "God of surprises," and many of us will no doubt have experienced this at some point in our lives. For me, the year 2017 was where I too perceived this in a totally unforeseen way, surprising me greatly, by altering drastically the plans I had envisioned.

In mid-2015, I had completed my second book, *Communion of Saints*. It had taken me the best part of eighteen months of fairly constant writing—in between teaching and my other duties as a husband and father—and as autumn turned to winter, I thought perhaps my short writing career was at an end. I had written about my favorite subjects of eschatology, ecclesiology, and Mariology and wondered if I had said everything I wanted to say. When people asked me "what book is next then?" my response was "nothing, at least for the foreseeable future." I truly meant it.

My intention was to spend more of my free time in the following years working on some of the great piano repertoire that I had not had chance to learn in the past. Instead, I believe the Lord had other plans for me—meaning Ravel, Rachmaninov, and Kapustin would have to wait a while longer.

Like many Catholics throughout the world, I had kept a close eye on the two Vatican Synods of 2014 and 2015 in which the "family" was discussed at length; I was thus aware of the controversy surrounding the question of the possible reception of Holy Communion for the divorced and remarried. Similarly, I was attentive to the way Pope Francis and his magisterium had been portrayed in some sections of the Catholic media; in fact, I had addressed the charism of Pope Francis in my most recent book, arguing that his pontificate was based on a radical and evangelical living of the Gospel that must be embraced in its totality. Thus prayer and piety had to go hand in hand with "touching the flesh of the poor," the marginalized and the "sinners" of society. It felt to me like the Holy Spirit was ramping up the process of stripping everything that hinders the Church from imitating her Bridegroom—something which had begun with the loss of the Papal States in the latter part of the nineteenth century, and continued in various ways in the twentieth, most notably with the Second Vatican Council.

Something began to change for me in November 2016 when the four "dubia" cardinals revealed they had presented the Holy Father with five questions in which they asked for "clarification" on certain aspects of *Amoris Laetitia*. Instead of keeping this initiative confidential—as requested by the Congregation for the Doctrine of the Faith[1]—the public revelation of this act soon led to an increase in criticism of Pope Francis, and it was no longer just traditionalists— the usual suspects—who were firing the shots. I began to notice on various Catholic websites, forums, and blogs, Catholics similar to me—those who have always accepted papal teaching, understood the reforms of Vatican II, and recognized the need for pastoral sensitivity in todays' wounded world—who were being swayed by the angry rhetoric of some dissenters of the papal magisterium.

Over the following couple of months, I began to feel more and more alarmed at this turn of events, and things came to a head for me personally when I saw an article by the American canon lawyer Dr. Edward Peters in January 2017. Peters was responding to an article by a fellow American, Fr. Paul Keller, CMF,[2] who had been invited by cruxnow.com to provide a case study, where he would envision allowing the reception of Holy Communion for a divorced and remarried woman. Dr. Peters took it upon himself to respond,[3] and respond he did in a virtuoso display of scolding and correction. After informing Fr. Keller of seven mistakes (there were others apparently), Dr. Peters invited anyone who thought they could show him where he was mistaken, to do so. (The point seemingly being that this was a remote possibility at best.)

For me, the tone of the article and the invitation at the end was like red rag to a bull, and so I set about writing an essay; substantial in content and with the sole aim to prove that Fr. Keller had correctly interpreted the Holy Father's pastoral teaching in *Amoris Laetitia*. I wanted to explore several areas that were interconnected:

the correct concept of Tradition as something alive and active now, two thousand years after Christ; the historical case of how the Church had at times utilized the internal forum for these cases; the role of conscience and canon law. Upon completion of the text, I approached the famous Vaticanista, Andrea Tornielli, coordinator of *VaticanInsider*, part of the Italian newpaper, *LaStampa*. In all honesty, I didn't even expect to hear a reply, but Mr. Tornielli very kindly emailed me back and said he was interested. Upon reviewing the essay, he was, I believe, very happy to see that I had written a careful and fully researched piece, and so promptly published it as a *VaticanInsider* "Editorial" on *Amoris Laetitia*. Of course, I was deeply humbled by this, and even more so by the reaction to it. Yes, there were plenty of critics, including Dr. Peters, but in the following days, I was contacted by moral theologians, priests, and laypeople all across the world. My essay was retweeted by Fr. Antonio Spadaro, SJ, with the hashtag "mustread" and by bishops and journalists. For many, my essay seemed to ease concerns and shed a bit of light on what Pope Francis had done.

In the following months, I wrote several other essays and an open letter to the "dubia" cardinals in late June that received a great amount of publicity. But it was after a third essay in late March that a friend from the United States, Mike Lewis, had suggested to me that I use these writings as the foundations for a book on the subject. I contemplated the idea—considering in part the length of time my previous book had taken—but finally, taking into account the seriousness of the subject, and especially my burning desire to defend our beloved Pope Francis, I decided I had to write it.

Since working on this book, I have prayed much about it before the Blessed Sacrament, and have certainly noticed the Lord opening many doors for me in answer to specific prayers—especially among those cardinals and theologians who helped me so graciously in one way or another. One intervention, however, stood out in a quite remarkable way: the Holy Father granting me his preface. Something I could never have dreamed of happening actually did happen, and even now, I still cannot quite believe it.

In spite of the severe criticism I have faced in defending Pope Francis' teachings in *Amoris Laetitia*, some of which have been blatant lies of the sort no Catholic should ever be accused of,[4] I am deeply grateful to the Lord for having granted me an opportunity to be part of the defense of the authentic papal magisterium. I consider it essential to speak the truth even if others are made to feel uncomfortable. We live in a time of great tribulation and the world has many wounded souls in need of compassion and mercy. The Church as Mother has the ability to defend the doctrines on the indissolubility of marriage, the Holy Eucharist, confession, and mortal sin, while at the same time finding merciful ways to approach those brothers and sisters who have found themselves in a second, civil union.

The Lord continually goes in search of these souls and with great patience; His Bride exists precisely to extend His gentle hands toward them. We must love them, love them very much and leave all judgments to God. Only in this way can we begin to reflect the love and compassion of God, and to such an extent that it meets the Lord's expectations in this extraordinary era of divine mercy. It is my ardent desire that this short book can contribute in some small way to bring hope to those suffering souls in complex relationships, and to those who have been affected by the "manufactured confusion" of papal dissenters. The realization that Pope Francis teaches with the authority of Christ, confirmed by the divine words, "Whoever listens to you listens to me" (Lk 10:16), must be fearlessly proclaimed now more than ever.

NOTES

1. See Donum Veritatis: *On the Ecclesial Vocation of the Theologian*, no. 30, www.vatican.va.

2. See https://cruxnow.com/commentary/2017/01/06/case -study-communion-divorcedremarried/.

3. See https://canonlawblog.wordpress.com/2017/01/07/is -kellers-essay-really-the-way-amoris-should-be-read/.

4. For instance, that I believe adultery is "good" in some cases, or that I am trying to find a loophole to allow sin.

I THE MARRIAGE CRISIS: A MATERNAL RESPONSE

One of the most disconcerting elements of modern life, affecting countless millions of people across the globe, is the breakdown of the family and, more specifically, marriage. This reality, unparalleled in its scale in any previous generation, has contributed to the loss of hope and sense of despair that many experience in their daily lives. Love is, at times, nothing more than a distant dream; a fantasy that is beyond the reach of many. The sad truth is that in many homes, peace does not exist; relationships quickly fragment into chaos and couples become nothing more than lonely and resentful individuals who live under the same roof. Undoubtedly the social consequences of this terrible situation are vast and not always appreciated or understood. However, sober reality tells us that much of the turmoil around the world stems from a lack of love and commitment in the family. Large national problems have their genesis in far smaller ones. For every marriage that falls apart, or every family that is torn apart, evil gets the upper hand; children suffer in various ways, and God's plan—revealed through the creation of Adam and Eve—is frustrated.

What was once seen as a scourge plaguing primarily the "world," has now affected the Catholic Church as well. Within many ecclesial communities spanning various continents, marriages are failing; separation and divorce are lacerating families, while second, civil marriages are now not uncommon. There are many reasons for this troubling situation: a lack of true knowledge of the faith; impatience when faced with difficult situations; a defective understanding of Christian commitment; selfishness; and in some cases, lust. At the heart of it lies a silent apostasy; a kind of "practical

1

agnosticism and religious indifference"[1] whereby the faithful have, to a certain extent, fallen asleep to the faith. The lures of the world have made carrying the Cross of Jesus too heavy and thus developing a true loving relationship with the Lord has become a burden. Because of this, marriage, the bedrock of family life, is now suffering more than ever. When Jesus is no longer the center of the relationship, its foundations crumble; authentic, sacrificial love disappears and in its place comes a self-centerd attitude contrary to the message of the Gospel. The current marriage crisis reminds us of the Lord's words recounted in St. Matthew's Gospel: "And because of the increase of lawlessness, the love of many will grow cold" (Matt. 24:12).

The Church has had to confront a crisis in the last century that by and large it has never had to face before,[2] and theologically speaking, is a direct contradiction to the understanding that sacramental marriage mirrors the spousal love between Jesus Christ and his Bride, the Church. Under the guidance of the Holy Spirit, the popes have responded to this catastrophe in a variety of ways. Several popes have written Encyclicals on marriage and the family: Leo XVIII's *Arcanum* (1880); Pius XI's *Casti Connubii* (1930); Pius XII's *Ingruentium Malorum* (1951); Bl. Paul VI's *Humanae Vitae* (1968); and St. John Paul II's *Evangelium Vitae* (1995).

Various Synods of bishops have been held to discuss the issues and a constant stream of homilies, speeches, and letters have encouraged couples to seek help through their participation in the life of the Church and the Sacraments. The canonization of the parents of St. Thérèse of Lisieux—Sts. Louis and Zelie Martin—and the beatification of the married couple Luigi and Maria Beltrame Quattrocchi have also providentially provided married couples with exemplary role models and intercessors, heroic witnesses in the face of a growing, Christian, sociological crisis.

Pope Leo XIII was perhaps the first Pontiff to recognize with great prophetic insight the looming danger to Christian marriage and by extension, the family:

> But, now, there is a spreading wish to supplant natural and divine law by human law; and hence has begun a gradual extinction of that most excellent ideal of marriage which nature herself had impressed on the soul of man,

and sealed, as it were, with her own seal; nay, more, even in Christian marriages this power, productive of so great good, has been weakened by the sinfulness of man…it very often happens, as indeed is natural, that the mutual services and duties of marriage seem almost unbearable; and thus very many yearn for the loosening of the tie which they believe to be woven by human law and of their own will, whenever incompatibility of temper, or quarrels, or the violation of the marriage vow, or mutual consent, or other reasons induce them to think that it would be well to be set free.[3]

For Pope Pius XII, the new hedonism of the modern world exemplified by Hollywood was partly to blame, through its presentation of a warped and putrid version of marriage:

The entire conception of the field of life which is contained in the Sixth Commandment is infected by what might be called "movie marriages," which are nothing else but an irreverent and shameless show of marriage conflicts and conjugal unfaithfulness. The movies present marriage freed from any moral bond, as a setting and source of sensual pleasure only and not as the work of God, a holy institution, a natural office and candid bliss, in which the spiritual element always stands superior and dominates, a school and at the same time a triumph of a love faithful unto death, to the gates of eternity.[4]

Inevitably, a close connection must be seen between the problems affecting marriage, and a general loss of faith in the Western world. This sad state of affairs that began with the Enlightenment has grown exponentially in the past century, and suggests a collective temptation for Christianity mirroring that of Satan to Adam and Eve: "you will be like God" (Gen. 3:5). This temptation has centered around the idea that obedience to divine laws does nothing more than take away our true freedom and quest for real love—in whatever form or circumstance—and without doubt, the full force of this trial has led many to abandon their faith. In essence, we now find ourselves facing a counterreligion—anthropocentric secularism—that embraces moral relativism[5] with its understanding that there are no moral absolutes and that rejects the existence of God and Satan. Consequently, a new humanism has arisen that has essentially embraced and affirmed Satan's devious temptation.

But can it be said that all those who have left sacramental marriages have done so with an evil intention? Have they rejected the Lord's unequivocal teaching on the indissolubility of marriage? Should all cases of civil remarriage[6] be judged the same in terms of the guilt of adultery?

The Church has had to confront these complex questions over the past century in a careful and delicate way, because over time, it has become apparent that not all cases can be considered the same. There are some who will have rejected Catholicism in a defiant manner and embraced second unions with a similar attitude; others will have led private, promiscuous lives while outwardly, seemingly devout. Others still, will have been for all intents and purposes no more than baptized pagans who never knew or understood the teaching on marriage. Then there are those who were perhaps betrayed and abandoned at a very early stage of marriage—possibly with young children—and with the colossal struggle to remain single for possibly the rest of their life. For some—bearing in mind the economic difficulties of being a single parent—that scenario would have been too much to cope with. Others, after abandonment, may have fallen in love almost by accident, perhaps through caring for someone in great need. Thus when we compare these various cases, we must affirm that only someone truly heartless and lacking in mercy could fail to see huge discrepancies between them. Divorce and adultery have victims as well as culprits, and some of those victims will be in new relationships as well.

So what we can see from this trail of devastation caused by rampant secularization is that many factors must be taken into consideration when discerning the reasons why marriages fail. It is far too simplistic to say all these people are great sinners who have turned their back on God and shown contempt for his laws. We may recall Jesus' prayer upon the Cross: "Father, forgive them; for they do not know what they are doing" (Lk. 23:34). This plea of mercy from the Saviour is ample proof that some people act out of ignorance—even if to us, that doesn't seem possible. Yes, we can and *must* defend the permanence of marriage until death, but we must also seek to understand these situations and show a loving concern to those caught up in them. Special attention must be paid in particular to those who (1) either left the faith and subsequently returned with the grace of conversion or (2) who never experienced true faith and then found it at some stage after the breakdown of their first marriage. These are the souls to which I hope this book will be most beneficial; but of course, the Lord's arms are always open to *all* the divorced and remarried, and thus I hope they too can find in this book an invitation to seek the Lord's forgiveness and mercy, and a gradual path back to a beautiful friendship with him. There is nothing more precious than that!

At this point, I would like to trace the development of the Church's attitude to the divorced and remarried over the past century or so, and to see how we have arrived at the new situation whereby sacramental discipline has been altered for the divorced and remarried in certain cases. This will allow us to appreciate how organic growth inspired by the Holy Spirit has led to greater understanding and awareness—especially in moral theology—of individual cases.

In earlier centuries, adultery was at times considered an excommunicable offense[7] in different parts of the Catholic world. And in more recent times, divorce and civil remarriage also fell under the same canonical penalty. In the United States for instance, the Fifth Provincial Council of Baltimore of 1843 decreed that remarriage automatically incurred excommunication,[8] and in 1884, the Bishops of the United States reaffirmed that declaration. The 1917 Code of Canon Law stated that Catholics who disregarded canonical form in attempting to marry before a non-Catholic minister were automatically excommunicated (1917 CIC 2319 §1, 1°). Things changed little from a canonical standpoint until 1977, when the National Conference of United States Bishops requested Bl. Pope Paul VI to repeal the penalty of excommunication for the civilly remarried. On October 22, 1977, the Holy Father graciously granted their request. This new atmosphere of clemency was soon enveloping the entire Universal Church when the 1983 Code of

Canon Law promulgated by St. John Paul II failed to mention excommunication for adulterers or the civilly remarried.

Apart from the judicial aspect, the tone has changed remarkably over time in magisterial teaching.[9] There is now recognition that the souls involved are still part of God's family; they are on the same journey of faith as everyone else, as St. John Paul II stated very clearly:

> However, let these men and women know that the Church loves them, that she is not far from them and suffers because of their situation. The divorced and remarried are and remain her members, because they have received Baptism and retain their Christian faith. Of course, a new union after divorce is a moral disorder, which is opposed to precise requirements deriving from the faith, but this must not preclude a commitment to prayer and to the active witness of charity....When a couple in an irregular situation returns to Christian practice, it is necessary to welcome them with charity and kindness, helping them to clarify their concrete status by means of enlightened and enlightening pastoral care. This apostolate of fraternal and evangelical welcome towards those who have lost contact with the Church is of great importance: it is the first step required to integrate them into Christian practice. It is necessary to introduce them to listening to the word of God and to prayer, to involve them in the charitable works of the Christian community for the poor and needy, and to awaken the spirit of repentance by acts of penance that prepare their hearts to accept God's grace.[10]

In terms of the pastoral care for the divorced and remarried, traditionally there have been four possibilities:

1. Seek a declaration of nullity through a diocesan tribunal.
2. Advise the couple to separate.

3. Leave in "good faith" if the couple are not aware of the gravity of their situation canonically and morally.[11]
4. Encourage the couple to live as brother and sister if separation is all but impossible with children involved.

Some of these possibilities have proved extremely difficult for many people to utilize in irregular situations. Marriage tribunals for instance, especially in the early decades of the past century were very slow in processing cases and very few annulments were ever granted. There was a perception that annulments were available only for those with money, power, or influence, not for the everyday Catholic on a working-class wage. For many couples, living as brother and sister would have caused intolerable stress, and considered only accessible to those of great virtue and holiness.

The "good faith" option began to be used more widely in the United States during the 1940s when an influx of African American migrants led to problems proving the validity of certain marriage unions. If after a marriage tribunal had investigated, doubts were still present about a particular case, they could issue a written "decree of good faith" which allowed prospective converts to be received into the Catholic Church while remaining in their existing marriage. The decree was only issued on the understanding that both parties were in good faith at the time of their wedding; that the union was stable, and that no scandal could arise from it. The decree was not a judicial decision or ratification of the marriage, and it was not a declaration of nullity for any former union; it was essentially administrative in nature with the aim to give some sort of moral assurance to the couple.[12] By the late 1960s however, the process was being questioned by tribunals who thought it better if priests just gave spiritual counsel to the couple—especially in relation to receiving the Sacraments.

It is this personal spiritual direction in the internal forum that formed the basis of a famous letter from Bishop Robert Tracy of the Diocese of Baton Rouge in June 1972. The Pastoral Letter on "Good Conscience Cases" was designed to unveil a plan in which the Diocesan priests would all follow the same pastoral practice. This would involve an administrative "decree of good conscience" that would be issued by the tribunal after an internal forum process had been undertaken. In essence, priests would help guide the conscience of those penitents where either their first marriage was considered of doubtful validity—but could not be proven—or where discernment had led to the conviction that the second marriage was in fact the real one. As Bishop Tracy stated: "It is a recognition by the Church in an official way of the right of a party involved in a second marriage by reason of his good conscience in the matter to receive the sacraments with no official decision being rendered one way or the other as to the validity or invalidity of a previous marriage or marriages."[13]

Interestingly, in precisely the same year, a professor of theology at the University of Regensburg, Germany by the name of Fr. Joseph Ratzinger was penning an essay *On the Indissolubility of Marriage*.[14] In the text, Fr. Ratzinger delved into the controversial issue of the divorced and remarried and their possible admittance to the Sacraments. He proposed a solution whereby Holy Communion could be received by persons within a second civil marriage *if* the relationship had proven itself over a long period of time with faith and "virtuous reality":

> When the second marriage produces moral obligations with regard to the children, the family, and even the wife and there are no analogous obligations stemming from the first marriage; when for moral reasons, therefore, the cessation of the second marriage is inadmissible and, on the other hand, abstinence is practically not a real possibility, ("magnorum est," Gregory II says), openness to Eucharistic communion, after a trial period, certainly seems to be just and fully in line with the tradition of the Church.[15]

On August 17, 1972, Cardinal Krol of Philadelphia and President of the National Conference of Catholic Bishops issued a statement saying that a study was underway concerning the question of access to the Sacraments for the divorced and remarried. The study was a joint effort by the Holy See in Rome and by the NCCB's Committee on Pastoral Research and Practices. Cardinal Krol also quoted from a Vatican Letter that stated: "dioceses are not to introduce procedures that are contrary to current discipline."[16] On April

11, 1973, the response came from Cardinal Franjo Seper, Prefect of the Congregation for the Doctrine of the Faith in Rome who stated:

> Regarding the administration of the Sacraments, local Ordinaries should strive, on one hand, to encourage the observance of the discipline in force in the Church, and on the other hand, to act so that pastors of souls show particular solicitude toward those who live in an irregular union, seeking to resolve these cases through the use of the approved practices of the Church in the internal forum, as well as other just means.[17]

When this Letter was received by the NCCB, questions began to be asked about what exactly the phrase "approved practices of the Church in the internal forum" actually meant. Was it simply affirming the good faith decree from the 1940s for marriages whose validity was uncertain? Was it only applicable to those couples choosing to live as brother and sister? Or did it envisage a path for those remarried who continued to engage in sexual relations? Because of the confusion, the decision was made to ask the Vatican for clarification, and two years later on March 21, 1975, Archbishop Jerome Hamer, Secretary of the Congregation for the Doctrine of the Faith responded by saying: "These couples [divorced and civilly remarried] may be allowed to receive the sacraments on two conditions, that they try to live according to the demands of Christian moral principles and that they receive the sacraments in churches in which they are not known so that they will not create any scandal."[18]

Of course, the question then was: what does "trying to live according to the demands of Christian moral principles" actually mean? Who can determine how hard someone is really trying? It seemed that in spite of two letters emanating from the doctrinal department of the Vatican Curia, the Bishops of the United States were no clearer on exactly what course to take in pastoral terms. Certainly, they were on the right lines in utilizing the internal forum—that much was clear—but the question remained as to which cases could be legitimately considered.

In October 1978, Bishop Bernard Ganter of Beaumont, Texas,

issued his own pastoral letter on the internal forum solution. He began by stating what the internal forum is not:

1. It is not a validation of a second marriage while the spouse of the first marriage is still alive.
2. It is not permission for a previously married person, whose spouse is still living, to remarry in the Catholic Church.
3. It is not permission for a priest to perform any kind of public or private ceremony that has the appearance of a marriage ceremony, validation, or blessing.
4. It is not a judicial procedure, but simply a pastoral decision, made in accordance with recognized moral-canonical principles that a divorced person who has attempted remarriage (and/or his or her second spouse) may use the Sacraments of Reconciliation and Eucharist, if feasible without scandal.
5. It is not a substitute for, or bypass of, external forum solutions of the Tribunal.

Bishop Ganter went on to explain what the internal forum solution is:

1. It is a pastoral judgment made by the parties, with the assistance of the proper ecclesiastical minister, in the internal forum, that they, even though the previous spouse is still alive, by reason of a properly formed conscience, have the right to receive the Sacraments, with no canonical decision being rendered by the Tribunal as to the validity or invalidity of the previous marriage or marriages.
2. For proper serious discernment, the process should not be rushed; it should ideally take place over a period of time in order to map out the correct way forward. It should not be assumed that the couple will fully understand the full implications of a good conscience solution.

3. In terms of the couple/person having a properly formed conscience, the priest should ensure they know the difference between a declaration of nullity and a civil divorce.

After laying out these foundations, Bishop Ganter stated that the internal forum solution could apply to

1. A Catholic who had remarried, but who had tried to live their Faith in a profound way, and where the second "marriage" had been proven over a long period of time.
2. A Catholic who had "married" a protestant who was already married, and who wished to resume a sacramental life; again with the proviso that the second marriage had been proven over time.
3. A Protestant who had remarried, and who subsequently desired to convert to the Catholic Faith—on the condition that their conversion was for genuine reasons—and that the marriage had been proven over a period of time.

Finally, seven conditions were to be applied before the internal forum solution could be utilized including: all external forum possibilities (marriage tribunal and appeals) would have to be exhausted first; scandal would have to be avoided; the remarried party would have to validate the marriage in the event of the death of their spouse; any children from the union would have to be raised as Catholic.[19]

Bishop Ganter's Pastoral Letter can be seen as one of the first examples of how the internal forum solution could work in practice. He recognizes the reality that many people even back in the 1970s were struggling to come to terms with the ponderous annulment procedure and the problem of believing in conscience that their first marriage was never valid—even though it could not be proved canonically and judicially. The text makes absolutely clear that his sole concern is to ensure that those souls struggling in irregular unions, and who desire to lead an authentic Catholic life, are given the sacramental means to grow in sanctifying grace. It cannot be seen as a step toward advocating divorce or weakening the doctrine on the indissolubility of marriage.

Although the situation of divorce and remarriage was perhaps worse in the United States than in other countries, there is no doubt that the internal forum solution was also known and utilized quietly in other countries. For instance Cardinal Christoph Schonborn, Archbishop of Vienna, recalled in 2016 how he had questioned Cardinal Joseph Ratzinger in 1994 about the use of the internal forum in discerning situations for the divorced and remarried: " Is it possible that the old praxis that was taken for granted, and that I knew before the [Second Vatican] Council, is still valid?"[20] Conversations with priests reveal that in the United Kingdom it also had tacit approval in the early decades of the twentieth century—even if cases were extremely rare. Missionary priests in Africa were also known to use it, especially in the case of polygamy.

At the beginning of the 1980s, the entire issue of pastoral support for the divorced and remarried became a dominant theme for the Church. It took center stage at the fifth general assembly of the Synod of Bishops, which was held in the Vatican from September 26 to October 25, 1980. Interestingly, St. John Paul II appointed Cardinal Joseph Ratzinger—the future Pope Benedict XVI—to be the *relator* or guide of the Synod, and in his opening remarks he said:

> The problem of divorced and remarried persons, who are true faithful and desire to participate in the life of the Church, is one of the most difficult pastoral concerns in many parts of the world. It will be up to the synod to show the correct approach to pastors in this matter.[21]

Following Cardinal Ratzinger's invitation for discussion of this vexing question, bishops from Switzerland, Germany, Scandinavia, England, Canada, and Honduras all affirmed that the issue had to be dealt with. Initially, the focus fell on the marriage tribunal process with some suggesting a simplification of the system. Some bishops proposed a reexamination of the reasons for marriage nullity, while others asked if marriage should continue to enjoy the favor of the law in doubtful cases.

In terms of the pastoral, nonjudicial approach, two general cases were considered: the so-called *conflict* and *hardship* situations. The conflict situation referred to cases where the first marriage was invalid but could not be proven canonically, while the hardship situation referred to cases where the first marriage was definitely valid, but the second union could not be ended for various objective reasons. Within hardship situations, some bishops also separated cases involving abandoned spouses.

When it came to the question of readmitting these persons to the Sacraments of Confession and the Holy Eucharist, there was general disagreement. Within the language group discussions, the French and Italians suggested commissions to look into the question; the Latin group and a majority of the Spanish/Portuguese were opposed—although some Spanish speakers did support the idea—while the English groups were similarly divided. The Scandinavians encouraged the move. However, when it came to writing the proposition to be presented to the Holy Father, the Synod Fathers in Proposition 14 paragraph 3 reaffirmed the official practice of not admitting divorced and remarried persons to the Sacraments. The overriding feeling was that a much more positive pastoral approach should be undertaken to reintegrate these souls into the ecclesial community, but stopping short of full participation.[22]

St. John Paul II in his homily closing the Synod on October 25, 1980, more or less affirmed Proposition 14; he restated the ban on access to the Sacraments unless "they open themselves with a sincere heart to live in a manner which is not opposed to the indissolubility of marriage." This essentially meant two options remained: either separate or live in complete continence as brother and sister.

In 1981, the Holy Father published his Apostolic Exhortation *Familiaris Consortio*, which was his official response to the Synod. He addressed the issues facing the divorced and remarried in numbers 83 and 84. In the first of these, he focused on the separated and divorced who have not remarried, and notably, admits that in some cases, marriages are simply irreparable: "Various reasons can unfortunately lead to the often irreparable breakdown of valid marriages. These include mutual lack of understanding and the inability to enter into interpersonal relationships. Obviously, separation must be considered as a last resort, after all other reasonable attempts at reconciliation have proved vain."[23] The Pope also stressed the great Christian witness these souls give to the Church and the world through their fidelity and suffering.

In the following section, he reiterated once more the ban on Holy Communion for the divorced and remarried. Yet he also stressed that despite the "evil" of these situations, the Church would make "untiring efforts" to put at their disposal (for those in these irregular situations) "her means of salvation."[24] When speaking of the ban, St. John Paul II said it was based on Sacred Scripture—although he didn't provide a Scriptural text[25]—and proceeded to give two reasons explaining his decision:

1. Their state and condition of life objectively contradict that union of love between Christ and the Church that is signified and effected by the Eucharist.
2. The faithful would be led into error and confusion regarding the indissolubility of marriage.

The Holy Father continued by saying that the Sacrament of Confession was not a possibility while the relationship continued, and suggested that the brother/sister option was the only possible one that allowed the relationship to continue in some form and allow reception of the Sacraments. He concluded his teaching on the divorced and remarried by giving a message of great hope to those involved: "With firm confidence she [the Church] believes that those who have rejected the Lord's command and are still living in this state will be able to obtain from God the grace of conversion and salvation, provided that they have persevered in prayer, penance and charity."[26]

Although at the time, the brother/sister option seemed the only feasible one, it did present several problems: how would it affect the dynamics of the relationship? Would the couple have the strength to give up such an intense part of that relationship? Would allowing them to remain in the same house be inviting the proximate occasion of sin? What effect would this new situation have on any children within the home? And in terms of the issue of scandal for the Catholic parish community, how would they know the couple in question were now living in complete continence? Surely they would presume nothing had changed unless the couple made some general announcement.

Suffice it to say, in the ensuing years of the decade, it seemed as if the ban was unalterable. At the 1983 Synod of Bishops, the Japanese prelates, joined by bishops from Finland, East Germany, France, and the Central African Republic attempted to have the matter put up for discussion again but without success. St. John Paul II's Apostolic Exhortation *Reconciliatio et Paenitentia* of 1984 restated what he had taught three years previously. What should be stated categorically is that St. John Paul II instigated on a magisterial level a new path and a new openness to the divorced and remarried. In *Familiaris Consortio*, he advocated careful discernment for individual cases, reminding priests that this was for the "sake of truth." He emphasised that they remain part of the Church and therefore should involve themselves in the life of the parish, while striving to live lives centered on Jesus Christ. By encouraging them to implore God's grace day by day, the Pontiff also seemed to be recognizing in a discreet way that they cannot all be classed as mortal sinners.

Until the early 1990s, most of the discussion relating to the pastoral care of those in irregular situations was confined to theological journals. Nevertheless, by 1993 the question was back at the heart of Catholic debate, for on July 10th of that year, three bishops of the Upper Rhine region of Germany issued a joint pastoral letter in which they called for dialogue with the divorced and remarried, with the intention of discerning whether the general ban on access to the Sacraments could allow for exceptions. What made the Letter particularly significant was that its authors included two theologians of international repute: Walter Kasper of Rottenburg-Stuttgart, and Karl Lehmann of Mainz—both future cardinals. The third author, Archbishop Oskar Saier of Freiburg, was a canon lawyer, and vice-president of the German Bishops Conference.

The letter restates the official teaching of the Church that remarriage is an objective contradiction to the Sacrament of marriage, and that anyone who follows this path acts "contrary to the order of the Church."[27] However, the Bishops went on to suggest that although Canon Law can provide a generally valid sacramental discipline, it cannot cover the variety of complex and highly individual cases. In order to arrive at the correct conclusion for each case, the Bishops proposed an internal forum solution "in which the situation is thoroughly, candidly, and objectively brought to light."[28] The following criteria would form the basis of a careful discernment process:

1. When there is serious failure involved in the collapse of the first marriage, responsibility for it must be acknowledged and repented.
2. It must be convincingly established that a return to the first partner is really impossible, and with the best will, the first marriage cannot be restored.
3. Restitution must be made for wrongs committed and injuries done insofar as this is possible. This includes all obligations to the spouse and children from the first marriage.
4. If the person broke the first marriage and caused great scandal in the process.

For the Bishops, the aim of this discernment would be to arrive at a decision with a clear conscience; but for the priest, there would be no rubber stamping in a formal sense: "but to respect the judgment of that individual's conscience" and to "defend such a decision of conscience against prejudice and suspicion," while taking "care that the parish does not thereby take offense."[29]

Because of the stature of the theologians involved in this Letter, it wasn't long before the Congregation for the Doctrine of the Faith responded. Initially, this involved a series of meetings between the Congregation and the German Bishops, but on September 14, 1994, the CDF issued a letter entitled *Concerning the Reception of Holy Communion by Divorced-and-Remarried Members of the Faithful*. This document was sent to all the episcopacies worldwide and in reality slapped down the German proposal. While reaffirming St. John Paul II's ban from *Familiaris Consortio*, it also revealed a fundamental disagreement on the role of conscience:

Members of the faithful who live together as husband and wife with persons other than their legitimate spouses may not receive Holy Communion. Should they judge it possible to do so, pastors and confessors, given the gravity of the matter and the spiritual good of these persons as well as the common good of the Church, have the serious duty to admonish them that such a judgment of conscience openly contradicts the Church's teaching. Pastors in their teaching must also remind the faithful entrusted to their care of this doctrine.[30]

The German Bishops immediately responded to the Letter by stressing that "we do not find ourselves in any doctrinal disagreement," but "the difference has to do with the question of pastoral practice in individual cases." The Bishops maintained that there does "exist room, beneath the threshold of the binding teaching, for pastoral flexibility in complex individual cases that is to be used responsibly."[31]

The reality is that the German Pastoral Letter was not significantly different in substance to that of Bishop Ganter from 1978 or from suggestions made by other bishops during the various synods. It was an attempt, quite simply, to reengage theological debate at a time when divorce and remarriage was an ever growing problem, and where people in this situation desired to receive the Sacraments. The Church could no longer accept—in this particular area of life—that everything was "black and white" and leave it at that. More serious reflection needed to be accomplished under the guidance of the Holy Spirit.

After the death of St. John Paul II in April 2005, Cardinal Joseph Ratzinger was elected Supreme Pontiff and took the name Pope Benedict XVI. Although there was no change to sacramental discipline during his Pontificate, he certainly did revisit the question at various times; and perhaps his most significant contribution to the debate was to teach that the sufferings of the divorced and remarried can and should be offered for the benefit of the Church.[32] There is also little doubt that Pope Benedict XVI, and before as Cardinal Ratzinger, reflected on this problem greatly and did not rule out exceptions to the general rule. In 1980, as Archbishop of Munich and shortly after the synod, he allowed

Holy Communion to be given to people who were in second marriages but who were convinced their first union was invalid despite there being no judicial proof.[33]

March 13, 2013, saw the election to the papacy of Cardinal Jorge Mario Bergoglio, the Archbishop of Buenos Aries, Argentina, who took the name Francis. Almost immediately, he gave the impression of a Pope who would surprise, and one that would constantly pierce the conscience, striving to shake the dust off the soiled garment of the Church. Without any doubt, his greatest theme, even his *charism*, is the proclamation of divine mercy for the Church and the world. He made this clear on his first apostolic voyage when he visited Brazil for World Youth Day in July 2013. On the return flight he was asked whether his insistence on mercy meant a change in sacramental discipline would follow for the divorced and remarried:

> This is an issue which frequently comes up. Mercy is something much larger than the one case you raised. I believe that this is the season of mercy. This new era we have entered, and the many problems in the Church— like the poor witness given by some priests, problems of corruption in the Church, the problem of clericalism for example—have left so many people hurt, left so much hurt. The Church is a mother: she has to go out to heal those who are hurting, with mercy....And I believe that this is a kairos: this time is a kairos of mercy. But John Paul II had the first intuition of this, when he began with [St.] Faustina Kowalska, the Divine Mercy.... He had something, he had intuited that this was a need in our time. With reference to the issue of giving communion to persons in a second union (because those who are divorced can receive communion, there is no problem, but when they are in a second union, they can't...), I believe that we need to look at this within the larger context of the entire pastoral care of marriage.... Cardinal Quarracino, my predecessor, used to say that as far as he was concerned, half of all marriages are null. But why did he say this? Because people get married lacking maturity, they get married without realizing that

18

it is a life-long commitment, they get married because society tells them they have to get married. And this is where the pastoral care of marriage also comes in.[34]

Several months later, on October 8, the Vatican announced the calling of an Extraordinary Synod (for only the third time since the 1960s) that would take place in October 2014 on the theme of "Pastoral Challenges of the Family in the Context of Evangelization." This would then be followed a year later by an Ordinary Synod (with many more bishops present) along the lines of the one held in 1980. Both meetings were designed to study the issues surrounding family life in the light of the signs of the times.

The 2014 Extraordinary Synod took place against the backdrop of division between two opposing groups: those opposed to any change in sacramental discipline, and those who, like Cardinal Walter Kasper,[35] saw the need for clemency toward those in difficult marital circumstances. During the Synod, Cardinal Christoph Schonborn compared proceedings to a mother and father giving advice: the mother says "watch out, be careful," while the father says "no, that's fine, go ahead."[36] Even before the Synod had got underway, five Cardinals had penned a book essentially dismissing any chance of a disciplinary alteration. Of the ten small groups of bishops, two were opposed to the idea according to the Italian newspaper *Corriere della Sera*, while only one group explicitly endorsed the idea. Two more groups approved with some reservations, while the other five didn't address the issue at all.[37] It must be said that at the end of the Synod, no consensus had been reached and the overriding opinion was that the issue needed further study.

Pope Francis, in addressing the bishops at the closing of the Synod sought to frame the meeting in the context of a journey bound by the spirit of collegiality. He expressed joy and appreciation for the frankness with which the participants spoke, and encouraged mature reflection in preparation for the 2015 Synod. There can be no mistaking, however, his rejection of a rigid traditionalism that was evident during and before the Synod when he described it thus:

...a temptation to hostile inflexibility, that is, wanting to close oneself within the written word, (the letter) and not allowing oneself to be surprised by God, by the God of surprises, (the spirit); within the law, within the certitude of what we know and not of what we still need to learn and to achieve. From the time of Christ, it is the temptation of the zealous, of the scrupulous, of the solicitous and of the so-called—today—"traditionalists" and also of the intellectuals.[38]

It must also be stated that the Pope clearly rejected a "deceptive mercy" that binds the wounds without first treating and curing them. This, he said, was a temptation for the "so called progressives and liberals." From reading between the lines, it is clear that the correct attitude Pope Francis envisages from this address is one where the faithful Catholic remains somewhere in the middle between rigidity and laxity; one who adheres to all the teachings of the Church, yet who is humble enough to realize that the "letter" of the law may at times be deficient in particular circumstances. It is also noticeable in the address that the Holy Father—perhaps for the first time in his Pontificate—quite forcefully reminds us of the authority of the Pope (under the protection of the Holy Spirit) to guide the Church along the path Jesus desires, and thus the faithful Catholic should always humbly submit to his decisions based on the knowledge that "all acts of the magisterium derives from the same source, that is, from Christ."[39]

The Fourteenth Ordinary General Assembly of the Synod of Bishops took place from October 4 to 25, 2015, and prior to its commencement, Pope Francis had called the Church to pray for its success: "I ask you to pray fervently for this intention, so that Christ can take even what might seem to us impure, like the water in the jars scandalizing or threatening us, and turn it—by making it part of his "hour"—into a miracle. The family today needs this miracle."[40]

In his opening remarks before the Synod Fathers, Pope Francis reminded them that the Synod is

neither a convention, nor a "parlour," a parliament nor senate, where people make deals and reach a consensus. The Synod is rather an ecclesial expression, i.e., the Church that journeys together to understand reality with the eyes of faith and with the heart of God; it is the Church that questions herself with regard to her fidelity to the deposit of faith, which does not represent for the Church a museum to view, nor just something to safeguard, but is a living spring from which the Church drinks, to satisfy the thirst of, and illuminate the deposit of life.[41]

The Holy Father stressed the point that the Holy Spirit acts within the Synod and urged the participants to put on *apostolic courage, evangelical humility,* and *trusting prayer* in order for the Synod to be fruitful. As in the Address he gave at the conclusion of the Extraordinary Synod, he again warned against certain temptations: being worldly, by seeking to extinguish the light of truth; judgmental toward the views of other bishops, and not listening to the voice of the Holy Spirit.

No doubt, Pope Francis wanted to ensure that the three weeks of deliberations would take place with peaceful and serene debate; not hostility and rancour. Certainly from the media reports at the time, it is difficult to suggest that calmness and tranquillity ruled over the entire proceedings, but of course, with such a serious issue at stake, the chances of that happening were always going to be slim.

There were suggestions from the beginning that the Synod had already been "rigged" in order to approve Cardinal Kasper's proposal to allow Holy Communion for the divorced and remarried. The key moment came on the first day when Cardinal George Pell handed Pope Francis a letter that had been signed by thirteen Cardinal participants[42] of the Synod. The letter objected to the Kasper proposal and also questioned the way the Synod process was going to work. Several days later, Cardinal Dolan of New York revealed more about the contents of the letter:

We're worried first of all that if the *instrumentum laboris,*[43] which has a lot of good things...if that's the only document that we're going to be talking about at the synod. Number 2, we're a little worried about the process, there seems to be some confusion, and 3, we're a little worried about if we're going to have a say in the people who are going to be on the final drafting committee.[44]

At the press conference at the end of the first day, Italian Archbishop Bruno Forte was clear that no doctrine would be tampered with: "It will not lead to doctrinal changes, because it is about pastoral attention, pastoral care. We are about resonating pastorally."[45] Cardinal Erdo, the Synod's General Relator said that the Synod Fathers would listen to each other, paying special attention to the Church's doctrinal heritage: "Development is not unlimited; we have to look at Tradition."[46] Archbishop Mark Coleridge of Brisbane opined that the Synod was split on the issue of Holy Communion for the divorced and remarried by about 65 percent against and 35 percent for—although those figures were at the beginning of the Synod, and related to the Kasper proposal specifically. When asked about the idea of decisions being made on a local level, by individual bishops, his view was that it would be a 50/50 split: "My sense is that there would be significantly greater interest in a proposal of that kind. Some would want a confirmation from the Holy See to ensure checks and balances."[47]

As the Synod continued, it became clear that there was still a divergence of opinion concerning the matter. The Polish Bishops maintained that no change in discipline could occur because it would display a defective theology of grace and a false compassion, while the German Bishops were in favor. Archbishop Paul-Andre Durocher of Gatineau, Quebec, stated that there were differing opinions on whether any change was doctrinal or disciplinary.[48] Within the working groups, Italian Group C suggested an internal forum discernment process under the guidance of a bishop, while Group B rejected a general change, but again suggested the local bishop could discern individual cases. English Group D exhibited quite differing views, with one Father suggesting that an Ecumenical Council was the only way the question could be dealt with due to doctrinal complexity, while another Father talked of the "power of the keys," saying that the Pope can, in effect, "twist the hands of God."[49] English Group C was evenly split, but voted to keep St. John Paul II's teaching from *Familiaris Consortio* no. 84. These deliberations, along with many other aspects of the family led to the formulation of the Synod's Final Report, which was to be presented to Pope Francis as a guide for the writing of his forthcoming Apostolic Exhortation and magisterial response to the Synod. The 94 paragraph report, approved on the last working day of the three-week Synod, highlighted the role of priests in explaining doctrine to couples and helping them proclaim the Gospel in their own unique circumstances. It also emphasized how "pastoral accompaniment" should involve discernment in order to judge the moral culpability of people not fully living up to the Catholic ideal. Bishops and other full participants of the Synod voted separately on each paragraph, and the votes were duly published. The paragraph dealing specifically with guiding divorced and remarried Catholics on a path of discernment passed with one vote beyond the necessary two-thirds.

In his closing address for the Synod, Pope Francis recalled what it was about:

> Certainly, the Synod was not about settling all the issues having to do with the family, but rather attempting to see them in the light of the Gospel and the Church's tradition and two-thousand-year history, bringing the joy of hope without falling into a facile repetition of what is obvious or has already been said. Surely it was not about finding exhaustive solutions for all the difficulties and uncertainties which challenge and threaten the family, but rather about seeing these difficulties and uncertainties in the light of the Faith, carefully studying them and confronting them fearlessly, without burying our heads in the sand…it was about showing the vitality of the Catholic Church, which is not afraid to stir dulled consciences or to soil her hands with lively and frank discussions about the family. It was about trying to view and interpret realities, today's realities, through God's eyes, so as to kindle the flame of faith and enlighten people's hearts in times marked by discouragement, social, economic and moral crisis, and growing pessimism. It was about bearing witness to everyone that, for the Church, the Gospel continues to be a vital source of eternal newness, against all those who would 'indoctrinate'

it in dead stones to be hurled at others....It was about making clear that the Church is a Church of the poor in spirit and of sinners seeking forgiveness, not simply of the righteous and the holy, but rather of those who are righteous and holy precisely when they feel themselves poor sinners.[50]

As the Synod ended, attention inevitably turned to what the Pope would teach in the eagerly awaited Apostolic Exhortation. Would he reinforce St. John Paul II's ban from 1981? Would he endorse the Kasper proposal? Would he ignore the issue entirely? Or would he promote a discreet, individual internal forum solution while keeping the general ban on Holy Communion for those in irregular relationships?

For the Catholic world, the five months between the end of the Synod and the publication of the Apostolic Exhortation, *Amoris Laetitia* was a time, not only of great apprehension, but also of lively anticipation. In the following chapters, we will seek to delve deeply into the significance of this magisterial document, and to discuss issues related to it, so that we can, in time, arrive at a greater appreciation of the teachings contained within it, along with a holy zeal to help struggling families, especially those who do not conform fully to the ideals of the Gospel.

NOTES

1. St. John Paul II, Apostolic Exhortation, *Ecclesia in Europa*, no. 7, June 28, 2003, www.vatican.va.

2. At times, powerful rulers have demanded (unsuccessfully) papal approval of their divorce: we may recall Henry VIII's confrontation with Popes Clement VII and Paul III; Philip I's with Popes Urban II and Paschal II, and Napoleon's battle with Pope Pius VII.

3. Pope Leo XIII, Encyclical Letter, *Arcanum*, no. 27, February 10, 1880, www.vatican.va.

4. Pope Pius XII, "Allocution to Lenten Preachers," February 23, 1944. *The Pope Speaks* (New York, Pantheon Books, 1957), 230.

5. Relativism, especially moral or ethical, lies at the heart of this temptation, and the recent Popes have continuously spoken out against it. Bl. Paul VI taught: "Relativism, too, seeks to justify everything, and treats all things as of equal value. It assails the absolute character of Christian principles." Bl. Paul VI, Encyclical Letter, *Ecclesiam Suam*, no. 49, August 6, 1964. For Pope Benedict XVI, it was a constant theme: "We live at a time that is broadly characterized by a subliminal relativism that penetrates every area of life. Sometimes this relativism becomes aggressive, when it opposes those who say that they know where the truth or meaning of life is to be found. And we observe that this relativism exerts more and more influence on human relationships and on society. This is reflected, among other things, in the inconstancy and fragmentation of many people's lives and in an exaggerated individualism. Many no longer seem capable of any form of self-denial or of making a sacrifice for others. Even the altruistic commitment to the common good, in the social and cultural sphere or on behalf of the needy, is in decline. Others are now quite incapable of committing themselves unreservedly to a single partner. People can hardly find the courage now to promise to be faithful for a whole lifetime; the courage to make a decision and say: now I belong entirely to you, or to take a firm stand for fidelity and truthfulness and sincerely to seek a solution to their problems." Pope Benedict XVI, "Address at the Seminary of Freiburg im Breisgau," September 24, 2011, www.vatican.va.

6. We will use the term *remarriage* to describe, Catholics who have entered into a second union for convenience, but it should be clarified that these civil unions do not constitute marriage.

7. See chapter 8 on the Internal Forum and Canon Law.

8. *Pastoral Letters of the American Hierarchy: 1792-1970*, ed. Nolan (Huntington, OSV, 1971), 112.

9. Bl. Pius IX referred to nonsacramental civil marriages between Christians as "nothing else than a disgraceful and death-bringing concubinage." Bl. Pius IX, "Allocution *Acerbissimum vobiscum*," September 27, 1857 (Denzinger, 1640). Pope Leo XIII stated: "It is easily understood how harmful—as much for the home as for public life—are these divorces that proceed from a degradation of customs, and that lead in turn to the most extreme

licentiousness." Pope Leo XIII, "Allocution Afferre iucundiora," December 16, 1901, *Acta Sanctae Sedis* 34 (1901–2), 262.

10. St. John Paul II, "Address to the Pontifical Council for the Family," January 24, 1997, www.vatican.va.

11. This concept is discussed in chapter 8.

12. R. Carey, "The Good Faith Solution," *Jurist* 29 (1969), 428–38. The good faith solution was at first used for the marriages of two non-Catholics, but later began to appear in cases involving only one Catholic. In the latter case, the Catholic may have entered the new union in good faith on the understanding that the first marriage was null even if it could not be proven canonically.

13. Bishop Robert Tracy, "Divorce, Re-Marriage and the Catholic," *Origins* 2, July 27, 1972, 135–36.

14. Fr. Joseph Ratzinger was to become Pope Benedict XVI in 2005. Over time, he changed his opinion on granting Holy Communion to the divorced and remarried. For instance, in 2014, he returned to this 1972 essay and revised the final section to encourage the practice of "spiritual communion" rather than sacramental. However, in his 1996 book *Salt of the Earth*, he acknowledged that "individual questions" were still a possibility.

15. Joseph Ratzinger, "On the Question of the Indissolubility of Marriage," originally published in German: "Zur Frage nach der Unauflöslichkeit der Ehe: Bemerkungen zum dogmengeschichtlichen Befund und zu seiner gegenwärtigen Bedeutung," *Ehe und Ehescheidung: Diskussion unter Christen* (Kösel-Verlag, München, 1972), 35–56.

16. Cardinal Jon Krol, "Good Conscience Procedures," *Origins* 2, September 7, 1972, 176–77.

17. Congregation for the Doctrine of the Faith, "Letter regarding the indissolubility of marriage," April 11, 1973, http://www.vatican.va/roman_curia/congregations/cfaith/documents/rc_con_cfaith_doc_19730411_indissolubilitate-matrimonii_en.html.

18. Congregation for the Doctrine of the Faith, "Letter of Clarification to Archbishop Joseph Bernardin," Prot. No. 1284/66, March 21, 1975.

19. Bishop Bernard Ganter, "Pastoral Letter," October 17, 1978. A copy of this letter is kept on file.

20. See http://www.chicagocatholic.com/cnwonline/2016/news /0707b.aspx.

21. Giovanni Caprile, *Il Sinodo dei Vescovi, Quinta assemblea generale 26 settembre-25 ottobre 1980* (Rome: La Civilta Cattolica, 1982), 755.

22. For a thorough study of the events at the 1980 Synod on the Family, see James Provost, "Intolerable Marriage Situations: A Second Decade," *The Jurist* 50 (1990): 573–612.

23. St. John Paul II, Apostolic Exhortation, *Familiaris Consortio*, November 22, 1981, www.vatican.va.

24. Ibid, no. 84.

25. Pope Benedict XVI mentioned in his own Apostolic Exhortation *Sacramentum Caritatis* that the Scriptural text in question was Mk. 10:2–12, which speaks of divorce and adultery; however there is no mention of the Holy Eucharist. St. Paul, of course, warns against eating the Body of Christ unworthily (cf. 1 Cor. 11:27–29), but as we shall see in chapter 5, this refers to mortal sin, which as Pope Francis teaches, will not be the state of soul for all remarried people.

26. *Familiaris Consortio*, no. 84.

27. "Pastoral Ministry: The Divorced and Remarried," *Origins* 23, March 10, 1994, 670–76.

28. Ibid.

29. Ibid.

30. Congregation for the Doctrine of the Faith, Letter "Concerning the Reception of Holy Communion by Divorced-and-Remarried Members of the Faithful," September 14, 1994, www.vatican.va.

31. "Response to the Vatican Letter," *Origins* 24, March 10, 1994, 341–44.

32. Cf. Pope Benedict XVI, "Evening of Witness Address, World Meeting of Families," June 2, 2012, www.vatican.va.

33. Cardinal Joseph Ratzinger, "Pastoral Letter for Advent 1980," in *La Documentation Catholique* 78, 1981, 389.

34. Pope Francis, "Press Conference during the return flight from Rio," July 28, 2013, www.vatican.va.

35. Cardinal Kasper had been invited by Pope Francis to address the Extraordinary Consistory of Cardinals in February 2014. His lecture was entitled "The Gospel of the Family." In the

text he renewed the appeal he had made jointly with his two brother Bishops from the Upper Rhine region in 1993.

36. See https://cruxnow.com/church/2014/10/16/synod-is-mo re-and-more-like-a-soap-opera/.

37. See https://cruxnow.com/church/2014/10/17/further-stu dy-likely-result-on-communion-for-divorced-remarried/.

38. Pope Francis, "Address at the Conclusion of the Third Extraordinary General Assembly of the Synod of Bishops," October 18, 2014, www.vatican.va.

39. Congregation for the Doctrine of the Faith, *Donum Veritatis on the Ecclesial Vocation of the Theologian*, no. 17, May 24, 1990, www.vatican.va.

40. Pope Francis, "Homily at Mass for Families," Samanes Park, Guayaquil, Equador, July 6, 2015, www.vatican.va.

41. Pope Francis, "Introductory Remarks for the Synod of Bishops," October 5, 2015, www.vatican.va.

42. The signatories included Cardinals Caffara, DiNardo, Dolan, Muller (Prefect of the Congregation for the Doctrine of the Faith), Pell, Sarah, and Collins among others.

43. The working document for the Synod.

44. See https://aleteia.org/2015/10/13/cardinal-dolan-gives -details-re-controversial-13-cardinals-letter/.

45. See http://en.radiovaticana.va/news/2015/10/05/synod_ on_the_family_press_briefing_day_1/1177020.

46. Ibid.

47. See https://cruxnow.com/church/2015/10/07/archbishop -coleridge-says-synod-6535-against-communion-for-the-divorced -and-remarried/.

48. See http://www.news.va/en/news/synod-on-the-family -press-briefing-day-2.

49. See https://zenit.org/articles/synod15-report-from-small -circle-english-d-3/.

50. Pope Francis, "Address at the Conclusion of the Synod for the Family," October 24, 2015, www.vatican.va.

II *AMORIS LAETITIA*: THE FAMILY JOURNEYING TOWARD GOD

Amoris Laetitia–The Joy of Love, was signed by Pope Francis on the Feast of St. Joseph, March 19, 2016, although not released until several weeks later, on April 8. The document is a lengthy exposition on the family set over 325 paragraphs within 9 chapters. In his introduction to the text, Pope Francis gives two reasons why the understanding of the document should be placed firmly in the context of the Jubilee of Mercy that was being celebrated throughout the Catholic world at the time:

> First, because it represents an invitation to Christian families to value the gifts of marriage and the family, and to persevere in a love strengthened by the virtues of generosity, commitment, fidelity and patience. Second, because it seeks to encourage everyone to be a sign of mercy and closeness wherever family life remains imperfect or lacks peace and joy.[1]

It is this second reason that really illuminates the entire Exhortation and places it firmly at the heart of Pope Francis' entire magisterium. In *Amoris Laetitia* no. 297, for instance, we read:

> It is a matter of reaching out to everyone, of needing to help each person find his or her proper way of participating in the ecclesial community and thus to experience being touched by an "unmerited, unconditional and gratuitous" mercy.[2]

This mercy, for the Holy Father, stems from the boundless love of God that accompanies the human family (as a whole and individually) on a journey of grace toward eternal life. The Divine Word is no less than a travelling companion, in which the Gospel episode of the "Road to Emmaus" is replicated constantly throughout history. Pope Francis is clear that all families and relationships—even those with complex situations—are not "problems" in the eyes of God but "opportunities," opportunities for spiritual growth that can in time, with God's grace and patience, manifest the victory of divine love and mercy over sin and evil.

Amoris Laetitia is striking for several reasons: (1) it offers a refreshing realism that does not hide from the multitude of problems ordinary families encounter. (2) It rejects an abstract application of doctrine that does not take into account the truth that only an encounter with the Risen Christ can bring forth a true metanoia. (3) It moves away from a "them and us" mentality to family situations, reminding us that we are all sinners and all in great need of mercy. (4) It teaches responsibility to be sympathetic to the plight of others—especially those in second civil marriages—and as a consequence, we must "remove our sandals before the sacred ground of the other" (cf. Ex. 3:5).[3]

Before we look more closely at the individual chapters,[4] we can say that Pope Francis underpins the entire text with a call to welcome, accompany, discern, and integrate each and every family into the bosom of the Church. His dream is of a Church that caresses and reaches out to those suffering families with a maternal tenderness that imitates that perfect love of the Holy Family. *Amoris Laetitia* invites the entire people of God to foster new attitudes of love, respect, and compassion to those on the fringes; it also challenges a greater and more authentic living of the Gospel as a way to heal the wounds that many families experience.

Chapter 1 of *Amoris Laetitia*, entitled "In the Light of the Word," places the family firmly within a biblical context. The Holy Father desires to return the reader to the roots of God's plan, an invitation to discover the true meaning of marriage and the family, one that is centerd on love and communion, mirroring the love and union present within the Holy Trinity. In the case of parents, Pope Francis states: "They embody the primordial divine plan clearly spoken of by Christ himself: 'Have you not read that he who made them from the beginning made them male and female?' (Matt 19:4)."[5] In their fruitfulness, they are a "living image" of God the creator, "living icons" capable of reflecting the salvific love of God.

In the beautiful Psalm 126, the Holy Father sees the imagery of structures and city life as reflecting the presence and gift of children, building blocks for the continuation of the family through salvation history. These children, whom the psalmist describes as "live shoots around your table" (Ps. 127:3) are the living stones (cf. 1 Pet. 2:5) upon which the true faith is passed on:

> Things that we have heard and known, that our ancestors have told us. We will not hide them from their children; we will tell to the coming generation the glorious deeds of the Lord, and his might, and the wonders that he has done. He established a decree in Jacob, and appointed a law in Israel, which he commanded our ancestors to teach to their children; that the next generation might know them, the children yet unborn, and rise up and tell them to their children. (Ps 78:3-6)

Pope Francis reminds us that parents have a duty to educate their children (cf. Prov. 3:11–12; 6:20–22; 13:1; 22:15; 23:13–14; 29:17), while children are called to honor and obey their parents (Ex. 20:12). In such a way will sins be forgiven and blessing bestowed: "Those who honor their father atone for sins, and those who respect their mother are like those who lay up treasure" (Sir. 3:3–4).

At no. 19 of *Amoris Laetitia,* the Holy Father takes up the grim reality of suffering and evil that has stained the history of the human family since Cain's murder of his brother Abel:

> We read of the disputes between the sons and the wives of the Patriarchs Abraham, Isaac and Jacob, the tragedies and violence marking the family of David, the family problems reflected in the story of Tobias and the bitter complaint of Job: "He has put my brethren far from me... my kinsfolk and my close friends have failed me... I am repulsive to my wife, loathsome to the sons of my own mother." (Job 19:13–14, 17)[6]

The Pontiff then proceeds to show how Jesus, in his ministry of healing, and storytelling through the parables, draws close to the anxieties and tribulations of everyday families; he reaches out in a myriad of ways to dispel the darkness of corruption wrought by sin. We can think of the wailing of the widow of Nain for her deceased son (Lk. 7:11–15), the death of Jairus' daughter (Mk. 5:22–24, 35–43) and the raising of Lazarus (Jn. 11:1–44). In all these and so many other instances of Jesus touching the flesh of a bruised human family, we are invited to see in him a divine physician who doesn't temporarily bind up wounds but applies a medicine of everlasting quality—baptism—which is the first resurrection (cf. Rev. 20:5–6).

In the following paragraphs, Pope Francis deals with the issue of labor, where he says work "is an essential part of human dignity....Labour also makes possible the development of society and provides for the sustenance, stability and fruitfulness of one's family: 'May you see the prosperity of Jerusalem all the days of your life! May you see your children's children!' (Ps. 127:5–6)." The terrible issues of unemployment and social degeneration are also taught with a biblical perspective.

The latter part of chapter one deals with a most beautiful consideration: the tenderness of God's love. The Pope weaves his way through the various fruits of authentic love: mercy, forgiveness, selflessness, and tenderness; all are concrete expressions of the law of love that Jesus commanded us to follow. But in tenderness we find the idiosyncratic way God desires union with his children, as the Holy Father explains:

> As in other biblical texts (e.g., Ex 4:22; Is 49:15; Ps 27:10), the union between the Lord and his faithful ones is expressed in terms of parental love. Here we see a delicate and tender intimacy between mother and child: the image is that of a babe sleeping in his mother's arms after being nursed. As the Hebrew word *gamûl* suggests, the infant is now fed and clings to his mother, who takes him to her bosom. There is a closeness that is conscious and not simply biological. Drawing on this image, the Psalmist sings: "I have calmed and quieted

my soul, like a child quieted at its mother's breast" (Ps 131:2).[7]

Tenderness on the part of God dispels any notion that an unholy fear should mark the relationship between Creator and created. In fact, this divine attribute should be the rule for the manifestation of parental love in such a way that peace, joy, and trust are the lasting aftereffects; a sanctifying ambience that pervades the home. Pope Francis encourages us to look to Mary, whose Immaculate Heart is a "treasury" in which are stored the experiences faced by all families. The Mother of Jesus can come to the aid of all seeking solace; a tender Mother who never abandons her children.

Chapter 2 of *Amoris Laetitia* is entitled "The Experiences and Challenges of Families." It seeks to understand the variety of concrete realities that afflict families right across the globe. Pope Francis says from the outset that it is a demand of the Holy Spirit that the Church confront these challenges in order to "be guided to a more profound understanding of the inexhaustible mystery of marriage and the family."[8]

The Holy Father begins by stressing the danger of an "extreme individualism which weakens family bonds and ends up considering each member of the family as an isolated unit, leading in some cases to the idea that one's personality is shaped by his or her desires, which are considered absolute."[9] The fast pace of modern life, coupled with an evolutionary development of flexible work hours and social organization, has meant that the modern family no longer eats or shares quality time together. The Pontiff expresses concern that an overly individualistic culture that promotes greater freedom of choice could degenerate into an inability to give of oneself generously, if "noble goals" are not sought. Nowhere do we experience this more than the modern crisis of marriage:

> The ideal of marriage, marked by a commitment to exclusivity and stability, is swept aside whenever it proves inconvenient or tiresome. The fear of loneliness and the desire for stability and fidelity exist side by side with a growing fear of entrapment in a relationship that could hamper the achievement of one's personal goals.[10]

Strikingly, the Holy Father moves on to a healthy dose of self-criticism for the Church, in the way it has historically presented the ideal of marriage. Too often, he says, Catholic marriages have been presented as little more than baby-making factories, ignoring the critical foundation of the unitive aspect—of growing ever deeper in love and mutual support:

> At times we have also proposed a far too abstract and almost artificial theological ideal of marriage, far removed from the concrete situations and practical possibilities of real families. This excessive idealization, especially when we have failed to inspire trust in God's grace, has not helped to make marriage more desirable and attractive, but quite the opposite.[11]

This is the refreshing realism of this Pontificate. It would be hard to imagine any previous pope being so self-critical, and yet he goes even further in one of the most enlightening passages of the entire Exhortation:

> We have long thought that simply by stressing doctrinal, bioethical and moral issues, without encouraging openness to grace, we were providing sufficient support to families….We find it difficult to present marriage more as a dynamic path to personal development and fulfilment than as a lifelong burden. We also find it hard to make room for the consciences of the faithful, *who very often respond as best they can to the Gospel amid their limitations, and are capable of carrying out their own discernment in complex situations. We have been called to form consciences, not to replace them.*[12]

The Holy Father continues his survey of the causes of family problems by addressing the "culture of the ephemeral" whereby people treat relationships along the lines of social networking; they connect and disconnect on a whim without ever allowing a deeper emotional attachment to take root. The fear of permanent commitment, the obsession with free time, and a narcissistic attitude are also highlighted: "cultural tendencies in today's world seem to set no limits on a person's affectivity; indeed, a narcissistic, unstable or changeable affectivity does not always allow a person to grow to maturity."[13]

Concern is also expressed for the "world politics" of reproductive health, which gives rise to a mentality in which children are seen as a hindrance to personal freedom and lifestyle. Alongside this repressive influence, several other social factors are also seen as contributing to this crisis: industrialization, the sexual revolution, fear of overpopulation, economic problems, and Consumerism. For Pope Francis, this alarming decline in the birth rate risks creating a generational gap between young and old and a further destabilization of the family unit.

One problem, which many young adults especially will experience, is the cost of affordable housing that in turn inevitably leads to the postponement of marriage. Pope Francis is clear, "Families and homes go together."[14] Furthermore, with the lack of job security in many parts of the world, young couples do not have the confidence to "take the plunge" and cement their union through sacramental marriage. This must be especially painful for those in love, who desire the most intimate union, and who would gladly welcome children, yet who feel they do not have sufficient economic security to create a family. This vexing problem must surely be on the agenda at the 2018 Synod that is devoted to the youth.

Pope Francis also tackles other issues relevant to contemporary challenges to the family: children born out of wedlock, sexual abuse, violence due to organized crime and war, migration and human trafficking, the persecution of Christian families, families with special needs, the vulnerability (euthanasia and assisted suicide) of the elderly, drug abuse, alcoholism, and gambling.

Toward the end of the chapter, the Holy Father approaches the subject of equality between men and women. He refers to the "shameful ill-treatment" to which women are sometimes subjected; verbal, physical, and sexual violence are all condemned as contradictions to the very nature of conjugal union. Also condemned in the strongest terms is the practice of genital mutilation that mars certain cultures. Interestingly, Pope Francis, while not endorsing all forms of feminism, nevertheless sees the action of the Holy Spirit in the women's movement that works "for a clearer recognition of the dignity and rights of women."[15]

The Holy Father's final words are devoted to the menacing development of gender theory, which "envisages a society without sexual differences, thereby eliminating the anthropological basis of the family."[16] He warns:

> This ideology leads to legislative enactments that promote a personal identity and emotional intimacy radically separated from the biological difference between male and female. Consequently, human identity becomes the choice of the individual, one which can also change over time. It is a source of concern that some ideologies of this sort, which seek to respond to what are at times understandable aspirations, manage to assert themselves as absolute and unquestionable, even dictating how children should be raised.[17]

We are reminded that we must not "fall into the sin of trying to replace the Creator....Creation is prior to us and must be received as a gift."[18]

The overall impression given in chapter 2 of *Amoris Laetitia* is that the Church faces a huge challenge in helping the modern family overcome its considerable trials. However, hope and missionary creativity are the key driving forces that can inject new energy and enthusiasm amidst the realism of contemporary life.

Chapter 3, entitled "Looking to Jesus: The Vocation of the Family," is dedicated to the Church's teaching on marriage. It seeks to reveal the full truth of this beautiful Sacrament and the mystery of Christian family life as proclaimed in the Gospels.

Pope Francis begins by stating that marriage is a gift (cf. 1 Cor. 7:7) that should not be seen as a yoke imposed, but a generous offering to partake of God's salvific plan; one which benefits from a divine indulgence that binds the indissoluble union of man and woman. He reaffirms the truth that Jesus restores marriage to its original meaning by giving it sacramental dignity; thus becoming a path of sanctification not only for husband and wife, but also their children, who "share not only genetically but also spiritually in the 'flesh' of both parents."[19]

The Holy Father invites the reader to delve into the magisterial documents of the Church on marriage and the family in order to fathom the depths of this great gift. He emphasizes the grounding of both spouses in Christ:

> Christ the Lord "makes himself present to the Christian spouses in the sacrament of marriage" and remains with them. In the incarnation, he assumes human love, purifies it and brings it to fulfilment. By his Spirit, he gives spouses the capacity to live that love, permeating every part of their lives of faith, hope and charity. In this way, the spouses are consecrated and by means of a special grace build up the Body of Christ and form a domestic church.[20]

The Encyclical *Humanae Vitae* of Blessed Paul VI is promoted by Pope Francis as a document that contributes to the doctrinal development of marriage by "bringing out the intrinsic bond between conjugal love and the generation of life,"[21] while St. John Paul II's magisterial documents, notably *Familiaris Consortio*, recalls the truth that marriage is an authentic path to holiness; the starting point for a "community of life and love."[22] Finally, Pope Francis refers to Benedict XVI's magnificent Encyclical *Deus Caritas Est* in which the German Pontiff taught that the love of man and woman is illuminated by the love of the crucified Christ; marriage becomes an "icon" for the reciprocal love between God and his people.

Pope Francis returns to Benedict XVI's theology of marriage and the Cross later in the chapter where he states:

> Christian marriage is a sign of how much Christ loved his Church in the covenant sealed on the cross, yet it also makes that love present in the communion of the spouses. By becoming one flesh, they embody the espousal of our human nature by the Son of God. That is why "in the joys of their love and family life, he gives them here on earth a foretaste of the wedding feast of the Lamb."[23]

Turning to other forms of marriage—natural and those forms from other religious traditions—the Holy Father still sees the active presence of the Holy Spirit, even if the absence of Christ's sacramental grace deprives these unions of the true beauty of marriage from a redemptive perspective:

> We can readily say that "anyone who wants to bring into this world a family which teaches children to be excited by every gesture aimed at overcoming evil—a family which shows that the Spirit is alive and at work—will encounter our gratitude and our appreciation. Whatever the people, religion or region to which they belong!"[24]

Toward the end of the chapter, Pope Francis turns to the critical issue of transmission of life and respect for children. He states that the conjugal union of man and woman is ordered to creation by its "very nature," and that the child who is born "does not come from outside as something added on to the mutual love of the spouses, but springs from the very heart of that mutual giving, as its fruit and fulfilment."[25] The Holy Father further teaches that true love "refuses every impulse to close in on itself" and thus "no genital act between husband and wife can refuse this meaning."[26] Also reconfirmed is the Catholic teaching that children must be conceived through the sexual act rather than artificial means such as IVF.

Finally, Pope Francis discusses the scourge of abortion:

> Here I feel it urgent to state that, if the family is the sanctuary of life, the place where life is conceived and cared for, it is a horrendous contradiction when it becomes a place where life is rejected and destroyed. So great is the value of a human life, and so inalienable the right to life of an innocent child growing in the mother's womb, that no alleged right to one's own body can justify a decision to terminate that life, which is an end in itself and which can never be considered the "property" of another human being.[27]

The overriding message from chapter 3 is that the "domestic church"—the family—is intimately linked to the Church itself, in that the holiness of these little cells strengthens the Mystical Body overall and contributes to the fulfilment of God's saving plan. From an eschatological point of view, each family formed by grace and love acts like a prophetic beacon for the full manifestation of the Communion of Saints that will come at the Lord's return.

Chapter 4 of *Amoris Laetitia* entitled "Love in Marriage," should be seen, along with the following chapter, as the heart of the entire document. It is a magnificent treasure trove of wisdom and magisterial teaching that will be beneficial for all who meditate on it pages. Sadly, due to its length and the confines of this book, it will only be possible to give a brief outline of its contents; however, a full and reflective rumination on the actual text will be most beneficial and a sound investment for all married couples.

The Holy Father takes as his guide the "Hymn to Love" found in St. Paul's 13th chapter of his First Letter to the Corinthians. He breaks the text down, dissecting what love is, and isn't: love is patient, love is kind, it is not arrogant or rude, and so on. Quoting St. Ignatius of Loyola,[28] Pope Francis teaches that love is more than just a feeling; it is the ability and desire to do good: "It thus shows its fruitfulness and allows us to experience the happiness of giving, the nobility and grandeur of spending ourselves unstintingly, without asking to be repaid, purely for the pleasure of giving and serving."[29] Envy, on the other hand, is a form of sadness that is provoked by another person's prosperity; it forces one to be closed off from the happiness of others.

Moving through the Hymn, we discover dazzling insights from the Pontiff that presents a grand Christological vision on love. For instance, concerning forgiveness, he invites us to "pray over our past history," to accept and forgive ourselves as a way of learning to forgive others: a generous spirit full of love can "transcend and overflow the demands of justice," expecting nothing in return. Pope Francis also tells us that "the Lord especially appreciates those who find joy in the happiness of others," thus family members should always rejoice at the success of each other.

While discussing "love bears all things," the Holy Father says this is more than just putting up with evil. It also entails holding one's peace, of keeping the tongue quiet when the temptation to judge arises. Gossip and slander are types of terrorism in the mind of Francis, and the tongue "is a world of iniquity" that "stains the whole body." Love, however, cherishes the good name of another and always seeks to uphold divine law.

Pope Francis' realism is evident when he turns to how couples should treat each other:

> We have to realize that all of us are a complex mixture of light and shadows. The other person is much more than the sum of the little things that annoy me. Love does not have to be perfect for us to value it. The other person loves me as best they can, with all their limits, but the fact that love is imperfect does not mean that it is untrue or unreal. It is real, albeit limited and earthly.[30]

"Love believes all things." The Holy Father explains that rather than taking this in a strict theological sense, it actually refers to trust; trust that leads to freedom, where one's spouse is not being controlled or imprisoned by suspicion and jealousy. Sincerity and transparency become the fruits of this attitude, enabling the couple to share their lives unconditionally in a spirit of fraternal charity. Along the same lines comes the virtue of hope, and for the Holy Father, hope does not disappoint because it draws each person into a supernatural perspective, seeing eschatological light at the end of life. For themselves and their spouse, hope tells them that weaknesses, sin, and vice will be erased forever in the glorious transformation wrought by Christ's resurrection.

Pope Francis next turns his attention to the subject of conjugal love: "It is an 'affective union', spiritual and sacrificial, which combines the warmth of friendship and erotic passion, and endures long after emotions and passion subside."[31] For the Holy Father, it is the Holy Spirit who infuses love within marriage as a powerful reflection of the unbroken Covenant between Christ and humanity. In essence, "God is, as it were, 'mirrored' in them; he impresses in them his own features and the indelible character of his love. Marriage is the icon of God's love for us."[32]

Looking at joy and beauty in marriage, Pope Francis warns that an obsessive search for physical pleasure can be detrimental to the experience of other satisfactions; real joy on the other hand breaks away from that temptation and results in an "expansion of the heart," where even sorrow and tribulation cannot smother its flames. And beauty, far from being the impoverished understanding modern society has today, is that "great worth" in which we see the innate majesty and sacredness of the other, no less than the image and likeness of God.

Dialogue, on many levels, is always at the forefront of papal teaching, and in the context of marriage it is no different. The Holy Father, ever the realist, reminds that a long apprenticeship will be required to master the essential communications skills: the tone we use, self-discipline in knowing when to speak, patience, ensuring we have listened carefully, quality time, respect for other opinions, and so on. All will contribute greatly to a healthy and peaceful family environment.

One of the most significant and rich teachings of *Amoris Laetitia* concerns the role of sexuality in marriage. Undoubtedly, this is one of the most remarkable manifestations of authentic doctrinal development in recent times; no longer is marriage seen as just a baby-making factory, but a place where passion truly symbolizes the love God has for his people.[33] Pope Francis is clear that sexuality is a "marvellous gift of God"; not a form of entertainment of gratification, but "an interpersonal language wherein the other is taken seriously, in his or her sacred and inviolable dignity. As such, the human heart comes to participate, so to speak, in another kind of spontaneity."[34] Eroticism, as a dimension of sexuality, becomes a blessed and specifically human manifestation of it, which must never be seen as a permissible evil or even just tolerated:

> As a passion sublimated by a love respectful of the dignity of the other, it becomes a "pure, unadulterated affirmation" revealing the marvels of which the human heart is capable. In this way, even momentarily, we can feel that "life has turned out good and happy."[35]

Amoris Laetitia is also clear that couples should not view marriage and its sexual element as just generous donation or self-sacrifice. Authentic love is concerned with the love that can be received and welcomed "with sincere and joyful gratitude the physical expressions of love found in a caress, an embrace, a kiss and sexual union." Man and woman are not just spiritual beings but physical too, thus the full dignity of human sexuality incorporates a variety of aspects where the erotic and the physical play essential parts in strengthening the bond of true love. This magnetic pull of mutual attraction should forever be the wellspring that brings vitality to the relationship.[36]

In conclusion, the central teaching of the Holy Father is that true love will always shun selfish gratification or an attitude that places one's opinions or desires above another. True love is not ephemeral; it perseveres through sufferings and trials where it is refined even further. It models its charity on the love of God and thus always seeks its joy in the joy of others. For Pope Francis, this is the recipe for a good lasting marriage that will withstand the storms of life that will inevitably come.

Chapter 5 of the Apostolic Exhortation is entitled "Love Made Fruitful" and concerns the growth of the family through the gift of children. Pope Francis tells us from the outset that "each new life allows us to appreciate the utterly gratuitous dimension of love, which never ceases to amaze us. It is the beauty of being loved first: children are loved even before they arrive."[37] The Pontiff intuits here a reflection of the primacy of God's love for us due to its unconditional nature: he loves us without us having first deserved it. We can go even further and state that God has loved each child from all eternity, patiently waiting for the moment when conception arrives, and then, as the Holy Father beautifully states, "the Creator's eternal dream comes true."

Pope Francis, as is his unique style, offers kind words of encouragement to expectant mothers. He invites them to pray to God, asking for the wisdom to know their child; he urges them to remain happy and not let their interior joy be robbed by useless worries or comments from others. He warns against obsessing over unnecessary things and suggests imitating Mary's serene excitement proclaimed so wondrously in the *Magnificat*. Turning to the role of mothers post birth, the Holy Father touches on the modern phenomenon of feminism, and while acknowledging a certain value, eschews a form that would weaken a maternal dimension of the feminine genius: "Mothers are the strongest antidote to the spread of self-centered individualism....It is they who testify to the beauty of life."[38]

Addressing fathers, the Pope stresses their ability to help the child to perceive the limits of life, to be open to everyday challenges, and to see the necessity of hard work (cf. Gen. 3:19). He reveals his concern at the rejection of the father figure in Western culture—which stems in part from an authoritarian and repressive model of the past—and recognizes that we have now gone from one extreme to the other. Sure and solid guidance for children is now more than ever in jeopardy, warns Francis, because of fathers who are absent for one reason or another.

After encouraging the adoption of children with no home as a great and generous act of love, the Holy Father turns to the reality of the family as an "expanding fruitfulness" of marriage. He states that families must play their part in society; and for Christian ones in particular, a summons to transform the world from within, thus preparing it for the coming of the Kingdom: "Families should not see themselves as a refuge from society, but instead go forth from their homes in a spirit of solidarity with others."[39] The Pope points out that the Holy Family of Nazareth did not live apart from the world or from extended family; they were in fact quite normal. So much so that many couldn't grasp Jesus' wisdom: "What deeds of power are being done by his hands! Is not this the carpenter, the son of Mary" (Mk. 6:2–3).

The radicalness of Christianity is to see in each person a brother or sister, especially the marginalized and less fortunate; it is the fundamental teaching of the Gospel subordinate only to loving God. Pope Francis invites "open and caring families" to adopt this command as a way of evangelizing and speaking of Jesus. He sees it as a witness to the luminosity of the Gospel message, an attraction that will allow God's love to penetrate into the hearts of the poor and vulnerable. He warns however that to ignore the pleas of the destitute is to wound the Body of the Lord; they "eat and drink judgment against themselves" (1 Cor. 11:29). Due to this danger, the celebration of the Eucharist must be a summons for each Catholic to examine their conscience; ensuring that the Body is totally united on a mystical and social level.

Moving on to the extended family, the Pontiff has special words for grandparents and the elderly in general. He sees their wisdom and history as a beautiful way of instructing the young on life's pilgrimage, especially the spiritual aspect of it:

The lack of historical memory is a serious shortcoming in our society. A mentality that can only say, "Then was then, now is now," is ultimately immature. Knowing and judging past events is the only way to build a meaningful future. Memory is necessary for growth: "Recall the former days" (Heb 10:32). Listening to the elderly tell their stories is good for children and young people; it makes them feel connected to the living history of their families, their neighbourhoods and their country. A family that fails to respect and cherish its grandparents, who are its living memory, is already in decline, whereas a family that remembers has a future.[40]

Overall, Pope Francis sees the family as a tremendous asset to humanity, where the bond of fraternity is a great school of freedom and peace. This fraternity seeps into society, bringing with it unity that is capable of breaking down barriers. Sadly, as we see so often in our modern world, the opposite occurs and fissures appear within families that then have repercussions in the wider population. Only through God's grace and intervention can the tide be turned, but we must hope and pray that love in the end will prevail.

Chapter 6 of *Amoris Laetitia* is entitled "Some Pastoral Perspectives" and presents a variety of methods to aid the family in its present difficulties. To begin with, Pope Francis turns to the formation of priests, deacons, religious, catechists, and seminarians. He suggests that it is not enough to have doctrinal formation; that the complexity of family life in the twenty-first century requires a thorough pastoral training that doesn't simply count on a textbook answer to harrowing problems. The presence of women, for instance, in priestly formation is one way the Holy Father suggests can be beneficial to promote a more rounded preparation for the challenges ahead.

A serious concern for the Pontiff is an inadequate marriage preparation. Since 2013, he has stated on several occasions the possibility that many sacramental marriages throughout the world are invalid for lack of understanding what it entails; thus he desires to address that problem urgently. He begins by listing various ways that can help couples achieve a greater awareness of the path they are venturing on: perceiving the attraction of complete union that perfects the "social dimension of existence," the proper meaning of sexuality, cultivation of the virtues (especially chastity), involvement of the community for support, rejection of a consumption society, and praying together.

The Pope wants couples to realize that marriage is a lifelong journey where each spouse must not expect perfection from the other, but make generous allowances for one another; trusting in God's grace that can and will accompany them if they invite him too:

> Another great challenge of marriage preparation is to help couples realize that marriage is not something that happens once for all. Their union is real and irrevocable, confirmed and consecrated by the sacrament of matrimony....Each must set aside all illusions and accept the other as he or she actually is: an unfinished product, needing to grow, a work in progress.[41]

The Holy Father warns that the first exciting years of marriage must not become stagnant like putrid water, but must be propelled forward, "dancing toward the future with immense hope."[42] Hope enables one to look past mistakes and arguments, seeing things in a broader perspective, and so a constant renewal of love and mercy can foster greater maturity and compassion when problems arise. Pope Francis teaches that generosity and sacrifice can ensure that there are always "two winners" in the home and that, based on that logic, decisions cannot and must not be made unilaterally.

In paragraph 221, the Pope describes wedlock in a particularly beautiful way: "Each marriage is a kind of 'salvation history,' which from fragile beginnings—thanks to God's gift and a creative and generous response on our part—grows over time into something precious and enduring."[43] He asks this question: "Might we say that the greatest mission of two people in love is to help one another become, respectively, more a man and more a woman?"

Love, for Pope Francis, is the ability to help shape the identity of one's spouse, to always be ready to open new possibilities for the relationship to grow, and to point the way to heaven. Perhaps the greatest way possible of nurturing the relationship is by being generous in bestowing life, and the Holy Father encourages pastoral care in this direction:

> In this regard, experienced couples have an important role to play. The parish is a place where such experienced couples can help younger couples, with the eventual cooperation of associations, ecclesial movements and new communities. Young couples need to be encouraged to be essentially open to the great gift of children.[44]

Pope Francis continues his exploration of pastoral care by encouraging pastors and those within the ecclesial community to promote the spending of quality time together, to plan routines, and to encourage prayer, confession, *lectio divina*, and spiritual direction. All these treasuries of the faith can enable the family unit to become the "domestic church;" they are magnificent witnesses to the truth of Christian love in a pagan world. Along these lines, the Holy Father states:

> Parishes, movements, schools and other Church institutions can help in a variety of ways to support families and help them grow. These might include: meetings of couples living in the same neighbourhood, brief retreats for couples; talks by experts on concrete issues facing families, marriage counselling, home missionaries who help couples discuss their difficulties and desires, social services dealing with family problems like addiction, infidelity and domestic violence, programmes of spiritual growth, workshops for parents with troubled children and family meetings.[45]

Pope Francis continues his survey by touching on the pastoral accompaniment for those whose marriages have broken down, but since we will look at this in much greater detail in several other chapters, we do not need to enter into that discussion here.

The final part of the chapter is devoted to the suffering caused by death in a family. The Holy Father states that we cannot fail to offer the light of faith to the grieving or turn our backs on them. Pastors especially must accompany these poor souls and adapt to the demands of each stage of grief: "At particular times, we have to help the grieving person to realize that, after the loss of a loved one, we still have a mission to carry out, and that it does us no good to prolong the suffering, as if it were a form of tribute."[46] Pope Francis is adamant that praying for the souls of the deceased can ensure the bond of love is maintained and that closeness to them can be experienced in a new and powerful way. Our prayers cannot only help them reach heaven, but make their intercession for us more effective; our Catholic Faith can give us great hope that as love is stronger than death we can look forward to the day when we meet again in the heavenly Kingdom. Pastoral care then should include the great doctrine of the Communion of Saints as a summons to look to the future with the glorious resurrection as our final destination.

Chapter 7 of *Amoris Laetitia,* entitled "Towards a Better Education of Children," aims to advise parents on ways to help their children prepare for the opportunities and dangers that will inevitably confront them in the years to come. The Holy Father stresses the importance of spending quality time with them; speaking with "simplicity and concern" about the serious issues of drug addiction, aggression, sexual abuse, and exploitation. However, he warns that parents cannot control every situation that a child may experience or obsess about their movements. Authentic education will allow them to grow in freedom and maturity, recognizing the need for discipline and prudence.

Concerning the ethical formation of children, Pope Francis invites parents to take this seriously and not presume that school education will arm them with the necessary knowledge:

> Parents are also responsible for shaping the will of their children, fostering good habits and a natural inclination to goodness. This entails presenting certain ways of thinking and acting as desirable and worthwhile, as part of a gradual process of growth....Moral formation should always take place with active methods and a dialogue that teaches through sensitivity and by using a language children can understand. It should also take place inductively, so that children can learn for themselves the importance of certain values, principles and

norms, rather than by imposing these as absolute and unquestionable truths.[47]

In the thought of the Pontiff, a good ethical education will seek to show a child it is in their own interests to do what is right; to see that effort and self-sacrifice can bring great pleasure and peace of soul, even if the prevailing opinion in society is contrary to that. Along these lines, the repetition of good moral acts will become the building blocks for a will resolved to seek the good of others, and always in obedience to the natural law. Not only that. The cultivation of the virtues will also inevitably flow from this interior disposition under the guidance of the Holy Spirit.

The Holy Father moves on to discuss the issue of correction for misbehavior. He suggests children should be encouraged to put themselves in the shoes of those they have hurt, and to have the humility to ask for forgiveness. He also teaches that parents should recognize and show appreciation for children's efforts in this regard, and thus these youngsters can perceive that growth and potential are being noted. This will serve as a stimulus for ever greater efforts to respond to divine grace.

Pope Francis is clear that in the education of morality, a patient and delicate approach must be utilized that takes into account the child's age, maturity, and abilities. Small steps will be far more helpful than demands that overawe, discourage, and are not realistic. Turning to "situated or real freedom," the Holy Father sees it as being limited by various factors that can take away its inherent facility:

A distinction is not always adequately drawn between "voluntary" and "free" acts. A person may clearly and willingly desire something evil, but do so as the result of an irresistible passion or a poor upbringing. In such cases, while the decision is voluntary, inasmuch as it does not run counter to the inclination of their desire, it is not free, since it is practically impossible for them not to choose that evil. We see this in the case of compulsive drug addicts. When they want a fix, they want it completely, yet they are so conditioned that at that moment

48

no other decision is possible. Their decision is voluntary but not free.[48]

At paragraph 280, Pope Francis introduces the pressing issue of an authentic sex education that is based not on the disgusting trivialization promoted far and wide today, but one that is based on true love and mutual self-giving in the context of marriage. He suggests that education in this area must be adaptable to the age and maturity of the young so that certain issues are not inflicted upon those not yet able to understand or deal with them. Modesty is something however that should be central to all discussion of sexual matters:

> A sexual education that fosters a healthy sense of modesty has immense value, however much some people nowadays consider modesty a relic of a bygone era. Modesty is a natural means whereby we defend our personal privacy and prevent ourselves from being turned into objects to be used. Without a sense of modesty, affection and sexuality can be reduced to an obsession with genitality and unhealthy behaviours that distort our capacity for love, and with forms of sexual violence that lead to inhuman treatment or cause hurt to others.[49]

The Pontiff goes on to make a very pertinent observation that young people should not confuse two levels of reality: sexual attraction and love. Sexual attraction can unfortunately serve as an illusion that makes one believe they are in love until something occurs to reveal its true shallow depth. This is a constant danger, especially in this hedonistic culture and with the peer pressure that goes with it; Pope Francis undoubtedly feels that this distinction needs to be clearly taught so that teenagers and young adults are not betrayed.

The final section of chapter 7 is devoted to passing on the faith. His Holiness describes the home as the fitting place for a developing appreciation of the Christian way of life, from praying with the heart, to looking after one's neighbor. Of course, in order for that to happen parents must first have their own deep faith and trust in God; one cannot pass on what one doesn't possess:

> Education in the faith has to adapt to each child, since older resources and recipes do not always work. Children need symbols, actions and stories. Since adolescents usually have issues with authority and rules, it is best to encourage their own experience of faith and to provide them with attractive testimonies that win them over by their sheer beauty. Parents desirous of nurturing the faith of their children are sensitive to their patterns of growth, for they know that spiritual experience is not imposed but freely proposed.[50]

Pope Francis' dream is that missionary and evangelization work can begin in family cells where a ripple effect seeps beyond the borders of the home. The children perhaps can begin to influence in a positive way their friends: an act of mercy, of generosity, hope for someone in despair, helping the poor. Many teachings can be taken off the page and put into practice and thus the domestic church can express clearly "in the world" the love God the Father has for all his children. Ultimately, this is what *Amoris Laetitia* is about, and in the context of today's crises, it is a message that must be promoted with utmost vigor and urgency. All families have the right to know the true joy of love and the Father's embrace.

Chapter 9[51] of the Exhortation is entitled "The Spirituality of Marriage and the Family" and looks at the ways God dwells within the home. The Pope invites us to see the Lord reigning in the family—especially when authenticity inspired by love prevails—despite the trials and tribulations that are the lot of us all:

> The spirituality of family love is made up of thousands of small but real gestures. In that variety of gifts and encounters which deepen communion, God has his dwelling place. This mutual concern "brings together the human and the divine," for it is filled with the love of God.[52]

The Holy Father makes the point that those seeking a true path toward holiness should not see the family environment as a stumbling block to spiritual growth, but the way chosen by the Lord to reach that goal of "mystical union." The pain of the Cross will be felt no doubt at times of great suffering such as bereavement, but the grace of the risen Christ will strengthen those and fill them with divine consolation. A startling yet profoundly beautiful passage relevant to married couples is found in paragraph 317, where Pope Francis states: "Moreover, moments of joy, relaxation, celebration, and even sexuality can be experienced as a sharing in the full life of the resurrection."[53]

Prayer is the essential ingredient for the spiritual life of the family, and the Holy Father encourages a variety of ways to accomplish this: praying for anyone in special need, thanksgiving for graces received, praying for the gift of charity, and asking for the protection of the Blessed Virgin. Added to these could be the Rosary, the Divine Mercy Chaplet, Novenas, and meditations on the Passion of Jesus. Of course all this is geared to participation in Holy Mass on Sunday, the day of great joy in the Resurrection. It would be hoped that married couples would benefit from meditation on the close bond between their marriage and the marriage of Christ to his Bride the Church, manifest most extraordinarily in the Eucharistic Sacrifice.

Pope Francis ends this chapter by reaffirming the truth that no family drops down from heaven already perfectly formed. Families need to constantly grow in love toward one another, trusting that with patience and the active presence of the Holy Spirit, difficulties can be overcome. What must never be lost is that eschatological vision, that journey toward the heavenly homeland in which the family will finally experience perfection. The Holy Father warns against demanding such high expectations in this life—even if we are commanded to be perfect as our Father in heaven is perfect (cf. Matt. 5:48)—because we cannot expect others to be something we ourselves will never be in this life. All we can do is strive to do our best, relying on God's grace and mercy, and praying for our other family members that the Lord will help them too. In that way will God's blessing fall like dew, and lead us toward that Sunday with no evening.

NOTES

1. Pope Francis, Apostolic Exhortation, *Amoris Laetitia*, March 19, 2016, www.vatican.va.

2. Ibid, no. 297.

3. Pope Francis, Apostolic Exhortation, *Evangelii Gaudium*, no. 169, November 24, 2013, www.vatican.va.

4. Due to the importance of *Amoris Laetitia's* chapter 8 (in the context of this book), I will devote an entire chapter of my own to it.

5. *Amoris Laetitia*, no. 9.

6. Ibid, no. 20.

7. Ibid, no. 28.

8. Ibid, no. 31.

9. Ibid, no. 33.

10. Ibid, no. 34.

11. Ibid, no. 36.

12. Ibid, no. 37. We shall return to the issue of conscience in a later chapter.

13. Ibid, no. 41.

14. Ibid, no. 44.

15. Ibid, no. 54.

16. Ibid, no. 56.

17. Ibid, no. 56.

18. Ibid, no. 56.

19. Ibid, no. 13.

20. Ibid, no. 67.

21. Ibid, no. 68.

22. St. John Paul II, Apostolic Exhortation, *Familiaris Consortio*, November 22, 1981, www.vatican.va.

23. *Amoris Laetitia*, no. 73.

24. Ibid, no. 79. Pope Francis here quotes from his own "Homily for the Concluding Mass of the Eighth World Meeting of Families," *L'Osservatore Romano*, September 28–29, 2015, 7.

25. Ibid, no. 80.

26. Ibid. Considering some recent concerns about the possible reversal of the ban on contraception, Pope Francis dismisses those with this reaffirmation of Blessed Paul VI's teaching in *Humanae Vitae*.

27. Ibid, no. 83.

28. "Love is shown more by deeds than by words." St. Ignatius of Loyola, *Spiritual Exercises*, Contemplation to Attain Love (230).

29. *Amoris Laetitia*, no. 94.

30. Ibid, no. 113.

31. Ibid, no. 120.

32. Ibid, no. 121.

33. St. John Paul II's "Theology on the Body" series of general audiences could be seen as the starting point for this doctrinal development, as well as being the magisterium's response to the sexual revolution.

34. *Amoris Laetitia*, no. 151.

35. Ibid, no. 152.

36. Although I have desired to present the positive elements of sexuality and marriage as taught by Pope Francis, nevertheless, he is adamant that abuse of this gift is an ever present danger through various forms: manipulation, domination, perversion, and violence. These must be condemned in the strongest terms.

37. *Amoris Laetitia*, no. 166.

38. Ibid, no. 174.

39. Ibid, no. 181.

40. Ibid, no. 193.

41. Ibid, no. 218.

42. Ibid, no. 219.

43. Ibid, no. 221.

44. Ibid, no. 223.

45. Ibid, no. 229.

46. Ibid, no. 256.

47. Ibid, no. 264.

48. Ibid, no. 273.

49. Ibid, no. 282.

50. Ibid, no. 288.

51. Although Pope Francis teaches that *Amoris Laetitia* must be read in order for it to be properly understood, because of the importance of chapter 8 and the necessity of giving it much more detail, it is appropriate that it has a chapter of its own, rather than a brief synopsis here.

52. *Amoris Laetitia*, no. 315.

53. Ibid, no. 317.

III *AMORIS LAETITIA* CHAPTER 8: POPE AND PASTOR OF MERCY

Chapter 8 will surely be remembered years from now as one of the most controversial things a Pope has written as part of the ordinary magisterium. In dealing with the pastoral care of those in irregular situations—such as the divorced and civilly remarried—it presents a substantial challenge to the reader, inviting all to step outside the comfort zone wrought by a general rule and discipline-based approach to complex moral issues. Most importantly I believe, it asks us to consider the entire truth about every person; not just the moral truths taught by the Church, but the truth of their particular situation. Individuals are no longer to be seen simply as a "case number" that has fallen into mortal sin. No, there is far more to the story than an objective situation of grave sin, and in our age it should no longer be acceptable to blindly label people without looking carefully at each set of circumstances. Justice demands that we seek the entire truth even if that makes us somewhat uncomfortable.

Pope Francis from the outset is keen to recognize the reality that God's grace is still able to work even in these difficult and possibly sinful circumstances:

> Illumined by the gaze of Jesus Christ, "she turns with love to those who participate in her life in an incomplete manner, recognizing that the grace of God works also in their lives by giving them the courage to do good, to care for one another in love and to be of service to the community in which they live and work."[1]

The Holy Father stresses that the Church "constantly holds up the call to perfection and asks for a fuller response to God," yet, "the Church must accompany with attention and care the weakest of her children, who show signs of a wounded and troubled love, by restoring in them hope and confidence."[2] In paragraph 292, while upholding perfectly the teaching that Christian marriage is a reflection of the betrothal between Christ and his Bride the Church, Pope Francis touches on the reality of irregular unions. While stating that some "radically contradict" the ideal of sacramental marriage, he recognizes that others realize it in a "partial and analogous way." Due to this fact, he explains that the Church's pastors must enter into pastoral dialogue with these souls to ensure that those good elements may lead to a more faithful embracing of the Gospel, and serve as a stimulus for evangelization and spiritual growth.

In this context, the Pontiff proposes the so-called "law of gradualness" taught by St. John Paul II in *Familiaris Consortio*. This doctrine, not to be confused with the erroneous "gradualness of the law," suggests that persons of goodwill can accomplish moral good through stages of growth in a step-by-step ascendency; it is a "gradualness in the prudential exercise of free acts on the part of subjects who are not in a position to understand, appreciate, or fully carry out the objective demands of the law."[3] However, Pope Francis is clear that the law is itself a "gift of God which points out the way, a gift for everyone without exception; it can be followed with the help of grace."[4]

At paragraph 296, the Successor of St. Peter turns his attention to the discernment of irregular situations. Immediately, he sets the tone for the discussion, lest anyone be in any doubt of the maternal duty of the Church:

> There are two ways of thinking which recur throughout the Church's history: casting off and reinstating. The Church's way, from the time of the Council of Jerusalem, has always been the way of Jesus, the way of mercy and reinstatement....Consequently, there is a need to avoid judgements which do not take into account the complexity of various situations.[5]

The Holy Father continues by explaining that it is a matter of reaching out to those in need of the medicine of mercy; of helping them to be reintegrated into the ecclesial community. They like everyone need to be touched by the "unmerited, unconditional and gratuitous mercy" of God, and the Catholic Church exists to facilitate that. "Nobody is condemned forever, because that is not the logic of the Gospel!" says Pope Francis,[6] and thus the most vulnerable and weak must find hope in that salvific message. On the other hand, he delivers a strong rebuke to those who would wallow in their sinful state in a way that would cause public scandal:

> Naturally, if someone flaunts an objective sin as if it were part of the Christian ideal, or wants to impose something other than what the Church teaches, he or she can in no way presume to teach or preach to others; this is a case of something which separates from the community (cf. Mt 18:17). Such a person needs to listen once more to the Gospel message and its call to conversion.[7]

One of the most significant teachings in this section of the text —drawing on St. John Paul II's call for discernment in Familiaris Consortio[8]—refers to the disparate nature of these irregular unions. Pope Francis warns against "overly rigid classifications" and pigeonholing when judgements are being made about these situations:

> One thing is a second union consolidated over time, with new children, proven fidelity, generous self giving, Christian commitment, a consciousness of its irregularity and of the great difficulty of going back without feeling in conscience that one would fall into new sins.[9]

Other situations that require careful discernment concern those people who try desperately to save their first marriage, those who enter a new relationship for the sake of their children's well-being, and those who are subjectively conscious their first marriage was invalid. In contrast to these circumstances, there are those where a new relationship has quickly followed a divorce, or the case of someone moving regularly between relationships with no regard for those left behind in turmoil. Each case must be carefully discerned by the pastor charged with guiding the spiritual lives of these fragile souls.

In this process of outreach, the Holy Father desires that the person or couple in the irregular (civilly remarried) union feel invited to participate in the life of the Church in whatever way their circumstances permit. He reminds them that they are baptized brothers and sisters to the rest of the community, they are still beneficiaries of the Holy Spirit's charisms (given for the good of the Church), and they are called to experience the full joy of being a Catholic Christian.

From paragraph 300 to the conclusion of the chapter at no. 312, we enter into the most controversial part of the Apostolic Exhortation. This section invites us to delve into the moral theology of the Church; to reject simplistic categories that herd all people guilty of adultery into the field of mortal sin. If we are tempted to think that justice and mercy "clash" rather than embrace, then in humility, we will need to think again.

Pope Francis sets the scene by stating (in light of the Synod debates about the possible change in sacramental discipline for the divorced and remarried) that

> it is understandable that neither the Synod nor this Exhortation could be expected to provide a new set of general rules, canonical in nature and applicable to all cases. What is possible is simply a renewed encouragement to undertake a responsible personal and pastoral discernment of particular cases, one which would recognize that, since "the degree of responsibility is not equal in all cases," the consequences or effects of a rule need not necessarily always be the same.[10]

The Holy Father then includes footnote 336, which states: "This is also the case with regard to sacramental discipline, since discernment can recognize that in a particular situation no grave fault exists." These two passages alone are vitally important because Pope Francis indirectly affirms that the *general* ban on the divorced and remarried receiving Holy Communion remains in force. Why do I say this? Because to have issued a new canonical ruling would have left the gates open for those in a state of mortal sin to receive the Lord sacrilegiously; there would have been no way, or even necessity, to discern individual cases that could rule out that scenario. Footnote 336 however offers a hand of mercy to those who, through a discernment process with their pastor, come to the decision that mitigating factors diminish their responsibility in committing objectively gravely sinful acts.

In order to ascertain the level of sin—venial or mortal—and thus also the level of guilt, Pope Francis suggests the accompanying pastor help the penitent through explaining the teachings of the Church and the guidelines of the local bishop. On top of that is the requirement to make a detailed examination of conscience:

> The divorced and remarried should ask themselves: how did they act towards their children when the conjugal union entered into crisis; whether or not they made attempts at reconciliation; what has become of the abandoned party; what consequences the new relationship has on the rest of the family and the community of the faithful; and what example is being set for young people who are preparing for marriage.[11]

The Pontiff encourages this last exercise not only to recognize the sin involved, but also as a means to strengthen hope in the divine mercy of God who always offers the possibility of a new beginning. Contrary to the opinion of some of his critics, the Holy Father states that this process occurring in the "internal forum"[12] is aimed at guiding the "faithful to an awareness of their situation before God."[13] He makes the crucial point that this cathartic process can contribute to the formation of a "correct judgment" on what hinders the possibility of participating more fully in the life of the Church. From there, steps can be taken to improve the situation, always relying on God's grace and mercy. The Pontiff further teaches that this discernment mechanism cannot be a cover for happily continuing in sin; there must be a firm desire to change, even if circumstances make that extremely difficult:

> "This discernment can never prescind from the Gospel demands of truth and charity, as proposed by the

Church. For this discernment to happen, the following conditions must necessarily be present: humility, discretion and love for the Church and her teaching, in a sincere search for God's will and a desire to make a more perfect response to it." These attitudes are essential for avoiding the grave danger of misunderstandings, such as the notion that any priest can quickly grant "exceptions," or that some people can obtain sacramental privileges in exchange for favours.[14]

Paragraph 301 introduces the reality of mitigating factors that may diminish the guilt of the penitent:

The Church possesses a solid body of reflection concerning mitigating factors and situations. *Hence it is [sic] can no longer simply be said that all those in any "irregular" situation are living in a state of mortal sin and are deprived of sanctifying grace.* More is involved here than mere ignorance of the rule. A subject may know full well the rule, yet have great difficulty in understanding "its inherent values," or be in a concrete situation which does not allow him or her to act differently and decide otherwise without further sin.[15]

Pope Francis reminds us that the *Catechism of the Catholic Church* gives various reasons why a person's responsibility for acting against the Ten Commandments may be reduced or erased altogether,[16] and because of this, a negative judgment about the objective sin does not imply a judgment about the imputability or culpability of the person in question. He goes on:

Under certain circumstances people find it very difficult to act differently. Therefore, while upholding a general rule, it is necessary to recognize that responsibility with respect to certain actions or decisions is not the same in all cases. Pastoral discernment, while taking into account a person's properly formed conscience, must take responsibility for these situations. Even the consequences of actions taken are not necessarily the same in all cases.[17]

This discussion naturally leads on to that of conscience and its role in formulating moral decisions. The Holy Father firmly states that individual consciences must be "better incorporated into the Church's praxis in certain situations which do not objectively embody our understanding of marriage. Naturally, every effort should be made to encourage the development of an enlightened conscience."[18] However, in a case of authentic doctrinal development, he affirms that

> conscience can do more than recognize that a given situation does not correspond objectively to the overall demands of the Gospel. It can also recognize with sincerity and honesty what for now is the most generous response which can be given to God, and come to see with a certain moral security that it is what God himself is asking amid the concrete complexity of one's limits, while yet not fully the objective ideal.[19]

At paragraph 304, the Pontiff turns to "rules and discernment." He states that "it is reductive simply to consider whether or not an individual's actions correspond to a general law or rule, because that is not enough to discern and ensure full fidelity to God in the concrete life of a human being."[20] His teaching—based on St. Thomas Aquinas—is that although general rules set forth a good that cannot be disregarded, they cannot cover every single situation requiring moral decisions. Thus at times, people have to use practical reason—making a judgment based on the specific circumstances, along with a good conscience, and the wisdom of the Church's teachings—to arrive at the decision they hope is the correct one.[21] At the same time, the Pope is clear that this discernment process in particular circumstances cannot be elevated to the level of a rule, otherwise it would lead to an "intolerable casuistry."

Due to the complexity of many irregular situations and relationships, the Pope reminds pastors that they cannot simply apply moral laws as if they were "stones to throw" at people's lives. They must not look down from the "Chair of Moses," judging superficially and "hiding behind the Church's teachings." The truth is that in some, if not many instances, persons living in a situation of objective grave sin may in fact be living in God's grace and responding to it through acts of charity and mercy. We are reminded by St. Peter that "love covers a multitude of sins" (1 Pet. 4:8), while the Book of Sirach states: "As water extinguishes a blazing fire, so almsgiving atones for sin" (Sir. 3:30):

> By thinking that everything is black and white, we sometimes close off the way of grace and of growth, and discourage paths of sanctification which give glory to God. Let us remember that "a small step, in the midst of great human limitations, can be more pleasing to God than a life which appears outwardly in order, but moves through the day without confronting great difficulties."[22]

It is in this context that we discover the famous footnote 351. Pope Francis says that for people such as he has described, they can also receive the help of the Church:

> In certain cases, this can include the help of the sacraments. Hence, I want to remind priests that the confessional must not be a torture chamber, but rather an encounter with the Lord's mercy....I would also point out that the Eucharist is not a prize for the perfect, but a powerful medicine and nourishment for the weak.[23]

This is (along with footnote 336) where Pope Francis has in fact altered sacramental discipline for the divorced and civilly remarried. He is quite clearly stating that for souls not in a subjective state of mortal sin, with a sincere desire to respond to grace, they can benefit from receiving absolution in Confession and the Holy Eucharist at Mass as long as this is done in a discreet way that avoids scandal for the faith community. The critical factor is that this eventuality can only come about through the use of the internal forum, where penitent and confessor can take the journey together, seeking the light of the Holy Spirit and compliance with the divine will.

At paragraph 307, the Holy Father, in order to avoid any misunderstanding, restates the point that "in no way must the Church desist from proposing the full ideal of marriage, God's plan in all its grandeur,"[24] for to fail in this duty would be to fail the young and betray the Gospel. Showing understanding to those in "exceptional situations" should never mean "dimming the light of the fuller ideal" or proposing a watered-down version of what Jesus offers humanity.

Pope Francis is adamant that the Church must be attentive to the "goodness which the Holy Spirit sows in the midst of human weakness."[25] She must be prepared to get soiled by the "mud of the street" in accompanying her struggling children—a Mother who cannot bear to leave her brood to fend for themselves. In this way the Church will imitate its Lord and Savior who always goes out looking for the lost sheep. Mercy must not be allowed to become a pious wish or a code word for defiling truth; it must be the tool of every Christian who seeks to pass on what God has given them:

> At times we find it hard to make room for God's unconditional love in our pastoral activity. We put so many conditions on mercy that we empty it of its concrete meaning and real significance. That is the worst way of watering down the Gospel. It is true, for example, that mercy does not exclude justice and truth, but first and foremost we have to say that mercy is the fullness of justice and the most radiant manifestation of God's truth. For this reason, we should always consider "inadequate any theological conception which in the end puts in doubt the omnipotence of God and, especially, his mercy."[26]

To conclude this chapter, we can say that Pope Francis marries three essential spiritual elements in his teaching on reintegrating the divorced and remarried into the life of the Church: (1) Ignatian discernment, (2) Thomistic doctrine on morality, and (3) a Franciscan love for the (spiritually) poor. He also reveals a beautiful manifestation of the charism of Peter: he is both teacher and pastor; one who sees no sense in leaving doctrine to go stale on the shelf. Instead, he utilizes everything at his disposal to produce a blueprint for accompanying, discerning, and integrating the weak sheep back into the fold. What he asks from those brothers and sisters living these complex situations is goodwill and good intention. That is the starting point for the Lord to get to work. For the members of the Church who prefer a rigid application of the law, he shows understanding, yet asks them to look beyond their own concerns, to see the necessity of touching the wounded flesh of these souls. No longer can the faithful ignore the growing problems caused by divorce, especially the effect on children.

Amoris Laetitia is a document that had to come, to show that as historical circumstances change, the Church has the adaptability to manoeuvre into a new position; one that is not powerless to help. It needed a Pope of great courage to accomplish this, and thanks to the Holy Spirit, in Pope Francis it was given one. Although it has caused great controversy, that was to be expected simply because many are being challenged to rid themselves of the comfort zone wrought by a strict disciplinary-based approach to moral issues. Time will surely heal however, and divine wisdom will be proved right once again. If the Church exists to bring healing to the sick, then it simply must have an adequate prescription for the divorced and remarried seeking a deep spiritual life. We must learn to have the patience of God and not expect instant results based on an immature understanding of the working of grace. There may be extraordinary "Damascus" moments now and again, but by and large, the Lord lets real life take its course with its ebb and flow of sin and repentance.

Amoris Laetitia speaks of the realism of God, who knows the daily struggle many face; and with its focus on subjective guilt, it balances the objective sin approach taken by St. John Paul II in *Familiaris Consortio*. Thus the Church now has at its disposal a magisterial document that rightly looks in the eye of each person and says "I will walk with you." It seems to me that this is the message the Holy Spirit would like engrained in our hearts as we proceed forward in the years ahead as the one family of God.

NOTES

1. Ibid, no. 291.
2. Ibid.
3. Ibid, no. 295.
4. Ibid.
5. Ibid, no. 296.

6. This passage of *Amoris Laetitia* has caused unnecessary concern among some Traditionalist Catholics. They seem to interpret this statement as if the Pope has rejected the doctrine on hell. However, that is far from the truth. Pope Francis simply reaffirms that while on earth, each person has the opportunity to turn away from sin and embrace the salvation won by our Lord Jesus Christ. Concerning the danger of eternal damnation, the Holy Father stated in Fatima on May 13, 2017, "Our Lady foretold, and warned us about, a way of life that is godless and indeed profanes God in his creatures. Such a life—frequently proposed and imposed— risks leading to hell," www.vatican.va. Pope Francis also warned the mafia of possible eternal damnation: "Convert, there is still time, so that you don't end up in hell. That is what awaits you if you continue on this path." Pope Francis, "Prayer Vigil for the Nineteenth 'Memorial and Commitment Day,'" March 21, 2014, www.vatican.va.

7. *Amoris Laetitia*, no. 297.

8. *Familiaris Consortio*, no. 84.

9. *Amoris Laetitia*, no. 298.

10. Ibid, no. 300.

11. Ibid.

12. For a detailed explanation of the Internal Forum, see chapter 8, *Internal Forum: Heart Speaks Unto Heart*.

13. *Amoris Laetitia*, no. 300.

14. Ibid.

15. Ibid, no. 301.

16. This and related areas of moral theology are discussed in chapter 5.

17. *Amoris Laetitia*, no. 302.

18. Ibid, 303.

19. Ibid, no. 303.

20. Ibid, 304.

21. We can recall here St. John Paul II's teaching in *Veritatis Splendor*: "The Council reminds us that in cases where such invincible ignorance is not culpable, conscience *does not lose its dignity*, because even when it directs us to act in a way not in conformity with the objective moral order, it continues to speak in the name of that truth about the good which the subject is called to

seek sincerely. St. John Paul II, Encyclical Letter, *Veritatis Splendor*, August 6, 1993, no. 62, www.vatican.va.

22. *Amoris Laetitia*, no. 305.
23. Ibid, 305, footnote 351.
24. Ibid, no. 307.
25. Ibid, no. 308.
26. Ibid, no. 311.

IV GRACE AND MERCY:
A BIBLICAL REVELATION

A frequent charge often heard in the months and years since Pope Francis' election, is that a false mercy is being proclaimed; a mercy which is not bound to truth and justice. It is implied that this greatest attribute of God[1] is being abused in a way that makes following the moral doctrines of the Church unnecessary, and to a certain extent even the required repentance and contrition. A suspicion emerging from this charge is that the Pope wants to water down doctrines—especially those related to sexual morality—and the easiest way of doing this is to tell the faithful that it doesn't really matter if they fail in one way or another. God's mercy is so rich, so benevolent that he will forgive anyway; after all, Scripture assures us that he "desires everyone to be saved" (1 Tim. 2:4).

It is unquestionable that Pope Francis has advanced the doctrine of divine mercy a step further than St. John Paul II. For the great Polish Pontiff, it was also a recurrent theme (although not to the same extent) throughout his pontificate, but it was always strictly allied to the objective moral truths, thus there was little danger, or risk of misunderstanding. For Pope Francis, however, the situation in the Catholic world today, especially the West, is drastically different to what St. John Paul II encountered in his early years, and because of that, a more intense and urgent proclamation is necessary. In the late 1970s, the apostasy that has taken root now in many areas was still in its relative infancy, and thus the expectation was probably that most Catholic Christians accepted what was expected from them, notwithstanding falls through weakness.

A balance had to be found in which mercy was not seen to usurp moral teachings such as contraception and divorce. Accelerate four decades forward, and the Pope "from the ends of the earth"[2] has taken charge of a flock that to a large extent has now rejected these moral teachings, and thus Francis cannot preach just parrot fashion as if nothing has changed. The focus has had to shift to meeting people where they are—with all the moral mess that comes with it—and to use the message of mercy as a starting point to reintegrate lost souls back into the fold. Undoubtedly, the ability of Francis to cut through the doctrinal nettles but without jettisoning them is a charism given him by the Holy Spirit, and which is helping to open closed hearts. The question then is this: Just how far can mercy be stretched before reaching the breaking point?

In this chapter, I will seek to answer this vital question through a detailed examination and application of biblical texts, to ascertain whether the accusations against Pope Francis are in fact correct. If we are to truly grasp the concept of mercy in its totality, then we must first consider how God himself utilizes it through salvation history; how it is manifested in the life and ministry of Jesus. Only then can we say yes, this is truly the work of the Holy Spirit, or no, it is the work of the devil.

When we read the Old Testament, we are usually captivated by the history of Israel; God's chosen who left enslavement in Egypt, bound for the Promised Land. Viewed through the lens of the New Testament and the Catholic Church, we discover a typological significance to many people and events that point toward a greater escape from a wider captivity and future salvation. But essentially, the message is that the old Israel and the new are God's people; the rest are outside mired in original sin. What is striking however is that there are exceptions: pagans who find themselves chosen by the Lord to fulfil his divine will and make a significant contribution to salvation history.

One such figure is Melchizedek, the priest-king of Salem, a pagan who had blessed Abraham and offered him bread and wine after the military campaign in which the patriarch had rescued his nephew Lot from the hands of his enemies (cf. Gen. 14). Melchizedek, as the Letter to the Hebrews states, was "Without father, without mother, without genealogy" (Heb. 7:3), hence not a priest according to the prescripts of the Levitical priesthood. Prophetically, he became a prefiguration of Christ, the perfect High Priest who "has become a priest, not through a legal requirement concerning physical descent, but through the power of an indestructible life" (Heb. 7:16). The early Fathers thus viewed Melchizedek as a "holy pagan," the one through whom the pagan world could embrace salvation history. In his veneration and worship, and being a king of righteousness and peace, we can understand that the spirit of God was guiding him on the path toward full freedom in some mysterious way. Thus we see how mercy could be applied to those still with the stain of original sin.

Although Melchizedek is a good example for the more straight forward case of a "holy pagan," what interests us here is the idea of a pagan whose life is publicly sinful, someone whom we would consider to be in a state of objectively grave, or even subjectively, mortal sin. There is one figure, perhaps unique in Sacred Scripture who meets the requirements for our discussion here: Rahab the prostitute.

The remarkable story of Rahab is found in the Book of Joshua, and there we read how Joshua had sent two spies to reconnoiter the land of Jericho. They lodged in a house belonging to Rahab, a prostitute. The King of Jericho became aware of their presence and ordered Rahab to bring them out. Rahab lied by insisting they had left, while actually hiding them on the roof. Later, she approached the two spies and asked them to spare her and her family, knowing that Israel would soon bring death and destruction to the entire city. The two men said: "Our life for yours! If you do not tell this business of ours, then we will deal kindly and faithfully with you when the Lord gives us the land" (Josh. 2:14). They told her to hang a scarlet cord from her window (the same one they would use to escape) so that when the army besieged the city, they would know to spare Rahab's house. This all came to pass and Rahab and her entire family were spared by Joshua. From that day they dwelt in the company of Israel (cf. Josh. 6:25).

Rahab's importance is such that she takes her place in St. Matthew's genealogy of Jesus, one of only four women other than the Mother of Jesus. Paradoxically, as Benedict XVI points out,[3] rather than including the great women of Israel's history—Sarah, Rebecca, Leah, and Rachel—St. Matthew includes four pagan women: Rahab, Ruth, Bathsheba, and Tamar. All tainted by great sin in some way or another. The reason is undoubtedly to show how God's mercy was always centered on entering into the lives of the pagan world also; to bring them the salvation that for the time being was seen as the exclusive property of Israel.

If we look closer at the particular circumstances of Rahab, it may help to bring greater understanding to the situation facing some divorced and remarried, especially those who desire a loving relationship with the Lord. First, it cannot be denied that she was living a life of utter sexual immorality; she wasn't even a "good" pagan. Surely she was dicing with eternal death, and yet she displays something highly unusual. In her conversation with the two spies, we can perceive the presence of the three theological virtues: faith, hope, and charity. Faith, that she and her family would be spared the destruction of Jericho (cf. Heb. 11:31); hope, that a new life could begin under the protection and blessing of Joshua (who in turn is a type of Jesus); and charity, through her protection of the two spies. In fact, what is astounding is that in some magnificent inversion, turning logic completely on its head, it is the sinful harlot who saves the chosen ones. Rahab actually becomes a prototype of the Church. It is a mystery that we can only marvel at, and one that demonstrates the absolute futility in trying to decide how and when God's grace can work. It is a lesson that we must always learn anew, especially in our dealing with people we consider to be "living in sin."

In her saving of the two spies, we should also note that she actually lied in order to aid them; something that is intrinsically evil,[4] and yet, through that act that undoubtedly kept them alive, salvation history could move forward. What this tells us is that God looks beyond the objective sin and judges the heart of a sinner. Rahab's intention was good, even if the way she accomplished it was wrong. The symbolism of Rahab and the Church goes even deeper. The scarlet cord that both she and the Israelites used to escape is like the umbilical cord, the precious blood of Christ that brings forth salvation for all. In this way, Israel and the pagan world merge into the one people of God. St. Cyprian of Carthage also explains that when the spies told Rahab to ensure all her family were safely in the house during the destruction of Jericho, they were prophetically speaking of the Church:

> In which mystery is declared, that they who will live, and escape from the destruction of the world, must be

gathered together into one house alone, that is, into the Church; but whosoever of those thus collected together shall go out abroad, that is, if any one, although he may have obtained grace in the Church, shall depart and go out of the Church, that his blood shall be upon him.[5]

The story of Rahab then is one that should cause us to ponder greatly on the mystery of sin, the subjective guilt of the sinner, and the unfathomable mercy of God. It is an invitation to accept that the Lord seeks out those who appear lost, and not to judge those who from the outside appear as public sinners. The most significant point however, in relation to the objective state of sin for those who maintain a sexual relationship in an irregular union, is that Rahab accomplished this act while in a sinful state herself. For most if not all the other cases of great sinners in the Bible, conversion came first and then the ascent toward holiness, but not so in this fascinating case. It allows us to understand that in the secret depths of one's individual conscience God's light and grace can still be working and influencing even when the rule book tells us it shouldn't be possible.

Another female pagan that is listed in St. Matthew's Genealogy is Tamar, the daughter-in-law of Judah. Her story, while not having quite the same rich symbolism as Rahab's, is nonetheless remarkable in its own way.

After seeing her two husbands (Er and Onan) die one after the other because of their wickedness, Tamar was promised a future marriage to their younger brother, Shelah. In the meantime, she was told by Judah to live as a widow with her father. Some years later, Judah's wife, Shua died, and Tamar, disgruntled by now that she had not been given in marriage to the grown up Shelah, hatched a plot. Upon hearing that Judah was going to Timnah to shear his sheep, Tamar took off her widow's garment and disguised herself as a harlot. Judah, not realizing who she was, asked her for intercourse. Tamar, agreed, but asked for payment. Judah offered a young goat, and as a form of deposit, gave her his seal, cord, and staff. Tamar became pregnant, and three months later, word got to Judah that Tamar was with child, through prostitution. Upon hearing this, he demanded she be burnt to death, and while the locals brought her out, she revealed the seal, cord, and staff. Judah accepted they were his, stopped the impending execution, and said: "She is more in the right than I, since I did not give her to my son Shelah" (Gen. 38:26). Tamar gave birth to twins, Perez and Zerah.

The crux of this story is that Judah was not respecting the Old Testament covenant concerning special relationships. Tamar felt betrayed—especially her desire for children—and through deceit, took matters into her own hands. But as St. Augustine points out, God's mercy is evident even in this sinful act:

> We have next to consider the prophetic significance of the action of Judah in lying with his daughter-in-law. But, for the sake of those whose understanding is feeble, we shall begin with observing, that in sacred Scripture evil actions are sometimes prophetic not of evil, but of good. Divine providence preserves throughout its essential goodness, so that, as in the example given above, from adulterous intercourse a man-child is born, a good work of God from the evil of man.[6]

St. Ephraim goes even further in his seventh Hymn on the Nativity:

> For holy was the adultery of Tamar, for Your sake. You it was she thirsted after, O pure Fountain. Judah defrauded her of drinking You. The thirsty womb stole a dew-draught of You from the spring thereof.
>
> She was a widow for Your sake. You did she long for, she hasted and was also a harlot for Your sake. You did she vehemently desire, and was sanctified in that it was You she loved.
>
> May Tamar rejoice that her Lord has come and has made her name known for the son of her adultery! Surely the name she gave him (Gen. 38:29) was calling unto You to come to her.[7]

Now of course we must place these words in their proper context. St. Ephraim is in no way advocating the evil of adultery; his words instead express in a rather robust (and it may be said profound)[8] way, the truth that Tamar's intention was "holy" even if the way her child came to be was sinful. She was sanctified through her desire for true love. Her heart was open, and yet she had been robbed of heaven's blessing through the sinful actions of others. As in the case of Rahab, the Lord was still close, still manifesting his mercy in spite of gravely sinful acts. These biblical accounts should give us all hope that as long as purity of intention is there, and in spite of extremely difficult circumstances that may involve sinful acts, God's grace can still navigate a path toward sanctity.

If the Old Testament contains only periodic interventions of divine mercy alongside the more conspicuous rigors of divine justice, then in the New Testament we discover its full revelation. Mercy is no longer just a concept, it is a divine person: Our Lord Jesus Christ. Through his Incarnation, Death, and Resurrection, the divine plan first announced in the aftermath of Adam and Eve's fall comes to fruition. It is a plan of merciful love; one that destroys the power of the devil and plunders his house (cf. Matt. 12:29). This "house" now becomes a place where mercy can gradually transform its inhabitants until a time when the full, universal restoration is complete (cf. Acts 3:21).

The portrait of Jesus from the Gospel accounts portrays someone who has great concern for the poor and marginalized; not just the materially poor, but those in spiritual poverty too. Sinners are those he is determined to save, seeking them out, binding up their wounds, and giving them the water of new life. Various passages bear this out: His dinner at the house of Matthew the tax collector where he said: "Those who are well have no need of a physician, but those who are sick. Go and learn what this means, 'I desire mercy, not sacrifice.' For I have come to call not the righteous but sinners" (Matt. 9:12–13). And a similar lesson is also given to Simon the Pharisee while dining at his house (cf. Lk. 7:36–50). St. Luke also recounts the three parables on mercy: the lost sheep, the lost coin, and the prodigal son. So, should we understand this compassion as a more lax approach to the moral code demanded by the Ten Commandments? And if not, how then do we interpret this radical stance that upset the religious authorities so much?

In order to answer these questions, we must first recall what the author of the Letter to the Hebrews tells us concerning Jesus: "For we do not have a high priest who is unable to sympathize with our weaknesses, but we have one who in every respect has been tested as we are, yet without sin" (Heb. 4:15). Sympathizing with our weakness is to know the entire truth of our individual existence, every factor that influences the decisions that we make, especially those relating to faith and morals. This is where the fault line exists between Jesus and the Pharisees. For them, the law is everything: a strict adherence that doesn't look past appearances and thus is easy to judge; looking at the heart is an irrelevance. For Jesus however, looking at the heart is the critical factor, precisely because he knows the weakness brought about by Adam's sin. Concupiscence, for instance, in sexual matters has always been and will forever be a terrible fruit of original sin. The Lord knows that; he was tempted "as we are," and thus empathy equals mercy. This is the key factor and lies at the heart of the Gospel. In justice we were doomed, in mercy we are saved.

The reality of Jesus' approach is twofold. His proclamation of mercy does not affect his proclamation of truth. At no stage in the Gospels are we told sin is not so bad. One need only look at the Passion, and all the tortures endured by the Savior to know the terrible price of sin. In fact, St. Matthew recounts the unequivocal words of Jesus, leaving no room for "liberal" interpretations:

> Do not think that I have come to abolish the law or the prophets; I have come not to abolish but to fulfill. For truly I tell you, until heaven and earth pass away, not one letter, not one stroke of a letter, will pass from the law until all is accomplished. Therefore, whoever breaks one of the least of these commandments, and teaches others to do the same, will be called least in the kingdom of heaven; but whoever does them and teaches them will be called great in the kingdom of heaven. For I tell you, unless your righteousness exceeds that of the scribes and Pharisees, you will never enter the kingdom of heaven. (Matt. 5:17–20)

Let us then never be tempted to ignore the gravity of sin, for the more one strives to reach the heights of holiness, the more one sees even the tiniest sin as an offence against God and his law of love. Jesus tells us: "Be perfect, therefore, as your heavenly Father is perfect." (Matt. 5:48), and thus we must place that commandment at the center of our spiritual lives. Having said that, the clear teaching from the Lord is that no matter how harsh we are on ourselves—and even at times that may not be the correct way forward—we must not judge others; we must show mercy, accepting that we are all sinners and that we cannot possibly know what lies beyond the outward appearance of someone else.

Three episodes from the Gospels reveal Jesus' dealings with adulterous women, and for the purposes of this book, and the general criticism aimed at *Amoris Laetitia*, they are essential to our understanding of an authentic theology of mercy.

St. Luke records one episode, the woman with ointment, and St. John records two: the meeting with the Samaritan woman at Jacob's Well; and the case of the woman caught in the act of adultery. We shall follow the chronological order.

In chapter 7 of St. Luke's Gospel, he tells the story of Jesus' dinner at Simon the Pharisee's house. While at table, a "sinful woman" who had learned of the Lord's presence arrived with an alabaster flask of ointment. She stood behind him weeping and began to bathe his feet with tears. She then proceeded to wipe them with her hair, kiss them, and finally anoint them with the ointment. Simon was saying to himself: "If this man were a prophet, he would have known who and what kind of woman this is who is touching him—that she is a sinner" (Lk. 7:39). Jesus replied:

> "Simon, I have something to say to you." "Teacher," he replied, "speak." "A certain creditor had two debtors; one owed five hundred denarii, and the other fifty. When they could not pay, he canceled the debts for both of them. Now which of them will love him more?" Simon answered, "I suppose the one for whom he canceled the greater debt." And Jesus said to him, "You have judged rightly." Then turning toward the woman, he said to Simon, "Do you see this woman? I entered your house; you gave me no water for my feet, but she has bathed my feet with her tears and dried them with her hair. You gave me no kiss, but from the time I came in she has not stopped kissing my feet. You did not anoint my head with oil, but she has anointed my feet with ointment. Therefore, I tell you, her sins, which were many, have

74

been forgiven; hence she has shown great love. But the one to whom little is forgiven, loves little." (Lk. 7:40–47)

Certain things are immediately apparent in this story. First, the woman is a public sinner; maybe not strictly an adulterer but certainly highly promiscuous. She is happy to offer herself without regard for God's law; perhaps someone we would refer to today as having a sexual addiction. No doubt even if she were not married, she would have been with men who were. The woman has almost certainly known of Jesus before; she seeks him out and displays no regard for interrupting Simon's hospitality. Shocking as it may seem to us, there appears to be an almost sexually charged atmosphere with what she proceeds to do. She brings her baggage—her way of acting toward men—with her. But there is a huge difference this time; no longer a seductive temptress, but a sorrowful, repentant woman in search of true love. Tears are shed, releasing possibly years of guilt at her way of life. Simon the Pharisee doesn't get it. In his eyes she is still damaged goods—and acting like it—and he cannot therefore see Jesus as a prophet since he doesn't realize what she is up to.

The real significance of the story, however, is Jesus' approach to her and his teaching on forgiveness and mercy. No conversation takes place between them, thus no questions are asked about how sorry she may be. In his silence, the Lord allows her repentance to speak for itself (which is implied through this act of pure love toward him). The suggestion is that her desire to do good has initiated the forgiveness that only God can offer; no words were necessary. Jesus however doesn't downplay her past in any way, in fact he reaffirms it to Simon, speaking of her "sins which were many," but still, her true love—as displayed in a few brief minutes—has been enough to erase from history her sinful past.

Relating this episode to that of Rahab, once again we can see how the grace of God began working through this woman even in the midst of serious sexual sin. At some stage before her entry into Simon's house, she had received the grace to desire a new start based on pure love. Divine mercy had begun moving her, and quite possibly long before this act of love had proved it, and thus for Jesus, she was never damaged goods ready to be abandoned to the eternal fire, but a soul in need of spiritual medicine.

Moving to St. John's Gospel, the first episode related occurs in chapter 4, and is the most relevant of the three to the situation concerning so many today in irregular relationships. The story begins with Jesus, who, while passing through Samaria, stops at Jacob's Well, in the town of Sychar. A Samaritan woman then arrives ready to draw water. Jesus says to her: "Give me a drink." The story then unfolds thus:

> The Samaritan woman said to him, "How is it that you, a Jew, ask a drink of me, a woman of Samaria?" (Jews do not share things in common with Samaritans.) Jesus answered her, "If you knew the gift of God, and who it is that is saying to you, 'Give me a drink,' you would have asked him, and he would have given you living water." The woman said to him, "Sir, you have no bucket, and the well is deep. Where do you get that living water? Are you greater than our ancestor Jacob, who gave us the well, and with his sons and his flocks drank from it?" Jesus said to her, "Everyone who drinks of this water will be thirsty again, but those who drink of the water that I will give them will never be thirsty. The water that I will give will become in them a spring of water gushing up to eternal life." The woman said to him, "Sir, give me this water, so that I may never be thirsty or have to keep coming here to draw water." Jesus said to her, "Go, call your husband, and come back." The woman answered him, "I have no husband." Jesus said to her, "You are right in saying, 'I have no husband'; for you have had five husbands, and the one you have now is not your husband. What you have said is true!" The woman said to him, "Sir, I see that you are a prophet. Our ancestors worshiped on this mountain, but you say that the place where people must worship is in Jerusalem." Jesus said to her, "Woman, believe me, the hour is coming when you will worship the Father neither on this mountain nor in Jerusalem. You worship what you do not know; we worship what we know, for salvation is from the Jews. But the hour is coming, and is now here, when the true worshipers will worship the Father in spirit and truth,

for the Father seeks such as these to worship him. God is spirit, and those who worship him must worship in spirit and truth." The woman said to him, "I know that Messiah is coming" (who is called Christ). "When he comes, he will proclaim all things to us." Jesus said to her, "I am he, the one who is speaking to you." (Jn. 4:9–26)

At this point, with the apostles returning from buying food in the town, the woman leaves her water jar, goes back to her townsfolk and says: "Come and see a man who told me everything I have ever done! He cannot be the Messiah, can he?" (Jn. 4:29).

This passage is incredibly rich in theological content and demands that we place ourselves within the scene, in the place of this woman. And for those struggling in an objectively sinful relationship, we may hope there is extra significance that will bring great spiritual benefits.

The first thing to take note of is the importance of the Well. It was built by Jacob, the great Patriarch of Israel, as a constant source of water for his family. Jesus, thirsty himself, sits down by it and awaits the woman he knows will soon come by. Both need water and both have water to give. The divine and human meet, not just in their persons, but in their activity. For Jesus, he is about to take the woman's water and reimburse her with a "new" water that's divine in origin. In essence the Lord's message is "Jacobs' Well is the past, I am the future." The meeting in itself is staggering; Samaritans and Jews did not mix, and on top of that, for Jesus to be alone with a Samaritan woman would also have been scandalous.[9]

Jesus instigates the conversation by asking for a drink, and upon the woman's stunned reply, he immediately reveals what this conversation is really about. He turns the attention on himself: "If you knew the gift of God, and who it is that is saying to you, 'Give me a drink.'" After a dialogue ensues in which Jesus opens her heart to desire his living water, he then tells her to go and get her husband and come back. Again, the motive is profound: to draw the woman's attention to the state of her parched soul. She answers by saying: "I have no husband," to which Jesus informs her of his knowledge about her previous five husbands—thus revealing his divine power. The conversation continues with the nature of true worship—that of spirit and truth—and the woman exclaims: "I know the Messiah is coming....When he comes, he will proclaim all things to us." At this point, something almost unheard of happens: Jesus reveals to this adulterous woman exactly who he is. When we bear in mind that throughout his three-year ministry, Jesus kept this fact a secret from virtually all but those closest to him, it is quite startling.

This revelation, we may presume, came from a deliberate choice to reward this woman's honesty and sincerity in desiring a change, and perhaps the joy in the Lord's heart at her conversion also had something to do with it. However, let us look at the woman herself. Again, as with the woman in St. Luke's Gospel, we are talking about a public sinner committing grave sins against the Ten Commandments, and yet she also displays signs of grace at work. She asks for the living water to bring her eternal life, she acknowledges that the present man in her life is not her true husband, and when she returns to her town, she exhibits evangelical zeal; in essence she becomes an instant missionary. From that work of love, a chain reaction occurs and many more Samaritans come to believe in Jesus; in fact, they beg him to stay with them.

So what can we deduce from Jesus' attitude toward her? Is there the presence of a cold legalist or a severe judge? On the contrary, we discover a God who instigates in a gentle and merciful way a process of engagement leading to conversion. His modus operandi is always to reach out no matter how evil the sinner and seek face-to-face encounters with patience and tender love. What we must realize is that if this is divine wisdom at work, then there is no better way to encourage sinners to return to the faith. Yes, at times in the past a fear of hell has done the trick, but did that produce the fruits Jesus wanted? Did that produce souls absolutely in love with him, or were they just fearful of his judgment?

Finally, if we look at this episode from the perspective of Holy Communion for certain divorced and remarried, we should consider carefully the initial exchange between Jesus and the woman. She is not waiting for him, it is he who is waiting for her. He tells her that if she had asked for living water he would have given it to her, emphasizing it as a "gift of God." Can we say that this Jesus is the same Jesus whom opponents of Pope Francis would have us believe does not want to enter the heart of a sinner like the Samaritan woman? This passage strongly suggests that for venial sinners in similar situations—those truly sorry for their present situation—Jesus desires to unite himself to them in order to help them attain the full measure of holiness to which he calls them. The dialogue presented to us reveals that Jesus didn't spend time subjecting her to an inquisition; rather, he manifests his love for her—this scandal-laden, public-sinning Samaritan woman—and focuses on showing her the way to worshipping how God the Father wants, and thus in time—on earth or eternity—she could be free from all sin.[10]

The final installment of this merciful triptych is probably the most famous of all and is surely the most impressive from a pastoral point of view. St. John recounts the story in chapter 8 of his Gospel. The story begins with Jesus teaching early one morning in the Temple area, when some scribes and Pharisees arrive with a woman caught in the very act of adultery. In order to test the Lord, they remind him that the Law of Moses "commands" them to stone her to death. What is his view they ask? Jesus bends down and begins writing on the ground with his finger. However, their persistence pays off and finally Jesus says: "Let anyone among you who is without sin be the first to throw a stone at her" (Jn. 8:7). Then he continues writing on the ground. Gradually they leave one by one beginning with the eldest until Jesus and the woman are left alone. The scene is now reminiscent of the beginning of the scene at the Well; Savior and adulterous sinner alone. As before, Jesus has no wish to condemn but to save, and thus he says: "Woman, where are they? Has no one condemned you?".... "Neither do I condemn you. Go your way, and from now on do not sin again" (Jn. 8:10–11).

If we descend down into the details of this episode, its importance becomes apparent. Primarily, the issue is about the Law. Yes, the Pharisees are putting Jesus on trial rather than the woman—who for them is finished anyway—but they want to see him enforce the law. What he does is provide a divine masterstroke that in effect renders that law of justice redundant. He certainly doesn't deny it, but he places an insurmountable obstacle in the way of those whose only interest is in "justice," and thus in effect, he introduces a new "canon" into the law; a clause that only he can utilize. At this point the woman's life is still in danger because this one man remains. But he has no interest in an outcome that will possibly jeopardize the woman's salvation. No, on the contrary his is a mission of mercy that will in time see him offer his life up for the sake of adulterers like this woman. The old Law of Justice becomes a new law of mercy; even Jesus' writing on the ground speaks of this. If we recall, the Law of Moses was written on stone tablets, but Jesus as "divine legislator" supersedes Moses, and thus we can see a symbolism where the "stone" of justice is now ground into the "dust" of mercy; the self-righteous pharisaical application of justice is obliterated by the greater attribute of God.

If we were to think that this event is solely aimed at compassion toward the woman, then we would be very much mistaken. Jesus is once again—as so often in the Gospels—highlighting the hypocrisy of the religious authorities, trying to get them to understand the meaning of the words "go and learn what this means, 'I desire mercy, not sacrifice'" (cf. Hos. 6:6, Matt. 9:13). This is a teaching for all times and should be reflected on by confessors, and in particular canon lawyers, for whom the temptation will be to administer or promote a law without ensuring the application does true justice to the situation and the souls involved; as if canon law stands on its own, rather than as a servant of truth. Humility must always be present, otherwise smugness, in thinking one has all the answers in a law book, could easily lead to a corrupt attitude that is divergent from the example of Jesus. Mercy and justice cannot be separated as they are bound together through the salvific actions of God; as St. Thomas Aquinas tells us: "From this it is evident that mercy does not weaken justice, but is the perfection of justice."[11]

One of the most contentious issues in the entire debate concerning Pope Francis' alteration in sacramental discipline surrounds the area of accepting in some cases that sexual relations may continue between a couple in an irregular situation. The argument says: How can there be a firm purpose of amendment if these activities continue? The theological response to this will be given in the next chapter, but from a biblical perspective, St. Paul seems to reveal an interior struggle similar to those who may feel, perhaps because children are now part of the family, that an ending to the physical element will cause so much resentment and pain that more evil will result, possibly even emotionally scarring those youngsters.

It is in his Letter to the Romans that the great apostle to the Gentiles draws back the veil of his soul; humbly admitting the sobering reality that confronts us all:

> For we know that the law is spiritual; but I am of the flesh, sold into slavery under sin. I do not understand my own actions. For I do not do what I want, but I do the very thing I hate. Now if I do what I do not want, I agree that the law is good. But in fact it is no longer I that do it, but sin that dwells within me. For I know that nothing good dwells within me, that is, in my flesh. I can will what is right, but I cannot do it. For I do not do the good I want, but the evil I do not want is what I do. Now if I do what I do not want, it is no longer I that do it, but sin that dwells within me. So I find it to be a law that when I want to do what is good, evil lies close at hand. For I delight in the law of God in my inmost self, but I see in my members another law at war with the law of my mind, making me captive to the law of sin that dwells in my members. Wretched man that I am! Who will rescue me from this body of death? Thanks be to God through Jesus Christ our Lord! So then, with my mind I am a slave to the law of God, but with my flesh I am a slave to the law of sin. (Rom. 7:14–25)

Surely the most pertinent part of this passage is St. Paul's declaration that he takes an interior delight in the law of God, yet his flesh rebels against that desire. It reminds us of Tamar's good intention versus evil action; unquestionably the intention is for a life that is oriented toward God, but the lures of Satan, the world, and the flesh are at times overwhelming. It is significant that the holy apostle refers to himself as a captive—one who is held against his will and deprived of his freedom—and so the question has to be asked: In the eyes of God, what takes precedence, the flesh or the spirit? Jesus gives us the answer as recounted in the Gospel of St. John: "It is the spirit that gives life; the flesh is useless" (Jn. 6:63). The great French thinker Blaise Pascal spoke in his *Pensees* of two natures battling for domination within, one good and one bad, and through original sin, the second evil nature has been able

81

to set up home. Of course, because all creation originates from God, and especially the soul, the good is always more prominent and certainly stronger because its source is divine, whereas evil, not being primal, only derives from the freedom to act as a consequence of original sin.

St. Paul, in chapter 8 of the Letter to the Romans, takes up these words—*the spirit* and *the flesh*—and offers the correct interpretation on how to discern which of these two natures has the upper hand; which way the will of the person is orientated. He endorses immediately, as a continuation from his words in the previous chapter ("With my mind I am a slave to the law of God, but with my flesh I am a slave to the law of sin" [Rom 7:25]), the firm principle that there is a "security" for those true believers who strive to be disciples of the Lord, notwithstanding their weaknesses: "There is therefore now no condemnation for those who are in Christ Jesus" (Rom. 8:1). He further explains the difference between two opposing wills, that of the faithful and faithless:

> For those who live according to the flesh set their minds on the things of the flesh, but those who live according to the Spirit set their minds on the things of the Spirit. To set the mind on the flesh is death, but to set the mind on the Spirit is life and peace. For this reason the mind that is set on the flesh is hostile to God; it does not submit to God's law—indeed it cannot, and those who are in the flesh cannot please God. But you are not in the flesh; you are in the Spirit, since the Spirit of God dwells in you. Anyone who does not have the Spirit of Christ does not belong to him. But if Christ is in you, though the body is dead because of sin, the Spirit is life because of righteousness. (Rom. 8:5–10)

So, taken together, there is no contradiction between these two chapters; what they describe is a significant ontological difference: someone who struggles with sins of the flesh, yet who desires to break free from them; and someone who lives by sexual pleasure as a "legitimate" alternative. For Catholics who have an irregular marital status and who recognize that reality of their situation—as did the Samaritan woman—there is hope that St. Paul's words can give some measure of comfort in their anguish. While sin is always sin, individual circumstances can render culpability much less; even nonexistent in some cases, and thus the mercy of God should always be trusted.

This takes us to our final point in this chapter: is there biblical evidence that Jesus preaches this theological concept of reduced culpability in matters of serious sin? In St. John' Gospel, we encounter two instances where this truth is proclaimed: the first occurs in chapter 9 after Jesus had cured the blind man. After hearing Jesus say: "I came into this world for judgment so that those who do not see may see, and those who do see may become blind" (Jn. 9:39), some Pharisees said: "Surely we are not blind, are we? (Jn. 9:40) to which Jesus replied: "If you were blind, you would not have sin. But now that you say, 'We see,' your sin remains" (Jn. 9:41). Later, in the presence of Pontius Pilate, Jesus told him: "You would have no power over me unless it had been given you from above; therefore the one who handed me over to you is guilty of a greater sin" (Jn. 19:11). Moving to St. Luke's Gospel, he recounts that while Jesus was suffering the terrible pain of his crucifixion, he implored God's mercy on those who had clamored for his death: "Father, forgive them; for they do not know what they are doing." (Lk. 23:34). And later, in the aftermath of Pentecost, St. Peter told the crowds at the Portico of Solomon that they and their leaders had acted out of ignorance in condemning Jesus (see Acts 3:17), while St. Paul's Letter to Timothy reinforces the point: "...even though I was formerly a blasphemer, a persecutor, and a man of violence. But I received mercy because I had acted ignorantly in unbelief" (1 Tim. 1:13).

Without doubt then, we can be certain that Jesus in his judging takes into account every single factor in deciding the amount of guilt a person has; thus when judgment arrives, it is perfect in its application. From this angle, it is also consoling to read these beautiful words of Sacred Scripture: "They look on the outward appearance, but the LORD looks on the heart" (1 Sam. 16:7). Reflecting on this axiom, we discover the gulf between divine and human judgment: the heart encourages mercy; the appearance encourages superficiality. Equally, the same idea applies to a gradation of expectation for those aspiring to follow the Lord. In the parable of the vigilant and faithful servants, Jesus says:

But if that slave says to himself, "My master is delayed in coming," and if he begins to beat the other slaves, men and women, and to eat and drink and get drunk, the master of that slave will come on a day when he does not expect him and at an hour that he does not know, and will cut him in pieces, and put him with the unfaithful. That slave who knew what his master wanted, but did not prepare himself or do what was wanted, will receive a severe beating. But the one who did not know and did what deserved a beating will receive a light beating. From everyone to whom much has been given, much will be required; and from the one to whom much has been entrusted, even more will be demanded. (Lk. 12:45–48)

Returning to the original question posed at the outset of this chapter, we can rightfully affirm that Pope Francis' conception of mercy is aligned perfectly with the notion of mercy found in the Canon of Sacred Scripture. In fact, the whole span of salvation history speaks of this, from the protoevangelium in Genesis chapter 3, where God reveals his plan to destroy the work of Satan and restore humanity to communion with God, through the Incarnation, Death, and Resurrection of the Savior, to the final Passover when evil will be destroyed forever at the end of time. By focusing deliberately on the great pagan sinners rather than the chosen ones like King David, or St. Paul, we have been able to decipher the mysterious yet marvellous way God's grace is still able to envelop a soul disfigured by original sin. This should give confidence and reassurance to those blessed with baptism in objective gravely sinful situations that as long as the will, the intention, is to cling to the Cross, then God will be close to them with his mercy.

Let us not forget the beautiful image of Jesus the Good Shepherd carrying the lost sheep on his shoulders. He deliberately goes in search of those furthest afield; those who are almost impossible to find because of the sinful distance they might have travelled. But it is precisely these for whom his joy is greatest, because only he can find and save them; only he can bandage the wounds that for the sheep may seem impossible. We must constantly remind ourselves that nothing is unachievable with God, no matter the complexity of a situation or the feeling of there being no way out. What the

Scriptures tell us is that we are all sinners, and just because a sin may be intrinsically evil—as in the case of adultery— as opposed to one that is not, does not change the fact that for God, our good intention can lessen greatly the guilt. Jesus knows very well the social and emotional factors that will undoubtedly affect many second civil marriages where children are involved, and what he asks above all is a sincere desire to work toward an eventual path where purity of intention is matched by purity of being. This perhaps explains why in the conversation with the Samaritan woman he doesn't dwell on the adultery question but changes the course of the conversation quickly toward a better prayer life. We don't have the answers, but perhaps he knew her case was far more complex than that of the woman caught in the act of adultery, and this would possibly explain the different tone and content.

One thing we can take away from this chapter is that the Bible speaks of Christian realism; it is littered with sinners committing some truly horrendous acts. It does not present or promote a fantasy ideal where grace works like magic and where Jesus is a divine wizard. The journey to our own personal Easter Sunday will be painful and gradual; it will have its ups and downs, but through it all, it will be accompanied by a God who is both merciful and patient. May that be our hope and our joy!

NOTES

1. "Some theologians affirm that mercy is the greatest of the attributes and perfections of God, and the Bible, Tradition and the whole faith life of the People of God provide particular proofs of this. It is not a question here of the perfection of the inscrutable essence of God in the mystery of the divinity itself, but of the perfection and attribute whereby man, in the intimate truth of his existence, encounters the living God particularly closely and particularly often." St. John Paul II, Encyclical Letter, *Dives in Misericordia*, no. 13, November 30, 1980, www.vatican.va.

2. Pope Francis, "First Greetings of the Holy Father," March 13, 2013, www.vatican.va.

3. Pope Benedict XVI, Homily at Mass for the Ninetieth Birthday of Cardinal Thomas Spidlik, December 17, 2009, www.vatican.va.

4. *Catechism of the Catholic Church*, no. 1753, www.vatican.va.

5. St. Cyprian of Carthage, Epistle 75, www.newadvent.org.

6. St. Augustine of Hippo, *Contra Faustum*, no. 83, www.newadvent.org. In no. 84, Augustine discusses the symbolism of Tamar's evil husbands, and Judah's third son to the Kingdom of Judah. The two husbands represent two classes of kings who govern either through evil (Er) or those who do nothing at all (Onan). The third son who never married Tamar represents the continued existence of the Tribe of Judah, but without a King.

7. St. Ephraim, Hymn on the Nativity, no. 7, www.newadvent.org.

8. We may recall the *Exultet* Easter chant joyfully proclaims: "O truly necessary sin of Adam…O happy fault."

9. Pope Francis explains this in his own inimitable way: "The Gospel says that the disciples marvelled that their Master was speaking to this woman. But the Lord is greater than prejudice, which is why he was not afraid to address the Samaritan woman: mercy is greater than prejudice. We must learn this well! Mercy is greater than prejudice, and Jesus is so very merciful, very!" Pope Francis, Angelus Address, March 23, 2014, www.vatican.va.

10. By revealing himself to the Samaritan woman as the Son of God and proclaiming the type of worship the Eternal Father desires, Jesus seems to anticipate the new stage of salvation history that is about to emerge through his Passion, Death, and Resurrection. The woman can thus become part of the New Israel, attaining salvation through baptism and conversion. It seems significant that the Lord, in his dialogue with the woman, does not discuss possible changes to her circumstances or order her to leave the man she is with. Is this a recognition of the reality of her situation, of the irreversibility of history because children are now a factor?

11. St. Thomas Aquinas, *Summa Theologiæ*, I, q. 21, a. 3 ad 2, www.newadvent.org.

V *CARITAS IN VERITATE*: THE MORAL THEOLOGY OF CHAPTER 8

I n chapter 2, we dissected the highly controversial eighth chapter of *Amoris Laetitia*. We discovered a fervent desire of Pope Francis to reintegrate back into the Church the divorced and remarried who seek to participate fully in the Sacraments, and that analysis has laid the foundations for what must come next. In essence, this present chapter on the moral theology behind the Holy Father's new pastoral application must be seen as the fulcrum of the entire debate. Without it, doubts will possibly remain; not only to the wisdom of this papal initiative, but possibly its validity from a faith and morals perspective. Thus it is essential to present an articulate and theologically accurate case for this courageous change in sacramental discipline.

To begin, let us look at what St. John Paul II taught concerning the ban on divorced and remarried receiving Holy Communion:

> However, the Church reaffirms her practice, which is based upon Sacred Scripture, of not admitting to Eucharistic Communion divorced persons who have remarried. They are unable to be admitted thereto from the fact that their state and condition of life objectively contradict that union of love between Christ and the Church which is signified and effected by the Eucharist. Besides this, there is another special pastoral reason: if these people were admitted to the Eucharist, the faithful would be led into

87

error and confusion regarding the Church's teaching about the indissolubility of marriage.[1]

The Scriptural passage that St. John Paul refers to and confirmed by Pope Benedict XVI in his Apostolic Exhortation *Sacramentum Caritatis* is Mark chapter 10 in which Jesus confirms: "Whoever divorces his wife and marries another commits adultery against her; and if she divorces her husband and marries another, she commits adultery" (Mk. 10:11–12). Adultery is a sin against the sixth commandment and thus a sin of grave matter. It has often been assumed through the past two millennia that all adulterers must be in a state of mortal sin and thus these words of warning from St. Paul would apply to them: "Whoever, therefore, eats the bread or drinks the cup of the Lord in an unworthy manner will be answerable for the body and blood of the Lord....For all who eat and drink without discerning the body, eat and drink judgment against themselves" (1 Cor. 11:27, 29).

In *Amoris Laetitia*, however, Pope Francis has given a more nuanced approach to this matter. He States: "It can no longer simply be said that all those in any 'irregular' situation are living in a state of mortal sin and are deprived of sanctifying grace."[2] So what is and what constitutes a mortal sin? A mortal sin is one that destroys charity; it rebels completely against God's grace and mortally wounds the soul. To die unrepentant in this state is to be consigned to hell for all eternity. According to the *Catechism of the Catholic Church*, three things must be met together in order for a mortal sin to occur: the object must be grave matter (sins against the Ten Commandments), it must be committed with full knowledge, and deliberate consent must also be given. If any of those three are missing, the sin is venial, which, although serious, does not lead to spiritual death. Mortal sin can only be forgiven in the Sacrament of Confession, or if that is not possible, a perfect act of contrition must be said expressing profound sorrow for committing an offense against the love of God. The constant teaching of the Church is that persons guilty of mortal sin must not receive Holy Communion; otherwise an even greater sin of sacrilege is imputed to their soul.

The entire theological framework for chapter 8 then is the possibly reduced culpability of the persons involved in irregular unions. For Pope Francis, the secular intrusions on Catholic moral principles in recent decades have left the flock—especially the young—very vulnerable to erroneous ideas about the indissolubility of marriage, true love, and commitment. There is no doubt that many Catholics in second civil marriages would be horrified at the accusation that they are committing adultery; and in the same way, contracepting couples would similarly dismiss the notion that they are not really "giving" themselves to each other. The Holy Father states: "More is involved here than mere ignorance of the rule. A subject may know full well the rule, yet have great difficulty in understanding 'its inherent values.'"[3]

So let us ask the question: Is this idea of subjective culpability a novelty that is designed to ease the conscience of those involved, in essence erasing the constant teaching on mortal sin? The short answer is no, but the seriousness of the matter necessitates that we sift through the body of traditional Catholic moral theology, allowing us hopefully, to come to the firm conviction that what Pope Francis teaches is absolutely correct.

We have already seen that in Sacred Scripture, there is unequivocal evidence that Jesus himself taught this moral principle; thus everything that has come since then has been geared to developing our understanding of this truth and incorporating it into the theology of sin and guilt. The *Catechism of the Catholic Church* teaches this in several sections concerning morality and the Ten Commandments: "Imputability and responsibility for an action can be diminished or even nullified by ignorance, inadvertence, duress, fear, habit, inordinate attachments, and other psychological or social factors."[4] And again: "To form an equitable judgment about the subjects' moral responsibility and to guide pastoral action, one must take into account the affective immaturity, force of acquired habit, conditions of anxiety, or other psychological or social factors that lessen or even extenuate moral culpability."[5] It is precisely to "guide pastoral action" that has led Pope Francis to promote a careful discernment process between confessor and penitent; one that would seek to discover the truth about the state of one's soul and the possibility that mortal sin may not be present.

One of the earliest extant Christian writings, the *First Letter to the Corinthians of Pope St. Clement I,* speaks of there being "less guilt upon you," in respect of the Corinthians partiality toward the Apostles and a man approved by them, during the time of "factions" of which St. Paul had spoken. St. Augustine in the fourth century taught that if consent was not given, no sin could be imputed to the person; for such guilt to be attributed, the free will to act would have to be in operation, thus making the decision voluntary.[6]

St. Thomas Aquinas, the great thirteenth-century Dominican theologian was perhaps the first to really explore the fundamentals of sin, guilt, and free will. In his *Summa Theologica*, he explains that an erring conscience cannot be excused through negligence when someone really should know how to act in a particular situation: "But if the error arise from ignorance of some circumstance, and without any negligence, so that it cause the act to be involuntary, then that error of reason or conscience excuses the will, that abides by that erring reason, from being evil."[7] Aquinas also states that other factors can come into play that would lessen the guilt; fear for example: "Yet one's sin would be extenuated somewhat, for what is done through fear is less voluntary, because when fear lays hold of a man he is under a certain necessity of doing a certain thing. Hence the Philosopher (Ethic. iii, 1) says that these things that are done through fear are not simply voluntary, but a mixture of voluntary and involuntary....Fear excuses, not in the point of its sinfulness, but in the point of its involuntariness."[8]

One of the most important aspects in discerning subjective culpability is the relationship between will and emotion. We can will that a sinful action does not take place and yet the emotions, the passions, can interfere to some extent. The lures of concupiscence can wreak havoc in a soul that is normally absolute in its desire to live a life of purity. This pull, garnered from the devastation of original sin, explains why certain temptations become persistent and debilitating. It is a power that can compel one to reconsider performing immoral acts that in a normal state would never be considered. St. Thomas Aquinas says that although the emotions cannot directly interfere with the will, they can do so indirectly through distraction, which in effect means that attention is diverted toward the immoral act in such a way that other options of avoidance are ignored.

Aquinas calls sin committed from the passions as "sins of weakness":

Therefore weakness of the soul is when the soul is hindered from fulfilling its proper action on account of a disorder in its parts. Now as the parts of the body are said to be out of order, when they fail to comply with the order of nature, so too the parts of the soul are said to be inordinate, when they are not subject to the order of reason, for the reason is the ruling power of the soul's parts. Accordingly, when the concupiscible or irascible power is affected by any passion contrary to the order of reason, the result being that an impediment arises in the aforesaid manner to the due action of man, it is said to be a sin of weakness.[9]

Traditionally, there are four kinds of sins of weakness that can render as sin of grave matter venial rather than mortal:

1. emotions causing a person to act in a manner contrary to their normal disposition
2. emotions causing a person to ignore a morally required choice
3. weakness stemming from distress, sadness, anger, concupiscence, etc.
4. quasi-compulsive, in which the penitent struggles in a continuous cycle of sin and repentance originating from a particular recurrent temptation such as certain sexual sins

St. Thomas Aquinas states that the amount of guilt is proportionate to the amount of voluntariness, and that in turn is determined by the way passions interfere with will and reason before a sinful act takes place.[10] In his view, it is also possible that no sin is present if the use of reason is taken away to such an extent that the "act" becomes wholly involuntary.

If we look at some recent interventions of the magisterium, over the past forty years, we discover a maturation of understanding in relation to factors governing the extent of guilt in matters of grave sin. Psychology, for instance, is one area that has opened up vistas of opportunity to comprehend emotional, habitual, immature, or imbalanced behaviour. In 1975, the Congregation for the Doctrine of Faith issued a document entitled *Persona Humana* that stated: "It is true that in sins of the sexual order, in view of their kind and their causes, it more easily happens that free consent is not fully given; this is a fact which calls for caution in all judgment as to the subject's responsibility."[11] In 1986, the Congregation published a Letter on the *Pastoral Care of Homosexual Persons* that struck a similar tone: "Here, the Church's wise moral tradition is necessary since it *warns against generalizations in judging individual cases. In fact, circumstances may exist, or may have existed in the past, which would reduce or remove the culpability of the individual in a given instance;* or other circumstances may increase it."[12]

The Congregation's warning about generalizations is exactly the point Pope Francis has highlighted in *Amoris Laetitia*, and reminds us that only God can be the true judge concerning matters that are so complex. Suffice it to say, in this era of Christian realism, most Catholics are well aware of the difficulties and temptations that constantly bombard them and thus, it may be that the natural reaction is no longer to assume that the divorced and remarried couple in the next pew are mortal sinners.[13]

If we return to the text of *Amoris Laetitia's* chapter 8, we can see the influence of Aquinas' moral theology on the Pope's teaching. Of the three principles utilized that we discovered earlier in the book—practical reason, mitigating factors, and the correlation between objective sin and subjective guilt—it is practical reason where we locate a convergence of understanding between Aquinas and the Holy Father. For Pope Francis, we can no longer consider individual actions (or lack of) separate from the rest of one's spiritual life. He is very careful to state that rules can never be "disregarded or neglected," but equally he states that they cannot cover every scenario, and if not allied to the truth of subjective guilt, this could give a superficial and error-strewn discernment of a person's soul. Aquinas admits this is the case:

> Although there is necessity in the general principles, the more we descend to matters of detail, the more frequently we encounter defects....In matters of action, truth or practical rectitude is not the same for all, as to matters of detail, but only as to the general principles;

and where there is the same rectitude in matters of detail, it is not equally known to all....The principle will be found to fail, according as we descend further into detail.[14]

The thrust of this argument is that while the general principles are known to all through natural law and divinely revealed truths such as the Ten Commandments, the existential factors of an individual's life can be such that a general absolute moral norm for all is not possible in every single scenario. What is expected by God is that each person makes a carefully judged decision on what is the right thing to do in a particular situation. Thus practical reason and the virtue of prudence are married together to form a judgment that in conscience can give moral certainty and peace of mind. However, it may be the case that someone else in the same situation arrives at a different conclusion, or that later, armed with other facts, we ourselves would have made a different choice. An example would be the case of driving a car at a junction, and letting another car out; it's a charitable thing to do, but it may be that we decide the car behind us is too close and not paying attention, thus by slowing we may collide. Another person in the same scenario may decide actually there is no danger from behind and slow down; or in the case of a seriously injured person on life support, the advice of doctors may be that there is no hope and the machine should be turned off. Most would reluctantly say "ok we don't want to, but we accept your expertise and judgment." Someone of great faith however may say "no leave it on for now. I trust in the Communion of Saints, God will provide a miracle." Both scenarios would be morally acceptable, but having different conclusions.

This is what Aquinas means when he refers to the principle failing as we descend further into detail. In essence, everyone acts on the amount of moral knowledge and wisdom they have, and even where good will is evident, the choice may be morally defective. On the other hand, Pope Francis is careful to state that this process of practical discernment in particular cases cannot be elevated to the level of a rule, otherwise an "intolerable casuistry" would ensue; nobody is exempt from following the natural law inscribed upon the human heart. This naturally invites us to contemplate the vital issue of conscience, that mechanism of decision-making where choices are made that affect the moral and spiritual life, and ultimately eternal salvation.

The Second Vatican Council began a new era for moral theology, one that moved away from a manualist approach where a rule book was consulted to ascertain the moral correctness of an act, to one centerd on the relationship between the individual and Christ; essentially a more rounded approach that was Christological and biblical. Conscience was now described as the "most secret core and sanctuary of a man. There he is alone with God."[15] Strikingly, *Gaudium et Spes* also taught that "conscience frequently errs from invincible ignorance without losing its dignity."[16] While in *Lumen Gentium*, we also discover a major doctrinal development applicable to the unbaptized: "Those also can attain to salvation who through no fault of their own do not know the Gospel of Christ or His Church, yet sincerely seek God and moved by grace strive by their deeds to do His will as it is known to them through the dictates of conscience."[17]

Traditionally, there are two levels of conscience: *anamnesis*, the memory of goodness and truth within our being, and *conscientia*, judgment and decisions then formulated. *Anamnesis* is the philosophical idea that deep within man is implanted an interior law of love and truth that guides one toward the divine. It is not something exterior, but an ontological tendency that gives proof to the theological belief that man is created in the image and likeness of God. Understood in this way, anamnesis acts like a divine torch that illuminates the pilgrimage through life; its "memory" impels each day—for those seeking the right path—the constant desire to reach out, to see oneself as a nomad in the world, seeking the true heavenly homeland. Consequently, anamnesis could be seen as an interior warning at the approach of evil. It knows the natural law; the Ten Commandments are rooted in its genetic code; it is a majestic force for good. *Conscientia*, on the other hand, is the process of decision-making. St. Thomas Aquinas explained it as consisting of three stages: recognizing, bearing witness, and judgment. All the factors surrounding an act are taken into consideration, and then the decision is made. Now, of course, that decision could be wrong, but in Catholic teaching, even the erroneous conscience binds: "A human being must always obey the certain judgment of his conscience. If he were deliberately to act against it, he would condemn himself. Yet it can happen that moral conscience remains in ignorance and makes erroneous judgments about acts to be performed or already committed."[18]

So if an erroneous conscience binds, where is the fault? The fault undoubtedly comes from the care and attention given to anamnesis. It is possible to ignore the divine promptings and dampen the inner fire that burns to such an extent that the moral compass goes wildly astray. Because of this we can never say that subjectivity takes precedence over objectivity; certainly it can affect the amount of guilt as we have already seen, but unless an act is completely involuntary, guilt will remain to a certain extent. This notion is essential to understanding how evildoers who are not Christian can still be guilty of mortal sin. Without knowing the theological definitions, their blatant disregard for anamnesis with full knowledge and deliberate consent can render them just as guilty as anyone else. If the natural law was not inscribed on every human heart, then mortal sin would be impossible in areas of morality.[19]

From what we have just described, we see how a modern understanding of freedom—one where each individual is an infallible judge guided by the subjective—is one that leads to the pit of atheism and descent into moral darkness. We cannot ever propose a system that betrays the dignity of man. In times as evil as ours, a bold proclamation of conscience as a means to encounter the truth and freedom of Jesus Christ (cf. Jn. 8:32) must be a constant message relayed to the souls entrusted to the Church. Anything other than that would be treachery of the worst kind. This explains why Pope Francis reminds pastors that "naturally, every effort should be made to encourage the development of an enlightened conscience."[20] Still, we must affirm that not everyone acts out of malice. Many divorced and remarried Catholics will have never really known the faith; in essence they will at some stage of their lives have been little more than baptized pagans. Is that their fault? Can they be blamed for not understanding the indissolubility of marriage? Does God makes allowances for honest mistakes?

It seems to me that in order to offer a genuine moral theology that is of real benefit for those couples in invalid second marriages, we must not be frightened to proclaim the entire truth; in fact, we have a duty to do it. Justice and mercy demand it; Jesus demands

it. This inevitably involves the nature of adultery. It has been suggested by some that perhaps Pope Francis, in his zeal for mercy,
has made the distinction between what is and isn't sin rather
murky. That by loosening the strictness of sacramental discipline
somehow the Church now condones adultery. In reality, nothing
could be further from the truth. We must maintain—as does Pope
Francis—that adultery is an intrinsically evil act; one that is always
wrong. St. John Paul II stated in his moral theology Encyclical *Veritatis Splendor*:

> Reason attests that there are objects of the human act
> which are by their nature "incapable of being ordered"
> to God, because they radically contradict the good of the
> person made in his image. These are the acts which, in
> the Church's moral tradition, have been termed "intrin-
> sically evil" (*intrinsece malum*): they are such always and
> per se, in other words, on account of their very object,
> and quite apart from the ulterior intentions of the one
> acting and the circumstances. Consequently, without in
> the least denying the influence on morality exercised by
> circumstances and especially by intentions, the Church
> teaches that "there exist acts which per se and in them-
> selves, independently of circumstances, are always seri-
> ously wrong by reason of their object."[21]

There are many other acts that come under the umbrella
of intrinsic evils: homicide, genocide, abortion, artificial contraception, euthanasia and voluntary suicide, mutilation, physical and mental torture, offences toward human dignity, such as
subhuman living conditions, slave labor, arbitrary imprisonment,
deportation, slavery, and prostitution and trafficking in women
and children. The teaching of the Church is that a good intention
can never transform an intrinsically evil act into something that
is good or morally defensible; thus a "Robin Hood" style stealing
from the rich to give to the poor is still wrong, regardless of the
intention of aiding the needy. However, in the case of a confessor
discerning levels of guilt, Blessed Paul VI did state that "sometimes
it is lawful to *tolerate* a lesser moral evil in order to avoid a greater
evil or in order to promote a greater good."[22] That doesn't alter

the fact that it is never lawful, even for the gravest reasons, to do evil that good may come of it; in the face of constant criticism from some conservative and traditionalist quarters, it must be reaffirmed that at no time does *Amoris Laetitia* suggest that adultery is no longer wrong in certain cases, or that it possess some moral good. What we come back to is the influences and circumstances that mitigate the guilt to such an extent that in some cases it is no longer present. St. John Paul II stated in *Veritatis Splendor*: "It is possible that the evil done as the result of invincible ignorance or a non-culpable error of judgment may not be imputable to the agent."[23]

One of the most interesting documents issued by the Congregation for the Doctrine of the Faith, and significantly from the era of St. John Paul II and Cardinal Ratzinger, is the "*Moral Norm of Humanae Vitae and Pastoral Duty.*" This letter of clarification is almost identical to *Amoris Laetitia* (nos. 301–2) and contains ample evidence that there is a hermeneutic of continuity where moral theology is concerned:

> The same Christian moral tradition just referred to [acts that are intrinsically evil], has also always maintained the distinction—not the separation and still less an opposition —between objective disorder and subjective guilt. Accordingly, when it is a matter of judging subjective moral behaviour without ever setting aside the norm which prohibits the intrinsic disorder of contraception, it is entirely licit to take into due consideration the various factors and aspects of the person's concrete action, not only the person's intentions and motivations, but also the diverse circumstances of life, in the first place all those causes which may affect the person's knowledge and free will. This subjective situation, while it can never change into something ordered that which is intrinsically disordered, may to a greater or lesser extent modify the responsibility of the person who is acting. *As is well known, this is a general principle, applicable to every moral disorder*, even if intrinsic, it is accordingly applicable also to contraception.[24]

Although the document specifically refers to contraception, it is noticeable that "every moral disorder" should be judged by the close connection of objective disorder and subjective guilt; thus the culpability of adultery must be discerned carefully, taking into account every fact possible. This is not the only point of theological continuity that interests us. We read:

> In this line, the concept of the "law of gradualness" has been rightly developed, not only in moral and pastoral theology, but also on the level of pronouncements of the Magisterium itself. However, this law must not in the slightest way be confused with the unacceptable idea of a "gradualness of the law," as is clearly and explicitly stated in the Exhortation *Familiaris Consortio* (no. 34).[25]

Although these terms may appear similar, there is a world of difference in their meaning, and thus it is necessary to clarify them, as much needless confusion has been created in the wake of *Amoris Laetitia*. The theory of "gradualness of the law" is one that teaches that there are stages in one's life where advancement toward accepting the divine moral law can occur step by step. Thus a couple may decide for instance, to use artificial contraception— as a legitimate choice—for a certain time, and then only later consider an acceptable moral option. This is in reality utilizing the "creative" conscience error. On the other hand, the "law of gradualness" is the premise that a person advances through life, deepening their appreciation and understanding of the moral law as they respond to grace. The difference between the two concepts is that in the first, a deliberate decision is made to ignore divine laws; whereas in the second, the heart is always open, and erroneous decisions come from ignorance or weakness.

So far, we have looked at a variety of issues that have given us the foundations of traditional Catholic moral theology. We have discovered that in order to ascertain the entire truth behind a person's spiritual state, it is not enough to just consider the objective grave sin in isolation. We must look to the circumstances, the motivation, and the will that led to an immoral act taking place. To ignore subjective guilt as part of the judgment is to deny a person their right to a defense. It is to condemn them without trial. We have also refuted suggestions that adultery may at times be morally good, and corrected the assumption that conscience can decide for itself what acts may be right or wrong. It is thus certain that Pope Francis is in perfect continuity with his predecessors in applying pastoral care to moral laws.

At this point, however, I want to delve deeper into the specific situations facing the many thousands if not millions of Catholics in second civil marriages. It seems to me that we must take these teachings off the page so to speak, and administer them to those situations especially where there is a real desire to live an authentic life of faith; to be part of the family of the Church and not treated as public "sinners." In this way, I hope to give encouragement to those brothers and sisters, to show them a path back full of hope for the future, and with the blessing of the Lord.

If we are to look into real life situations, naturally the question arises: Are all cases of adultery the same? Do circumstances really make a difference, or is everything black and white? St. John Paul II in *Familiaris Consortio* recognized there are certainly gray areas:

> Pastors must know that, for the sake of truth, they are obliged to exercise careful discernment of situations. There is in fact a difference between those who have sincerely tried to save their first marriage and have been unjustly abandoned, and those who through their own grave fault have destroyed a canonically valid marriage. Finally, there are those who have entered into a second union for the sake of the children's upbringing, and who are sometimes subjectively certain in conscience that their previous and irreparably destroyed marriage had never been valid.[26]

Pope Francis also accepted this is the case: "The divorced who have entered a new union, for example, can find themselves in a variety of situations, which should not be pigeonholed or fit into overly rigid classifications leaving no room for a suitable personal and pastoral discernment."[27] It seems certain, based on Jesus' teaching on subjective culpability in the Gospels, that we must not consider every act of adultery in the same way, even if objectively the sin is identical. Could we possibly say that the man who leaves his wife and young children for another woman out of lust, or lack of commitment to his family, is the same as the man, who, abandoned by his wife years previously, tries to live alone respecting the law and yet who almost accidently falls in love with a friend in the midst of a painful loneliness? The rigid will say yes, they are the same; and on one level they are correct. But the point is, does God see it that way? Does the Almighty have a pastoral side that, while recognizing the sin, sees the way the second woman has entered this man's life, not for sinister purposes, but to bring comfort and friendship? Does he take into account the love and compassion he gave these people as part of their spiritual and emotional make up, and that led to this second union? Does he balance on his scales of divine justice the adultery against the original innocent act of charity and friendship? In my view, that is precisely the way divine mercy works. The Lord will *deliberately* look for any mitigating factors, because his will is for all to be saved (see 1 Tim. 2:4).

At the risk of being misunderstood, we should clarify that the Church asks people in irregular unions who cannot separate for legitimate reasons to live as brother and sister. This is not an "ideal" in a formal sense, but may seem it in the practical circumstances of everyday life. This teaching remains unaltered, contrary to the belief of some opponents of Pope Francis. But what of the scenario where a couple in a second, civil "marriage" already have children and who know that this celibate life is not realistic? Is this a dilemma with no way out? Is it an impossibility for them to refrain?

In order to answer this question, we can turn to the teaching of the Council of Trent that stated:

> But no one ought to think that, because he is justified, he is released from obligation to keep the commandments; nor is that rash saying to be used, which the fathers have prohibited and anathematized, "that it is impossible for a justified man to keep God's precepts": for God does not enjoin impossibilities, but commands, and admonishes us to do what we can, and to ask his help for what we cannot perform, and by his grace we are strengthened.[28]

It is clear therefore that we cannot use as an excuse the idea that sufficient grace is not available. The real question that couples face in this situation is one of Christian realism and the possible knock on effects for others in the home, notably children. Christian realism doesn't deny that the sixth commandment is impossible to obey; rather, it recognizes that for ordinary Catholics who do not possess a high level of virtue or sanctity, the chances of avoiding sexual relations are slim. On this point we have an important teaching of Pope St. Gregory II. In 726, St. Boniface had written to the Pope with a series of questions, one of which related to a man whose wife was unable to have sexual intercourse. The Pope stated: "It were best if he could continue as he is and practise self-restraint. But since this demands exceptional virtue, the man who cannot live in continence had better marry."[29] St. Gregory stated that the man should still look after his first wife since her problems had arisen from health issues rather than anything else.[30]

So we see here how there is a subtle but truthful distinction; and it must be said that in all probability, those persons in possession of exceptional virtue would not be in a civil marriage in the first place; although that is not to discount the possibility that someone later finds their faith during a situation of objective grave sin. Even the young professor Joseph Ratzinger, the future Pope Benedict XVI, accepted this reality, for in a 1972 essay in which he proposed a way for Holy Communion to be given in certain cases for the divorced and remarried, he referred to cases where "practically speaking abstinence presents no real possibility."[31]

This leads us to the question of forgiveness of sin, and firm purpose of amendment. Until recently the Sacrament of Confession has not been available to persons engaged in continuous sexual relations within an invalid marriage because it has been assumed that there is no repentance, or desire to change sinful ways, and thus sins cannot be forgiven. So how is this now possible? The answer lies squarely in the intention of the person committing the sin. Before we proceed further though, a distinction needs to be made. St. John Paul II is clear that good intentions can never transform evil into good; there is no possibility that adultery in any form can be considered to have a divine blessing. But what about the intention itself, separate from the act? This seems to me where the crux of the issue lies. St. Alphonsus de Liguori, the great moral theologian and Doctor of the Church opines: "Not only does one who acts from an invincibly erroneous conscience not sin, he probably acquires merit."[32] St. Augustine also teaches good intentions are rewarded. In his *Confessions*, he refers to his pagan friend Verecundus who had refrained from baptism because of the thought that adult converts should practice continence.[33] Verecundus had very kindly offered the use of his home to Augustine whenever he was in the country, and thus the Saint of Hippo prayed: "You will reward him O Lord with the reward of the just, for you have already given him the lot of the just."[34] Verecundus received the grace of baptism on his deathbed: "Thus you have mercy not only upon him, but upon us too....You are faithful to your promises, and you will repay Verecundus for his country house at Cassiciacum, where we rested in You from the world's troubles...for you forgave him his sins upon earth in the mountain of abundance, Your mountain, the mountain of richness."[35]

Of course for most couples, invincible ignorance won't be the issue, but avoiding further evil in the home most certainly will, and therein lies the intention. It is in this context that Pope Francis references *Gaudium et Spes* concerning couples who feel that "faithfulness is endangered and the good of the children suffers" if sexual intimacy is absent.[36] In this case the danger of adversely affecting the spiritual lives of the children would be of utmost concern, because the rejection of their faith would become a real possibility and perhaps endanger their salvation.

So what exactly is this situation to which we allude? It would be the case where children are born out of a civil, invalid union. The couple have at some stage returned to the faith and seek a loving relationship with Jesus. They know and accept their union is wrong, but there is no going back. Former marriages are irreparably damaged. In this new union they have tried hard to live as brother and sister, but their attempts have caused great tension and constant arguments. The husband is now fighting temptations against impurity of various kinds. The peace of the home is fragmenting and the children are being affected. No longer are the arguments kept behind closed doors, but abuse is being hurled across the room while the children play. There is a real danger of the home becoming a quasi-war zone, and possibly a family break-up is imminent. Not only have the children had to experience this, but they have also not experienced for a considerable time any affection between their parents; on the contrary, coldness has been apparent even in the "good" times. They are confused; what they hear preached at Church is not replicated at home. The older ones are asking questions why mom and dad no longer love each other, and there is the distinct possibility they begin to see nothing beneficial in Catholicism based on their experience at home; in fact, there is the danger of blame being attributed to the faith.

At this point, the parents make the decision that living celibate lives is unworkable. They say to God: "We cannot continue like this, we don't have the strength even though we have tried. For our children, we are now witnesses for the devil more than you. We are spreading poison and it is ruining them. If we continue like this, we are causing greater evil, and we feel we may turn the children away from the faith. Our conscience tells us we risk breaking the fifth commandment and in a real sense, destroying their emotional and spiritual lives. It is our honest intention to flee from all these evils including the sexual relationship, and we long to live lives of purity. We ask your constant forgiveness even though our weakness means we cannot fulfill what you desire from us. We shall strive in whatever way we can to respond to your grace, knowing that your love and mercy will lead us toward salvation. As proof of our good intention, what we lack now, we will make up for in other areas; in almsgiving and fasting."

It is certain that this example is not fiction for many couples who are trying to balance obedience to the faith with obligations to their children, and there will be other scenarios that may not involve children, but a partner who is perhaps suffering from some emotional, mental, or physical illness that creates great problems in trying to live as brother and sister.

St. Thomas Aquinas, in his moral and philosophical work *De Malo* (On Evil), says some interesting things applicable to this question. He states that the more emotions are involved the less serious is the sin, and "one who sins out of malice sins most seriously and most dangerously and cannot be recalled from sin as easily as one who sins out of weakness, in whom there remains at least a *good intention*."[37] Perhaps his most important point though regards the issue of coercion:

The necessity resulting from coercion is absolutely contrary to the voluntary, and such necessity altogether
excludes moral fault. But there is a kind of necessity that
is compatible with the voluntary, for example when a
sailor is compelled to jettison cargo in order to keep the
ship from sinking. And things done out of such necessity
can have the nature of moral wrong insofar as they are
partially voluntary. For such deeds are more voluntary
than involuntary, as the Philosopher says in the Ethics.[38]

Now although we couldn't claim that the couple we described
above are suffering "coercion" in deciding to continue adulterous
relations; they do suffer something very similar. They are suffering
"constraint"[39] due to the complex nature of their situation. What
they desire to do, in good faith they cannot, because of the
escalating evil. They are in a situation with seemingly no moral
way out. In that sense, they may be very close to acting in an
involuntary capacity—they are doing what they sincerely do not
want to do—but of course only God can judge that. At any rate,
even if acting out of "necessity" with some small voluntary act of
will, this would still render their guilt much less; possibly almost
nonexistent.

To return then to the dispute over absolution for sinners
who fit this description, what may we conclude? The question
raised by dissenters of Pope Francis is: "How can you forgive
someone who has no intention of refraining in the future?" What
I have attempted to show is that that assumption is erroneous.
These people have every intention, even if at present it is not possible to carry out, and they desire the Sacrament of Confession
precisely because they are sorry for these sins. There are no mind
games being played with God, no futile attempt at deception. No,
there is sincerity, the same sincerity as the Woman of Samaria at
Jacob's Well, or that of the returning Prodigal Son. Can we hon-
estly claim there is no difference between this scenario, and that of
a person who cares not one bit about his or her irregular situation;
who is happy to flaunt their state of sin as if it were a badge of
honor? Only someone who does not understand the truth about
the human condition, grace, repentance, and the divine mercy of
God could fail to see the distinction. The overwhelming evidence

of traditional Catholic moral theology informs us that these people have picked up their cross again and are seeking the path of divine love.

Before we depart this particular theological area, there is one question critics of the Holy Father often raise that should be addressed: If adulterers who say they cannot refrain from sexual relations for the time being are told they can receive Holy Communion due to mitigating factors reducing culpability, why can't this principle not be applied to a serial killer who would like to stop but can't because of the pleasure he gets from murder? In the case of the couple, they are acting out of mutual attraction, and they consider it a loving act. For the serial killer, he acts alone in a deliberately cold-blooded way; he tortures an unwilling person. This implies a hierarchy of sin; and when we look at the *Catechism*, we find confirmation of this fact: "The gravity of sins is more or less great: murder is graver than theft. One must also take into account who is wronged: violence against parents is in itself graver than violence against a stranger."[40] I would suggest that God grants through conscience and the natural law, an abhorrence for certain particularly grave sins: rape and murder especially, which is why most people would never dream or even be tempted to commit such acts. Sexual sins committed by two consenting adults, however, while always sins of grave matter, could not be classified in the same horrific way as sexual sins committed against an unwilling victim. Based on these facts, the confessor, far from inviting the killer to receive Holy Communion would be urging him to face the reality of his wickedness and hand himself in to accept the consequences of his actions.

Our final part of this chapter takes us to the heart of sacramental theology. We should ponder several questions: What do these persons in irregular unions gain from participating in the Sacrament of Holy Communion? What is our motive in arguing against their inclusion in certain cases? Is it genuine charity toward them, or is it simply a mentality of sheep and goats? Of course, we need to remind ourselves that we are not referring to people in a state of mortal sin, for whom reception of the Holy Eucharist would be sacrilegious. For them, no mitigating factors exist rendering them less culpable. That being said, the doors of the confessional are always open to them to return to a state of grace and resume a journey of faith.

Let us begin this discussion by quoting Pope Benedict XVI:

> *Dear Brothers and Sisters, it is important to recognize how precious and indispensable for every Christian is the sacramental life in which the Lord transmits this matter in the community of the Church,* and touches and transforms us. As the *Catechism of the Catholic Church* says, the sacraments are "powers that come forth' from the Body of Christ, which is ever-living and life-giving. They are actions of the Holy Spirit" (n. 1116)....The sacraments are the great treasure of the Church and it is the task of each one of us to celebrate them with spiritual profit. In them an ever amazing event touches our lives: Christ, through the visible signs, comes to us, purifies us, transforms us and makes us share in his divine friendship.[41]

It is quite clear from these words of the great theologian Pontiff that a sacramental life for anyone in a state of grace is of paramount importance. If it wasn't, then why did God in his divine wisdom ordain that they should enter into history as part of our salvific journey? In St. Paul's Letter to the Ephesians, he considers the mystery of God's hidden plan from time immemorial, until its full revelation in Jesus Christ (see Eph. 1:3–14). The Greek word *mysterion*—which in Latin translates as *sacramentum*—is a central part of his theology,[42]and speaks of the manifestation of God's saving love. This is most evident in the sacrifice of his only Son, through his crucifixion and death, when the Church was born from the blood and water that flowed from his pierced side. The Church exists to bring into one family all those destined to be saved, and in an individual sense to nurture communion with Jesus. In reality, Christianity is far more than a purely spiritual religion; it has a very definite corporeal and cosmological aspect that is revealed most gloriously in the bodily Resurrection of Jesus. The Sacraments are thus visible signs of invisible grace (see Council of Trent, DS 1639) that are ordered to the sanctification and transformation of each believer. Essentially, in the case of baptism, confirmation, and the Holy Eucharist, they make possible the divinization of man through a life-long process of spiritual ascent. In this way, the faith is always oriented to the eschatological realities when the universe will flower into a new creation at the end of time. This, we will speak more of in the final chapter.

The importance of receiving Jesus' Body, Blood, Soul, and Divinity in Holy Communion can never be underestimated. Even though the Gospels make this clear, from Jesus own teachings[43] to the Jews, and at the Last Supper,[44] the Lord ensured the message was clearly understood by revealing to St. Paul through a special revelation the truthfulness of this doctrine (see 1 Cor. 11:23–25). Every reception of Jesus under the appearance of bread and wine is a strengthening of love and friendship; it is to assimilate us ever more into his divine life and thus allow us to clothe ourselves in the garments of the saints (see Rev. 19:8). Not only that. We also receive the gift of the Holy Spirit in an increasing way and thus St. Ephream can say: "He called the bread his living body and he filled it with himself and his Spirit....He who eats it with faith, eats Fire and Spirit....Take and eat this, all of you, and eat with it the Holy Spirit. For it is truly my body and whoever eats it will have eternal life."[45]

The truth of the matter is that a sacramental life will aid all those who desire it in the moral and spiritual formation of their lives. To know that Jesus lives within you and prompts you with his grace is to recognize a new possibility. It is to be in the world but not of the world. It is to see with the eyes of the Lord and to act like him. In essence, it is not so much he becomes part of us, rather we become part of him; and thus our lives are ever more oriented to living by the beatitudes.

There is also the unitive element of belonging to the Mystical Body of Christ; as St. John Paul II teaches:

> The gift of Christ and his Spirit which we receive in Eucharistic communion superabundantly fulfils the yearning for fraternal unity deeply rooted in the human heart; at the same time it elevates the experience of fraternity already present in our common sharing at the same Eucharistic table to a degree which far surpasses that of the simple human experience of sharing a meal.[46]

St. John Paul II also asks the vital question: "Were we to disregard the Eucharist, how could we overcome our own deficiency?[47] The simple answer is we cannot, and to suggest otherwise is to follow the antichrist. For these brothers and sisters struggling in complex situations, we must embrace truth *and* mercy; we must come down from our seats of judgment and recall the times that *we* have sinned greatly. To deny the opportunity for a repentant sinner—even one that may not be able to fulfill their good intention—to approach the Lord's Table is to place oneself in an exulted position that belongs to God alone. Pope Benedict XVI has stated: "A Eucharist without solidarity with others is a Eucharist abused."[48] With the divine assistance given to Pope Francis, we now have a new pastoral application that in some cases will allow divorced and remarried Catholics to receive Holy Communion. This requires a special humility from all of us, and especially those who have fought against this change. Regardless of personal opinions or understandings, we must ask ourselves: if these souls are not in a state of mortal sin, and possibly not even bearing much guilt—as authentic moral theology attests—what right do I have to demand that their own personal meeting with the Lord does not happen? What right do I have to stand in the way at Jacob's Well? (see Jn. 4:4–42).

The Church of the twenty-first century stands in the midst of an era of divine mercy, an era that arose precisely as an antidote to the onslaught of evil. There are many souls swimming in a sea of ignorance to moral truths, or crushed by the weight of slavery to sin. The Holy Spirit has sent a Pope who understands these problems; who has spent his life in the trenches with his people. His teaching does not seek to undermine marriage or the great mystery of the Holy Eucharist. On the contrary, he takes to heart the words Jesus spoke in the parable of the wedding feast: "Go out into the roads and lanes, and compel people to come in, so that my house may be filled" (Lk. 14:23). These words of course do not refer to a forcing against will, rather a command to go and find the sinners, the lost sheep, those considered not worthy. Pope Francis doesn't abandon anyone; like a faithful disciple of Jesus, he doesn't pay lip service but touches the wounded and administers mercy. Thanks to the inspiration of the Holy Spirit, certain souls will now have the joy to embrace their Lord and Master; to throw themselves at the feet of his mercy; and rather than feel bitterness at that possibility, may we all consider the great joy of Savior and sinner at that meeting. In such a way will the Communion of Saints exult and rejoice!

NOTES

1. St. John Paul II, Apostolic Exhortation, *Familiaris Consortio*, no. 84, November 22, 1981, www.vatican.va.

2. Pope Francis, Apostolic Exhortation, *Amoris Laetitia*, no. 301, March 19, 2016, www.vatican.va.

3. Ibid, no. 301.

4. *Catechism of the Catholic Church*, no. 1735, www.vatican .va.

5. Ibid, no. 2352.

6. Cf. St. Augustine of Hippo, *De Vera Religione, Augustine:The Earlier Writings* (Philadelphia, Westminster Press, 1953), 238.

7. St. Thomas Aquinas, *Summa Theologica*, I-II, 19.6, www .newadvent.org.

8. Ibid, II-II, 125.4.

9. Ibid, I-II, 77.3.

10. Ibid, I-II, 77.6. St. Thomas also makes the same point in *de malo* Article 11, q 3.

11. Congregation for the Doctrine of the Faith, *Persona Humana*, no. 10, December 29, 1975, www.vatican.va.

12. Congregation for the Doctrine of the Faith, *Letter on the Pastoral Care of Homosexual Persons*, no. 11, October 1, 1986, www .vatican.va.

13. On this point, it may be that the issue of scandal is no. longer as dangerous as was thought in 1981 when *Familiaris Consortio* was promulgated. However, we will consider this again in a later chapter.

14. Ibid, I-II, 94.1.

15. Pastoral Constitution on the Church in the Modern World, *Gaudium et Spes*, no. 16, December 7, 1965, www.vatican .va.

16. Ibid.

17. Dogmatic Constitution on the Church, *Lumen Gentium*, no. 16, November 21, 1964, www.vatican.va.

18. *Catechism of the Catholic Church*, no. 1790, www.vatican
.va.

19. Blessed Cardinal Newman, the great nineteenth century theologian once famously said: "I add one remark. Certainly, if I am obliged to bring religion into after-dinner toasts, (which indeed does not seem quite the thing) I shall drink—to the Pope, if you please—still, to Conscience first, and to the Pope after- wards." These words have been erroneously taken to mean con- science comes before obedience to the pope in moral questions. However, Blessed Newman is simply stating that conscience— through anamnesis—has the ability to know the moral precepts, and thus it has first place. The papacy is secondary in that it is an aid to help discerning consciences. Pope Francis' words in *Amoris Laetitia* reinforce this interpretation: "We have been called to form consciences, not to replace them." Cardinal Newman, *Letter to the Duke of Norfolk* (New York: Catholic Publishing Company, 1875), 86; *Amoris Laetitia* no. 37.

20. Pope Francis, Apostolic Exhortation, *Amoris Laetitia*, no. 303.

21. St. John Paul II, Encyclical Letter, *Veritatis Splendor*, no. 79, August 6, 1993, www.vatican.va.

22. Blessed Paul VI, Encyclical Letter, *Humanae Vitae*, no. 14, July 25, 1968, www.vatican.va.

23. *Veritatis Splendor*, no. 63.

24. Congregation for the Doctrine of the Faith, "The Moral norm of Humanae Vitae and Pastoral Duty," *L'Osservatore Romano*, English Edition, nos. 9, 7, February 27, 1989.

25. Ibid.

26. St. John Paul II, *Familiaris Consortio*, no. 84.

27. Pope Francis, *Amoris Laetitia*, no. 298.

28. Council of Trent, "First Decree on Justification," ch. XI, January 13, 1547, William Brownlee, *The Doctrinal Decrees and Canons of the Council of Trent* (New York: American and Foreign Christian Union, 1857), 19.

29. St. Gregory II, Ep.14 *Desiderabilem mihi*, 2, PL 89, 525–26.

30. It is important to realize that Pope Gregory was not approving divorce in this case. Although the Letter from St. Boni- face no longer exists, it seems most probable that the first mar-

riage was not consummated, or was invalid for some other reason. In strengthening this argument, we have the instruction of Pope Gregory II to his legates in Bavaria from 716 in which he affirms that as long as both spouses live, they are not permitted to enter into another marriage. See St. Gregory II, *Capitulare datum Martiniano episcopo, Georgio presbytero, etc,* in Bavariam Ablegatis, 6, PL 89, 533.

31. Joseph Ratzinger, "On the Question of the Indissolubility of Marriage," originally published in German: "Zur Frage nach der Unauflöslichkeit der Ehe: Bemerkungen zum dogmengeschichtlichen Befund und zu seiner gegenwärtigen Bedeutung," *Ehe und Ehescheidung: Diskussion unter Christen* (Kösel-Verlag, München, 1972), 35–56.

32. St. Alphonsus de Liguori, *Theologia moralis,* Lib. 1, Tract 1, De Conscientia, no. 6.

33. This attitude appears to have been influenced by St. Ambrose of Milan.

34. St. Augustine of Hippo, *Confessions,* Bk. IX, III (London, Sheed&Ward, 1948), 145 St. Thomas Aquinas also refers to this passage in ST I-II,17.9.

35. Ibid, 146.

36. There has been plenty of controversy over the use of this quote from *Gaudium et Spes* due to the fact that in the Vatican II document it is referring to legitimately married couples. However, the point is that the nature of sexual attraction is the same in both instances. To pretend that couples in an irregular situation do not feel the same emotions and passions is simply not realistic. See *Amoris Laetitia* no. 298 and footnote 329.

37. St. Thomas Aquinas, *On Evil,* trans. Richard Regan, Q III, 13 (New York: Oxford University Press, 2003), 182.

38. Ibid, Q II.3.4, 102.

39. In the *Oxford Dictionary,* constraint is a synonym of coercion, thus they present almost identical philosophical and moral problems.

40. *Catechism of the Catholic Church,* no. 1858, www.vatican .va.

41. Pope Benedict XVI, "General Audience on Peter Lombard," December 30, 2009, www.vatican.va.

42. For a detailed explanation of the semantic history of *sacramentum*, see the General Audience of St. John Paul II, September 8, 1982, *L'Osservatore Romano*, Weekly Edition in English, September 13, 1982, 1.

43. Jesus said to them, "Very truly, I tell you, unless you eat the flesh of the Son of Man and drink his blood, you have no life in you. Those who eat my flesh and drink my blood have eternal life, and I will raise them up on the last day; for my flesh is true food and my blood is true drink. Those who eat my flesh and drink my blood abide in me, and I in them. Just as the living Father sent me, and I live because of the Father, so whoever eats me will live because of me" (Jn. 6:53–57).

44. Matt. 26:26–28, Mk. 14:22–24, Lk. 22:19–20.

45. St. Ephram, *Sermo IV in Hebdomadam Sanctam*, ed. E. Beck, CSCO 413/Syr. 182, 55.

46. St. John Paul II, Encyclical Letter, *Ecclesia de Eucharistia*, no. 24, April 17, 2003, www.vatican.va.

47. Ibid, no. 60.

48. Pope Benedict XVI, "General Audience," December 10, 2008, www.vatican.va.

VI DOCTRINAL DEVELOPMENT: TIME IS GREATER THAN SPACE

In the five years since Pope Francis was elected Supreme Pontiff, one word has dominated the lexicon of his critics: *Tradition*. This is not so much in relation to liturgical or cultural traditions, but Tradition in its most sublime Catholic sense. So what exactly do we mean by Tradition? Why is it the essential yardstick by which Pope Francis is being judged? In order to answer these questions, we need to look beyond simplistic notions relating to how things were done in the past, and discover a far more profound concept where Tradition is ever young and vibrant; a manifestation of constant divine activity for the benefit of souls in search of God.

Theologically speaking, Tradition is intimately bound to the reality of the Church, the Mystical Body of Christ, and the living presence of the Holy Spirit, who guides and teaches the community of faithful throughout history. Beginning at Pentecost fifty days after the Lord's Resurrection, it remains forever a living, breathing reality that embraces universality in two ways: synchronically, as the church expands its mission to evangelize to all the nations (see Matt. 28:19), and diachronically—throughout the ages until the consummation of the world. A reductive definition of *Tradition* would see it merely as a transmission of teachings from the beginning of Christianity that is rigid and cold—a kind of manifesto with which people can proselytize—and at times, it seems as if this has been the general understating. In God's salvific plan, however, this is far from the case. If we remember Jesus told the Apostles: "But the Advocate, the Holy Spirit, whom the Father will send in my name, will teach you everything, and remind you of all that I have said to you" (Jn. 14:26). This tells us that an ongoing

113

process would be the way divine revelation would be proclaimed: first, through the ministry of the Apostles themselves—as the twelve foundational bishops of the Church—and, then, through apostolic succession, to their brothers in the episcopate. Tradition is therefore fully alive, making present to the faithful of all times the same message of salvation that was announced two thousand years ago. The Lord Jesus, through the power of the Holy Spirit, always ensures that the truths concerning faith and morals retain freshness and purpose, so that Tradition doesn't become stale and irrelevant.

The *Catechism of the Catholic Church* reminds us how Tradition, intimately linked to Sacred Scripture, is the providential means of ensuring that truth is passed from generation to generation:

> This living transmission, accomplished in the Holy Spirit, is called Tradition, since it is distinct from Sacred Scripture, though closely connected to it. Through Tradition, the Church, in her doctrine, life and worship, perpetuates and transmits to every generation all that she herself is, all that she believes. The sayings of the holy Fathers are a witness to the life-giving presence of this Tradition, showing how its riches are poured out in the practice and life of the Church, in her belief and her prayer.[1]

Several key questions arise at this point: if Tradition is always active, how does it relate to changing historical circumstances? Are the transmitted doctrines under its care essentially fixed; locked into a one-dimensional interpretation, or is there scope for maturation of understanding as salvation history develops? Can we consider the possibility of a refinement over time whereby the entire truth of a particular doctrine is gradually revealed? These are essential questions that can hopefully guide our discussion in the right direction and invite a new appraisal to the Holy Father's act of benevolence toward the divorced and remarried. In order to seek the necessary answers to these questions, I propose to study two Catholic masters, separated by nearly fifteen hundred years, but bound by a burning desire to see truth flower in the most perfect way possible. The first is St. Vincent of Lérins, the great fifth-century Gallic monk and theologian, and the second, Blessed Cardinal John Henry Newman, the nineteenth-century English Anglican convert who was beatified by Pope Benedict XVI in 2010.

The figure of St. Vincent of Lérins is little known today;[2] his theology, left to those deliberately scouring the far-flung regions in search of something a little alternate to the ever-present theologies of St. Thomas Aquinas and St. Augustine. His most famous work, the *Commonitorium* (c. 434)[3] deals with two aspects of doctrine: its preservation and its maturation, and the text can, in simple terms, be boiled down to two rules: the first, known as the Vincentian Canon: "*id teneamus Quod ubique, quod semper, quod ab omnibus creditum est,*" that is, "that faith which has been believed every-where, always, by all."[4] And the second: "*in eodem sensu eademque sentential,*" that is, "with the same sense and the same meaning."[5] The first canon—for which St. Vincent is most familiar—certainly appears rather restrictive; almost as if there is an exaggerated con-cern for doctrinal preservation. He states:

> This rule we shall observe if we follow universal-ity, antiquity, consent. We shall follow universality if we confess that one faith to be true, which the whole Church throughout the world confesses; antiquity, if we in no wise depart from those interpretations which it is manifest were notoriously held by our holy ancestors and fathers; consent, in like manner, if in antiquity itself we adhere to the consentient definitions and determi-nations of all, or at the least of almost all priests and doctors.[6]

Fr. Thomas G. Guarino points out that this axiom of St. Vincent is the probable reason why his theology fell out of fashion in more recent times; it appears immovable, and would seem to undermine the magisterial understanding of Tradition as alive and active, here and now. Both a young Fr. Joseph Ratzinger, and the eminent theologian Yves Congar stated that it was too "static," and because of this, could not be included in the documents of Vatican II—whose intention was to present an energized and fresh approach—in the words of St. John XXIII: "reformulated in contemporary terms."[7] However, something has been curiously missing in this theological stance against St. Vincent. It is apparent that this first rule primarily concerns the separation of truth from heresy, thus it is a means of discernment and guidance for the faithful; but if we look at St. Vincent's teaching on his second rule, we discover a much more revolutionary approach that far from endorsing a restrictive view of doctrine, actually does the opposite. In chapter 23, he writes:

> But some one will say, perhaps, Shall there, then, be no progress in Christ's Church? Certainly; all possible progress. For what being is there, so envious of men, so full of hatred to God, who would seek to forbid it? Yet on condition that it be real progress, not alteration of the faith. For progress requires that the subject be enlarged in itself, alteration, that it be transformed into something else. The intelligence, then, the knowledge, the wisdom, as well of individuals as of all, as well of one man as of the whole Church, ought, in the course of ages and centuries, to increase and make much and vigorous progress; but yet only in its own kind; that is to say, in the same doctrine, in the same sense, and in the same meaning.[8]

St. Vincent continues by explaining this concept by way of analogy. He describes how the human body grows over time, from the embryo to old age. Everything necessary for a human being created in the image and likeness of God is present from conception, and yet it develops in a variety of ways: physical, mental, and spiritual. He suggests that if extra limbs were added at some stage, this would no longer be legitimate natural progress, but deliberate malformation, a distortion of God's design. Doctrinal progress logically follows this same pattern; the truth may be present from all eternity, but it is only through living Tradition that its beauty becomes fully apparent:

> In like manner, it behooves Christian doctrine to follow the same laws of progress, so as to be consolidated by years, enlarged by time, refined by age, and yet, withal, to continue uncorrupt and unadulterate, complete and

perfect in all the measurement of its parts, and, so to speak, in all its proper members and senses, admitting no change, no waste of its distinctive property, no variation in its limits....For it is right that those ancient doctrines of heavenly philosophy should, as time goes on, be cared for, smoothed, polished; but not that they should be changed, not that they should be maimed, not that they should be mutilated. They may receive proof, illustration, definiteness; but they must retain withal their completeness, their integrity, their characteristic properties.[9]

So how should we understand the idea that doctrine can develop while maintaining the "same sense and same meaning"? Is it not contradictory? It seems that there are two approaches that can adequately solve the problem: reformulation and organic growth. Reformulation seeks to return the doctrine to its original meaning *if* over time theological distortions have clouded the essential element. On the other hand, it would also strive to represent the doctrine in a way that is understood more clearly in a certain historical and sociological context. St. John Paul II had this in mind when he quoted St. Vincent's second rule in *Veritatis Splendor*:

Certainly there is a need to seek out and to discover the most adequate formulation for universal and permanent moral norms in the light of different cultural contexts, a formulation most capable of ceaselessly expressing their historical relevance, of making them understood and of authentically interpreting their truth. *This truth of the moral law—like that of the "deposit of faith"—unfolds down the centuries*: the norms expressing that truth remain valid in their substance, but must be specified and determined *"eodem sensu eademque sententia"* in the light of historical circumstances by the Church's Magisterium, whose decision is preceded and accompanied by the work of interpretation and formulation characteristic of the reason of individual believers and of theological reflection.[10]

St. John Paul II also spoke of this approach in his Encyclical on Ecumenism, *Ut Unum Sint*: "The expression of truth can take different forms. The renewal of these forms of expression becomes necessary for the sake of transmitting to the people of today the Gospel message in its unchanging meaning."[11]

The second approach of organic growth should undoubtedly be seen as St. Vincent's raison d'être; it is the path to exacting an entire doctrinal truth, to fathoming the full richness of God's revelation. Of course, there is a danger that cannot be overlooked, and one which the holy Monk of Lérins was well aware of—that of veering away from the original teaching and meaning. On the contrary, organic growth does nothing more than seek out the variety of angles from which a doctrine can be truly appreciated. Let us take Mariology for example. The study of the Blessed Virgin Mary in the first instance, concerns her existence as the Mother of Jesus. For the Church, however, that was the starting point for a whole host of explorations that would shed light on her exulted salvific role: Mother of God, Mother of the Church, Mediatrix of Grace, Advocate, Co-Redemptrix, Immaculate Conception, Perpetual Virgin, Spouse of the Holy Spirit, etcetera. In fact, through the ecclesiology of the Patristic period, the Church began to perceive that Mary was a mirror image of itself, a perfect icon radiating God's glory. Through organic growth then, the faithful have benefitted greatly from the full revelation of this marvel of God's creation. It is, of course, essential to see how the Holy Spirit is the "conductor" in all this; if theologians are given insights, it is through the magisterium that the wheat can be separated from the chaff. The Holy Spirit can ensure that harmony exists between the original doctrine and its full flowering throughout history.

If separating truth from heresy, and promoting authentic doctrinal development was an indispensable part of St. Vincent's *Commonitorium*, it was no less so in the thought of Blessed Cardinal Newman. In fact, Blessed Newman's own life, especially his conversion experience, tells a similar story to the theology he articulated on doctrinal development: "To live is to change, and to be perfect is to have changed often."[12] The pull of the Catholic Church led him to investigate thoroughly the early Fathers, papal infallibility, and the heresies and controversies of the first centuries of Christianity. His 1833 book *The Arians of the Fourth Century* gave him a particular opportunity to assess how doctrinal formulations and definitions were at times the necessary response to heretical opinions. However, it is his 1845 *An Esssay on the Development of Christian Doctrine* that reveals his proximity to St. Vincent of Lérins.

In chapter 5, Blessed Newman contrasts genuine doctrinal developments with those of corruption and devises seven "notes" that together can distinguish truth from error: "There is no corruption if it retains one and the same type, the same principles, the same organization; if its beginnings anticipate its subsequent phases, and its later phenomena protect and subserve its earlier; if it has a power of assimilation and revival, and a vigorous action from first to last."[13] The notes are:

1. *Preservation of Type*: this is Vincentian in that organic growth must always measure itself against the original teaching, even if the external expression changes somewhat. However: "real perversions and corruptions are often not so unlike externally to the doctrine from which they come, as are changes which are consistent with it and true developments."[14] This suggests corruption is to cling too tightly to a particular stage of development and thus dismiss any possibility of further maturation.

2. *Continuity of Priniciples*: for doctrinal development to be authentic, the principle must be maintained, because principles unlike doctrine do not develop; they are "abstract and general…more immediately ethical and practical."[15] Blessed Newman states: "Principle is a better test of heresy than doctrine."[16]

3. *Power of Assimilation*: this would allow for certain external realities to be assimilated into doctrinal growth; for example, philosophical concepts such as *epikeia*.

4. *Logical Sequence*: this implies that a doctrine defined by the Church at some point historically distant from its original exposition can be considered a development, and not a corruption, if logic suggests a perfect link between the two. Thus the dogma of papal infallibility

is the logical outcome of theological reflection concerning Jesus' prayer for Peter, the indefectibility of the Church, and the necessity of having a single guarantor of truth in faith and morals.

5. *Anticipation of Its Future*: this is the case where doctrines imply a later development even in their nascent form. For instance, the dogma of Purgatory is implied through Sacred Scripture (2 Macc. 12:39–46; Rev. 21:27) and writings of the Patristic era.[17]

6. *Conservative Action upon Its Past*: this is where doctrinal developments build on the foundations already laid, added clarity being one hallmark, whereas corruption would disturb rather than illustrate a given doctrine.

7. *Chronic Vigor*: authentic doctrinal developments always maintain life and vigor, a freshness, whereas corruption soon decays and dies. This is evident in the usually short life span of heresies.

What is clear from these two theological giants is that doctrinal development is not only possible but desirable if the Church is to be faithful to its mandate in promoting and expounding the truths of our Faith. Historical circumstances will always invite the possibility for added growth, especially as the Holy Spirit reveals greater understanding of the complexity of man—in the light of grace and sinfulness—the majesty of God and his divine attributes, and the pilgrimage through salvation history. It is my firm conviction that until the Lord's glorious return, the Holy Spirit will continue teaching and revealing, inviting the community of the faithful to breath in the fullness of the truth as the Church proclaims it.

At this point, is seems appropriate to look at the thinking of Pope Francis in terms of doctrinal development, to see if his approach bears any similarity to St. Vincent of Lérins and Blessed John Henry Newman; and from there, we can look at specific examples where this approach has been utilized, as that may help us appreciate why certain elements of *Amoris Laetitia* can and must be considered within this category of legitimate organic growth.

In his first Apostolic Exhortation, *Evangelii Gaudium*—which can be seen as the Pope's program for his entire Pontificate—the Holy Father refers to four principles that he suggests can help foster peace, justice, and fraternity. They are *Time is greater than space, Unity prevails over conflict, Realities are more important than ideas,* and *the whole is greater than the part.* However, for our discussion, in the light of doctrinal development, it is the first principle that interests us, and the one that Pope Francis appears to regard the greatest:[18]

> This principle enables us to work slowly but surely, without being obsessed with immediate results. It helps us patiently to endure difficult and adverse situations, or inevitable changes in our plans. It invites us to accept the tension between fullness and limitation, and to give a priority to time. One of the faults which we occasionally observe in sociopolitical activity is that spaces and power are preferred to time and processes. Giving priority to space means madly attempting to keep everything together in the present, trying to possess all the spaces of power and of self-assertion; it is to crystallize processes and presume to hold them back. Giving priority to time means being concerned about initiating processes rather than possessing spaces. Time governs spaces, illumines them and makes them links in a constantly expanding chain, with no possibility of return.[19]

Pope Francis returned to this principle in *Amoris Laetitia:*

> Since "time is greater than space," I would make it clear that not all discussions of doctrinal, moral or pastoral issues need to be settled by interventions of the magisterium. Unity of teaching and practice is certainly necessary in the Church, but this does not preclude various ways of interpreting some aspects of that teaching or drawing certain consequences from it. This will always be the case as the Spirit guides us towards the entire truth (cf. Jn. 16:13), until he leads us fully into the mystery of Christ and enables us to see all things as he does.[20]

Some of the Holy Father's most interesting comments relating to time and space come from an interview he gave to Fr. Antonio Spadaro, SJ, in September 2013:

> God manifests himself in historical revelation, in history. Time initiates processes, and space crystallizes them. God is in history, in the processes. We must not focus on occupying the spaces where power is exercised, but rather on starting long-run historical processes. We must initiate processes rather than occupy spaces.... This gives priority to actions that give birth to new historical dynamics. And it requires patience, waiting.[21]

The Pope then talked of doctrinal rigorism:

> If the Christian is a restorationist, a legalist, if he wants everything clear and safe, then he will find nothing. Tradition and memory of the past must help us to have the courage to open up new areas to God. Those who today always look for disciplinarian solutions, those who long for an exaggerated doctrinal "security," those who stubbornly try to recover a past that no longer exists—they have a static and inward-directed view of things. In this way, faith becomes an ideology among other ideologies.[22]

So what can we conclude from these passages? What is the Pope trying to say? It seems to me that he invites us to see time as a gift on two levels: individually and collectively. Individually, for the virtue of patience to grow through trials and difficulties; where God is able to illuminate the way forward. This would, for example, allow a couple to discern through time a new appreciation for Church teaching in matters of sexual morality, or a new way of looking at people of other faiths. Time is able to broaden horizons that space cannot. In a collective sense—for the Church—time is there to help spread the Gospel in a way that is ever more conformed to the way of Jesus. As ages pass, the Church is gradually stripped of everything that hinders the most authentic witness possible. And in a maternal way, the Church understands her children more; she listens to their concerns, their struggles, without offering anathemas in return. Time, therefore, as it belongs to God is for the patient process of moving forward; of man becoming fully alive with the glory of God.[23] God's own patience is the model that we should follow, where maturation and wisdom are able to grow through the generations.

I believe that we can tie together the two strands of *Vincentian* doctrinal development and *Bergoglian* concept of time in such a way that no threat exists to authentic doctrine; on the contrary, both are geared toward narrowing the confines of error ever more. As an analogy, we could imagine a pianist learning some great sonata or concerto: Time allows for not only the correction of errors, but also a maturation of interpretation, thus eventually, through careful refinement, an authentic representation of the composer's original intention becomes possible. It is no different with the evolution of salvation history.

Returning to Pope Francis' views on doctrinal development, in the interview already cited with Fr. Antonio Spadaro, he spoke of St. Vincent of Lérins, and the need for the Church to advance on a path of continual maturation and development. And although the extract is quite lengthy, I believe it is beneficial to give his entire response:

> St. Vincent of Lérins makes a comparison between the biological development of man and the transmission from one era to another of the deposit of faith, which grows and is strengthened with time. Here, human self-understanding changes with time and so also human consciousness deepens. Let us think of when slavery was accepted or the death penalty was allowed without any problem. So we grow in the understanding of the truth. Exegetes and theologians help the church to mature in her own judgment. Even the other sciences and their development help the church in its growth in understanding. There are ecclesiastical rules and precepts that were once effective, but now they have lost value or meaning. The view of the church's teaching as a monolith to defend without nuance or different understandings is wrong.

After all, in every age of history, humans try to understand and express themselves better. So human beings in time change the way they perceive themselves. It's one thing for a man who expresses himself by carving the "Winged Victory of Samothrace," yet another for Caravaggio, Chagall and yet another still for Dalí. Even the forms for expressing truth can be multiform, and this is indeed necessary for the transmission of the Gospel in its timeless meaning.

Humans are in search of themselves, and, of course, in this search they can also make mistakes. The church has experienced times of brilliance, like that of Thomas Aquinas. But the church has lived also times of decline in its ability to think. For example, we must not confuse the genius of Thomas Aquinas with the age of decadent Thomist commentaries. Unfortunately, I studied philosophy from textbooks that came from decadent or largely bankrupt Thomism. In thinking of the human being, therefore, the church should strive for genius and not for decadence.

When does a formulation of thought cease to be valid? When it loses sight of the human or even when it is afraid of the human or deluded about itself. The deceived thought can be depicted as Ulysses encountering the song of the Siren, or as Tannhäuser in an orgy surrounded by satyrs and bacchantes, or as Parsifal, in the second act of Wagner's opera, in the palace of Klingsor. The thinking of the church must recover genius and better understand how human beings understand themselves today, in order to develop and deepen the church's teaching.[24]

It is quite obvious from our deliberations that Pope Francis envisages a calm, patient, and above all pastoral approach to the presentation and progression of doctrine.[25] At no stage does he suggest doctrines can be reversed or watered down—contrary to the claims of some over excitable souls. His modus operandi—based on his pastoral work in the trenches of Buenos Aires—is to meet people where they are, avoiding rash judgments and say:

"Let's walk together on this journey of faith, let's allow grace to lead the way. The Holy Spirit will take your goodwill as a stepping stone for future growth." The Pope of realism knows that you don't feed babies steak and roast potatoes; you give them what their stomach can take. The spiritual life is similar, especially for those bruised and hurting from serious sin. Doctrines must be presented in such a way as to invigorate the soul; to show them a clear way forward, much in the same way an expert in debt management would: First, make clear the lowest point has been reached and thus things can improve little by little. That is the only way despair can be dealt with, and surely the way God desires it.

Now that we have studied the theology behind doctrinal development, the question remains: How does it actually work in concrete situations? It would be no surprise if for some, there will remain a nagging suspicion that this is nothing more than an exercise in sophistry, a deliberate attempt to do exactly what St. Vincent of Lérins said must not be done.

A useful (controversial) starting point would be to look at the famous axiom: *"extra ecclesiam nulla salus—outside the Church there is no salvation.* This teaching originated in the writings of St. Cyprian of Carthage (Letters 4 and 73), and later in the decrees of the Fourth Lateran Council and the Council of Florence. Pope Boniface VIII also included it in his Bull *Unam Sanctam.* Initially—as Fr. Francis Sullivan points out[26]—St. Cyprian was directing his warning not at those pagans outside the Church, but those Catholics flirting with excommunication or schism. St. Ignatius, Origen, and St. Irenaeus all taught the same doctrine. In the fourth and fifth centuries, the idea took hold that Christian missionary activity had spread to such an extent that those who were not Catholic were deliberately rejecting the offer of salvation. For St. John Chrysostom, however, even the rare cases of ignorance of Christ could not be excused.[27] In 1302, Pope Boniface VIII wrote: "We believe in her firmly and we confess with simplicity that outside of her there is neither salvation nor the remission of sins....Furthermore, we declare, we proclaim, we define that it is absolutely necessary for salvation that every human creature be subject to the Roman Pontiff."[28] Other papal writings over the centuries followed this seemingly absolute and one-dimensional teaching— with the caveat that invincible ignorance could allow some (probably rare) non-Catholics into heaven. Things began to change at the Second Vatican Council. In *Lumen Gentium* we read:

> But the plan of salvation also includes those who acknowledge the Creator. In the first place amongst these there are the Muslims, who, professing to hold the faith of Abraham, along with us adore the one and merciful God, who on the last day will judge mankind. Nor is God far distant from those who in shadows and images seek the unknown God, for it is He who gives to all men life and breath and all things, and as Saviour wills that all men be saved. Those also can attain to salvation who through no fault of their own do not know the Gospel of Christ or His Church, yet sincerely seek God and moved by grace strive by their deeds to do His will as it is known to them through the dictates of conscience. Nor does Divine Providence deny the helps necessary for salvation to those who, without blame on their part, have not yet arrived at an explicit knowledge of God and with His grace strive to live a good life. Whatever good or truth is found amongst them is looked upon by the Church as a preparation for the Gospel.[29]

We can therefore see here a momentous shift—not the denial of the original doctrine—but the acknowledgment that there are others outside the visible confines of the Church who display visible signs of grace in their acceptance and worship of God. There is also an implicit acceptance here that conscience is a guiding light for the ignorant: "with His grace strive to live a good life." St. John Paul II in his Encyclical *Redemptoris Missio* stated:

> In Christ, God calls all peoples to himself and he wishes to share with them the fullness of his revelation and love. He does not fail to make himself present in many ways, not only to individuals but also to entire peoples through their spiritual riches, of which their religions are the main and essential expression, even when they contain "gaps, insufficiencies and errors."[30]

Similarly, in 2000, the Congregation for the Doctrine of the Faith's *Dominus Iesus* taught that

> outside of her structure, many elements can be found of sanctification and truth, that is, in those Churches and ecclesial communities which are not yet in full communion with the Catholic Church. But with respect to these, it needs to be stated that "they derive their efficacy from the very fullness of grace and truth entrusted to the Catholic Church."[31]

The document went on to state a significant development in the understanding of ecclesial communities who do not share a valid episcopate:

> However, those who are baptized in these communities are, by Baptism, incorporated in Christ and thus are in a certain communion, albeit imperfect, with the Church. Baptism in fact tends per se toward the full development of life in Christ, through the integral profession of faith, the Eucharist, and full communion in the Church.... Therefore, these separated Churches and communities as such, though we believe they suffer from defects, have by no means been deprived of significance and importance in the mystery of salvation. For the spirit of Christ has not refrained from using them as means of salvation which derive their efficacy from the very fullness of grace and truth entrusted to the Catholic Church.[32]

So what can we conclude from this exploration of the axiom of St. Cyprian? The doctrinal development that has occurred is one where a negative formulation has been organically reformulated into a positive one, thus salvation, in any instance, whether for a Catholic, Protestant, Buddhist, even Atheist, comes from Christ and through the Catholic Church. It still does not accept salvation can be found anywhere else, but mature theological reflection has come to recognize that God works outside the visible confines of his Holy Catholic Church, and that in some mysterious, yet tangible way, non-Catholics are bound to the one true Church even if in an imperfect manner. This is a beautiful manifestation of authentic doctrinal development. What may have seemed a terrible situation for millions if not billions, now through the inspiration and guidance of the Holy Spirit opens up the door to salvation.[33]

One of the most important areas of doctrinal development, and very close to that of our entire discussion within this book, concerns the doctrine of marriage itself. Jesus gave it sacramental dignity, and under divine law, it remains unbroken until one of the spouses dies: "So they are no longer two, but one flesh. Therefore what God has joined together, let no one separate" (Matt. 19:6). That truth, of course, needs no development whatsoever. But what about the question of what constitutes a valid marriage? Is it simply two unmarried heterosexual persons who exchange vows under any circumstances? The answer is no. Even Sacred Scripture tells us so:

> To the rest I say—I and not the Lord—that if any believer has a wife who is an unbeliever, and she consents to live with him, he should not divorce her. And if any woman has a husband who is an unbeliever, and he consents to live with her, she should not divorce him. For the unbelieving husband is made holy through his wife, and the unbelieving wife is made holy through her husband. Otherwise, your children would be unclean, but as it is, they are holy. But if the unbelieving partner separates, let it be so; in such a case the brother or sister is not bound. It is to peace that God has called you. (1 Cor. 7:12–17)

This teaching of St. Paul came to be known as the *Pauline Privilege*, which is effectively a decision in favor of the faith; thus in cases where one of the married parties receives baptism, and the other departs, the Christian is free to leave and form a new marriage. Although this doctrine was obviously known in the postapostolic age, it was not until the thirteenth century that it became a fully defined theological-canonical apparatus with which to resolve cases.[34] The *Petrine privilege* is also a doctrinal development based on the Pauline privilege. When new pastoral circumstances arose with the missionary growth of the sixteenth century, the Popes solicitously addressed the needs of polygamists who were being converted to the faith with "new and very broad privileges which went far beyond the limits of the pauline privilege."[35] This was effected primarily through the following Apostolic Constitutions: Paul III, *Altitudo*, June 1, 1537; St. Pius V, *Romani Pontifices*, August 2, 1571; and Gregory XIII, *Populis*, January 25, 1585. The 1917 Code of Canon Law, however, extended them to the entire Church (can. 1125). The papal prerogative to accomplish this—which may cause some to wonder about—derives from several angles: his divinely conferred power to bind and loose; the superiority of the faith within a sacramental marriage, and the duty to aid the salvation of souls.[36]

The other development in the doctrine of marriage concerns annulments. Pope Francis explained in his recent Apostolic Letter, *Mitis Iudex*:

> Through the centuries, the Church, having attained a clearer awareness of the words of Christ, *came to and set forth a deeper understanding of the doctrine of the indissolubility of the sacred bond of marriage*, developed a system of nullities of matrimonial consent, and put together a judicial process more fitting to the matter so that ecclesiastical discipline might conform more and more to the truth of the faith she was professing.[37]

So how do annulments fit into the doctrinal development of marriage? Far from weakening marriage—as long as the annulment process is not abused—gradual formulations of reasons for invalidity actually strengthen marriage by rooting out areas that risk obscuring the true beauty of sacramental marriage. In this way, the doctrine of marriage is pruned and purified; the couple who consider marriage are able to discern more carefully if their circumstances suggest marriage is a realistic possibility. It is a sad reality that this book is being written precisely because the true doctrine of marriage has not been understood by probably many thousands if not millions of people around the world. The doctrinal development seeks nothing more than to reflect in an ever greater way the marriage of Jesus and his Bride, the Church. Surely it is a betrayal of the Lord if the Church doesn't refine its understanding through time?

There are other areas of doctrinal development that we can briefly mention: Christological (one person, two natures); the *sensus fidei* (a supernatural instinct for the truth of the Gospel of all the faithful); the laity sharing in the priesthood of Christ (baptism); eschatology (the heresy of millenarianism); papal infallibility; and the unitive aspect of sexuality in marriage.[38] This list is not exhaustive, but it reveals how the "doctrine" of doctrinal development has been utilized throughout the past two thousand years.

In conclusion, we must return to *Amoris Laetitia*, to survey the clear maturation of doctrine present in the text. In this way, guided by the knowledge that the Holy Spirit assists the magisterium of the Pope, we can appreciate these new insights, and hopefully arrive at a fresh, empathetic perspective of these brothers and sisters and their sufferings.

To begin with, the most obvious development concerns moral theology, and as we have already analyzed that particular issue, we don't need to add too much more here. Suffice it to say, we can perceive that the Holy Father has taken the entire doctrinal development on subjective guilt and applied it to some of these individual cases: "Hence it is can no longer simply be said that all those in any 'irregular situation' are living in a state of mortal sin and are deprived of sanctifying grace."[39] Perhaps the most interesting development though concerns the role of conscience:

> Yet conscience can do more than recognize that a given situation does not correspond objectively to the overall demands of the Gospel. It can also recognize with sincerity and honesty what for now is the most generous response which can be given to God, and come to see with a certain moral security that it is what God himself is asking amid the concrete complexity of one's limits, while yet not fully the objective ideal. In any event, let us recall that this discernment is dynamic; it must remain ever open to new stages of growth and to new decisions which can enable the ideal to be more fully realized.[40]

It is hard to imagine that a teaching such as this on conscience would be found in earlier magisterial documents; until now, the focus has been centerd on the two opposite possibilities for conscience to decipher: something being either right or wrong. Pope Francis has nevertheless taught that "moral security" can be had when certain circumstances don't allow for the full objective ideal to be realized. In essence, this means that even if the sinfulness of an act remains, God will take into account our intention, and the other factors that affect a decision made in good conscience; again, the principle of "time is greater than space" would appear to be at play here. As long as the conscience is not closed off to seeking truth—with God's grace and patience—spiritual growth can certainly be made. We may recall Blessed Cardinal Newman's gradual acceptance of Catholicism as a prime example of this. It is within this context that the doctrinal development of the "law of gradualness" applies—originally taught by St. John Paul II—and reaffirmed by Pope Francis in *Amoris Laetitia* 295.

Another genuine doctrinal development relates to the way the Pope understands the nature of these civil marriages. Being a great Christian realist, he is not afraid to accept the love manifest within these relationships:

> In such cases, respect also can be shown for those signs of love which in some way reflect God's own love....The divorced who have entered a new union, for example, can find themselves in a variety of situations, which should not be pigeonholed or fit into overly rigid classifications leaving no room for a suitable personal and pastoral discernment. One thing is a second union consolidated over time, with new children, proven fidelity, generous self giving, Christian commitment, a consciousness of its irregularity and of the great difficulty of going back without feeling in conscience that one would fall into new sins.[41]

With Pope Benedict XVI, we also discover a significant doctrinal progression related to these families. Acutely aware of their trials, he states: "I am convinced that their suffering, if truly accepted from within, is a gift to the Church. They need to know this; to realize that this is their way of serving the Church, that they are in the heart of the Church."[42]

Finally, although not strictly doctrinal, but disciplinary, we must see the new sacramental possibilities for the divorced and remarried in the light of these magisterial developments. The recent recognition of the complexity of individual situations, allied to the advancement in moral theology, and the necessity of integrating these people back into the Church has led Pope Francis to make this bold decision. However, we should never expect, or desire a change to the general norm because some acts of adultery will almost certainly involve mortal sin, and thus the possibility of sacrilegious reception of Holy Communion. Everything contained in *Amoris Laetitia* conforms to authentic doctrinal development because at no stage are any of the doctrines concerning Holy Communion, marriage, conscience, or mortal sin tampered with. The Holy Father is clearly in line with Tradition that these souls are in a state of grace and thus can benefit greatly from the Sacraments of Confession and the Eucharist.

So as we conclude this chapter, we can see how important doctrinal development is to the understanding of sacred truths. It is wrong to become fixated with a particular way of understanding a doctrine unless it has been clearly interpreted definitively by the magisterium. We must trust in the Holy Spirit, who blows where he wills (see Jn. 3:8), to guide these new openings in a way that enhances spiritual lives and allows the Church to enter more deeply into the mystery of divine teachings. St. Vincent of Lérins and Blessed Cardinal Newman encourage us to trust in the power invested in St. Peter and his successors; to humbly submit to their magisterial teachings, knowing that decisions they make or teachings they proclaim are ratified in heaven. It seems fitting to end with a passage from a recent speech of Pope Francis where he warns of a one-dimensional approach to how things should be done; it seems appropriate in the light of his disciplinary change described in *Amoris Laetitia*:

> There's a phrase that should never be used: "It's always been done that way." That phrase, let me tell you, is bad. We must always be changing because time changes. The only thing that does not change is what's essential. What doesn't change is the announcement of Jesus Christ, missionary attitude, prayer, the need to pray, the need to be formed, and the need to sacrifice. That does not

change. You have to find the way, how to do it, but it does not change. But the "always done this way" phrase did so much damage in the Church, and continues to do so much damage to the Church.[43]

NOTES

1. St. John Paul II, *Catechism of the Catholic Church*, no. 78, www.vatican.va.

2. For the most detailed analysis of St. Vincent of Lérins and his relevance to doctrinal development today, see Thomas G. Guarino, *Vincent of Lerins and the Development of Christian Doctrine* (Grand Rapids: Baker Academic, 2013), 1.

3. St. Vincent uses a pseudonym—*Peregrinus*—a pilgrim, in the *Commonitorium*.

4. St. Vincent of Lérins, *Commonitorium*, ch. 2, www .newadvent.org.

5. Ibid, ch. 23.

6. Ibid, ch. 2.

7. St. John XXIII, "Opening Speech of the Second Vatican Council," October 11, 1962, www.vatican.va.

8. St. Vincent of Lérins , *Commonitorium*, ch. 23.

9. Ibid.

10. St. John Paul II, Encyclical Letter, *Veritatis Splendor*, no. 53, www.vatican.va.

11. St. John Paul, Encyclical Letter, *Ut Unum Sint*, no. 19, May 25, 1995, www.vatican.va.

12. Blessed John Henry Newman, *An Essay on the Development of Christian Doctrine* (London: Basil Montagu Pickering, 1878), 40.

13. Ibid, 171.

14. Ibid, 176.

15. Ibid, 178.

16. Ibid, 181.

17. See Stephen Walford, *Communion of Saints: The Unity of Divine Love in the Mystical Body of Christ* (Kettering, OH: Angelico Press, 2016), 151–250.

18. This is exemplified by the fact that it appears in *Amoris Laetitia* twice and in the Encyclicals *Lumen Fidei* and *Laudato Si.*

19. Pope Francis, Apostolic Exhortation, *Evangelii Gaudium*, no. 223, November 24, 2013, www.vatican.va.

20. Pope Francis, *Amoris Laetitia*, no. 3, www.vatican.va.

21. Pope Francis, "Interview with Fr. Antonio Spadaro S.J.," September 19, 2013, www.vatican.va.

22. Ibid.

23. Cf. St. Irenaeus, *Adversus Haereses*, Bk. IV, 20.7, www.newadvent.org.

24. Pope Francis, "Interview with Fr. Antonio Spadaro S.J."

25. It should be noted that Pope Francis is in perfect continuity with his predecessors in approving doctrinal development. Pope Pius XII stated: "For God has given His Church, together with these sacred founts, the living authority, also to illustrate and develop these truths which are contained only obscurely and, as it were, implicitly in the deposit of the faith." Pope Pius XII, Encyclical Letter, *Humani Generis*, no. 21, *The Pope Speaks* (New York: Pantheon, 1957), 239. The Second Vatican Council Dogmatic Constitution *Dei Verbum* relates the same teaching: "This tradition which comes from the Apostles develop in the Church with the help of the Holy Spirit. For there is a growth in the understanding of the realities and the words which have been handed down. This happens through the contemplation and study made by believers, who treasure these things in their hearts (see Luke, 2:19, 51) through a penetrating understanding of the spiritual realities which they experience, and through the preaching of those who have received through Episcopal succession the sure gift of truth. For as the centuries succeed one another, the Church constantly moves forward toward the fullness of divine truth until the words of God reach their complete fulfillment in her." *Dei Verbum*, no. 8, www.vatican.va. St. John Paul II in *Veritatis Splendor* 4 and 28 also promotes doctrinal development.

26. Fr. Francis Sullivan, *Salvation Outside the Church: Tracing the History of the Catholic Response* (Eugene, OR: Wipf and Stock Publishers, 2002), 20.

27. See St. John Chrysostom, "Homily 26 on Romans," www.newadvent.org.

28. Pope Boniface VIII, Papal Bull, *Unam Sanctam*, November 18, 1302, www.newadvent.org.

29. Second Vatican Council, Dogmatic Constitution on the Church, *Lumen Gentium*, no. 16, November 21, 1964, www.vatican.va.

30. St. John Paul II, Encyclical Letter, *Redemptoris Missio*, no. 55, December 7, 1990, www.vatican.va.

31. Congregation for the Doctrine of the Faith, *Dominus Iesus on the Unicity and Salvific Universality of Jesus Christ and the Church*, no. 17, June 16, 2000, www.vatican.va.

32. Ibid.

33. We should mention that the Second Vatican Council reaffirmed that those who deliberately do not join the Catholic Church, even though they believe it to be the true Church and necessary for salvation cannot be saved. See *Lumen Gentium*, no. 14.

34. The following chapter explores the events surrounding this initiative of Pope Innocent III. Cardinal Joseph Ratzinger states how this doctrine was refined at various times in order to get as close as possible to the exact circumstance in which the privilege could apply: "The Church over the years repeatedly furnished the pauline privilege with positive norms, particularly regarding the definition of the term 'depart,' the requirement that 'departure' be established in the ecclesiastical forum by means of the 'interpellations,' and the norm that a marriage is not dissolved until the moment another marriage is contracted by the baptised party.... This demonstrates clearly that the Church has always been entirely aware of the power it enjoys to define the limits of this privilege as well as to interpret it in a broader sense, as it did for example with regard to the meaning of the term 'to depart,' which is fundamental to the pauline privilege." Cardinal Joseph Ratzinger, "Norms on the Preparation of the Process for the Dissolution of the Marriage Bond in Favour of the Faith," April 30, 2001, www.vatican.va.

35. Ibid.

36. It is also noteworthy that the Pope can dissolve a sacramental marriage as long as it has not yet been consummated: "For a just cause, the Roman Pontiff can dissolve a non-consummated marriage between baptized persons or between a baptized party and a non-baptized party at the request of both parties or of one

135

of them, even if the other party is unwilling." Can. 1142, Code of Canon Law, www.vatican.va.

37. Pope Francis, Apostolic Letter, *Mitis Iudex*, August 15, 2015, www.vatican.va.

38. Of particular significance is Pope Benedict XVI's Encyclical *Deus Caritas Est*, in which he discusses *eros*: "From the standpoint of creation, eros directs man towards marriage, to a bond which is unique and definitive; thus, and only thus, does it fulfil its deepest purpose." Pope Benedict XVI, Encyclical Letter, *Deus Caritas Est*, no. 11, December 25, 2005.

39. Pope Francis, *Amoris Laetitia*, no. 301, www.vatican.va.

40. Ibid, no. 303.

41. Ibid, nos. 294, 298.

42. Pope Benedict XVI, "Address at the Evening of Witness for the World Meeting of Families," June 2, 2012, www.vatican.va.

43. Pope Francis, "Speech for the Second International Forum of Catholic Action," April 27, 2017, http://www.romereports.com/2017/04/27/pope-says-phrase-it-s-always-done-that-way-damages-the-church.

VII THE MAGISTERIUM OF POPE FRANCIS: FREEDOM OF THE HOLY SPIRIT

I f the question of authentic Catholic moral theology was of fundamental importance in concluding that sacramental discipline could be changed, no less important is the question of the papal prerogative to accomplish it. Some critics have maintained that Pope Francis does not have the authority to do it; others have said he has deliberately caused confusion in the hope that bishops will understand his real intention; and others still have accused him of error or even heresy. At any rate, there are questions that need to be addressed in order for a restoration of theological equilibrium, especially in matters pertaining to papal primacy. It is also my hope that by shedding light on these matters, a greater understanding and appreciation of Pope Francis' magisterium may be gained, and thus love and respect for him will deepen from those who until now have only seen him as a threat to traditional Catholic teachings on the Holy Eucharist, marriage, and mortal sin.

Any discussion of papal authority must first return to Sacred Scripture, to ascertain the truth that Peter and his successors inherited a divine mandate to govern the Church from Pentecost until the Lord's return at the end of time. As early as verse forty-two of St. John's Gospel, we encounter the will of Jesus in this matter: Andrew presented his brother Simon to the Lord who looked steadfastly at him and said: "You are Simon son of John. You are to be called Cephas" (Jn. 1:42). "Cephas" was later translated as *Petrus* in Latin—meaning "rock," and thus the Lord's decision to

137

change his name was a sign of the mission entrusted to him.[1] Throughout the Gospels, we are invited to perceive an especially intimate connection between Jesus and Peter: St. Mark records Jesus entering Peter's house and curing his mother-in-law (see Mk. 1:29– 31), St. Matthew recounts the miracle of the fish and coin whereby Jesus paid the temple tax for himself and Peter (see Matt. 17:27), and St. Luke tells how Jesus got into Peter's boat and preached to the crowds on the Lake of Gennesaret (see Lk. 5:3). Other instances reveal Peter's primacy: when Jesus took Peter, James, and John with him at the Transfiguration, in the Garden of Gethsemane, and the raising from the dead of Jairus' daughter, Peter is always named first. After the resurrection, John deliberately waited for Peter to enter the tomb first (see Jn. 20:4–6), and the angel instructed the holy women to tell Peter about the glorious happenings (see Mk. 16:7).

If we move to the specific conferral of this unique ministry upon Simon, we read in St. Matthew's Gospel: "And I tell you, you are Peter, and on this rock I will build my church, and the gates of Hades will not prevail against it. I will give you the keys of the kingdom of heaven, and whatever you bind on earth will be bound in heaven, and whatever you loose on earth will be loosed in heaven" (Matt. 16:18–19). This proclamation reminds us of Jesus' words at the Sermon on the Mount: "Everyone then who hears these words of mine and acts on them will be like a wise man who built his house on rock" (Matt. 7:24). So what can we read into these words of the Lord? Undoubtedly, the designation of Peter as "rock" is a deliberate choice, cementing him along-side Jesus the "cornerstone." The two go together as immovable objects: firm foundations that will endure until the last day. The image of rock itself has biblical foundations; if we recall, Isaiah spoke of Abraham our father in faith in this way: "Look to the rock from which you were hewn....Look to Abraham your father" (Is. 51:1–2). The image of "keys" is also rich in biblical symbolism, and just as with the rock and cornerstone, Jesus intends to reveal a unique relationship between himself and Peter. In the Book of Isaiah, we read: "I will place on his shoulder the key of the house of David; he shall open, and no one shall shut; he shall shut, and no one shall open" (Is. 22:22), and the Book of Revelation repeats this almost word for word (Rev. 3:7). Through his perfect sacrifice, Jesus has taken the keys, unlocked, and opened the door to salvation. By giving these same keys to Peter, he has placed in his hands authority over the Church to rule in his name; to bind and loose, ensuring that the door to salvation remains always open for those who desire to walk through it. The Church has only one key holder, and thus it is essential to remain close to him.

In terms of the spiritual power invested in Peter and his successors, St. Luke recounts the momentous words of Jesus that reveal the true extent of his uniqueness: "But I have prayed for you that your own faith may not fail; and you, when once you have turned back, strengthen your brothers" (Lk. 22:32). The significance of this promise of Jesus cannot be overstated in our quest to understand the papacy. The Lord spoke them on the eve of his Passion, at the Last Supper, and in the context of Satan sifting the apostles like wheat—words that he had specifically addressed to Simon (see Lk. 22:31). Thus Jesus was informing his chosen one that he would be the beneficiary of a particular special grace: to protect his faith—not his personal sanctity—but his faith from attacks by the devil. In this way, he would be able to strengthen the faith of those entrusted to his care. It seems to me the focus of this episode should not be so much on the protection of Peter's faith, rather from whom it derives. We need to constantly remind ourselves that it is the prayer of God himself who ensures this happens. It is a *perfect* prayer that speaks of the divine will emanating from the most Holy Trinity that *never* shall Peter or his successors fail in teaching the truth. Our faith then should be unshakable in this reality; if Jesus has promised it, then we can rest assured that it will always remain true.

But the question is this: How far does the promise extend? Is it restricted to certain dogmatic declarations, or does it exist in the ordinary magisterium? In order to answer these questions, it is perhaps desirable to begin with the First Vatican Council's teaching on papal infallibility. In the *First Dogmatic Constitution on the Church of Christ*, from July 18, 1870, the Council Fathers in union with Blessed Pius IX defined the following as a dogma of the faith:

> ...that the Roman Pontiff, when he speaks ex cathedra, that is, when carrying out the duty of the pastor and teacher of all Christians by virtue of his supreme apostolic authority he defines a doctrine of faith or morals

to be held by the universal Church, through the divine assistance promised him in blessed Peter, operates with that infallibility with which the divine Redeemer wished that His church be instructed in defining doctrine on faith and morals; and so such definitions of the Roman Pontiff from himself, but not from the consensus of the Church, are unalterable.[2]

The critical point in this text is the phrase "faith and morals." It is only within these parameters that the Pope is protected by Jesus' promise because the fundamental aspects of salvation are contained within them. Outside of these, there is no necessity for a pope to be correct because they do not impinge on the Church's ability to preach the Gospel or promote an authentic Christian way of life. This infallible form of papal teaching is known as the extraordinary magisterium, and it is utilized on the rarest of occasions, the last being in 1950 when Pope Pius XII defined the dogma of the Assumption of Mary, body and soul, into heaven. So what of the ordinary magisterium, in which is contained the day-to-day teaching office of the Pope? First, we need to know exactly what constitutes the ordinary magisterium. St. John Paul II explained it thus:

> The Successor of Peter fulfills this doctrinal mission in a continual series of oral and written interventions that represent the ordinary exercise of the Magisterium as the teaching of truths to be believed and put into practice (*fidem et mores*). The acts expressing this Magisterium can be more or less frequent and take various forms according to the needs of the time, the requirements of concrete situations, the opportunities and means available, and the methods and systems of communication. However, given that they derive from an explicit or implicit intention to make pronouncements on *matters of faith and morals,* they are *linked to the mandate received by Peter and enjoy the authority conferred on him by Christ.*[3]

When we consider the ordinary magisterium, we need to take into account the level of authority that a particular document or doctrine contains, because there are subtle differences that are significant for theologians and the faithful in general. There is an assumption in certain Catholic circles that infallibility is the only criterion for assent; thus everything that has not been declared such is open to debate or even dissent. That, however, is not the case. The truth and definitive nature of a doctrine depends on the deposit of faith transmitted by Scripture and Tradition, while infallibility refers only to the degree of certitude of an act of magisterial teaching. The Pope has at his disposal several ways of proclaiming the truth of a doctrine: an *ex cathedra* declaration from himself or through an Ecumenical Council (a defining act), or a definitive teaching through his ordinary magisterium that derives from Tradition, as something held *constantly* by the Church through the ages and transmitted by the ordinary universal magisterium[4] (nondefining act). This second element also utilizes the charism of infallibility, making the doctrine irrevocable; it was used most recently in St. John Paul II's Apostolic Letter *Ordinatio sacerdotalis* from 1994 in which he declared that the Church did not have the authority to ordain women to the priesthood and that the judgment was to be held "definitively."

So what level of assent is required for these two elements where infallibility is utilized? The Congregation for the Doctrine of the Faith gave the answer in its *Doctrinal Commentary on the Concluding Formula of the* professio fidei. For *ex cathedra* declarations: "These doctrines require *the assent of theological faith* by all members of the faithful. Thus, whoever obstinately places them in doubt or denies them falls under the censure of heresy, as indicated by the respective canons of the Codes of Canon Law."[5] For those doctrines to be held definitively through an act of the ordinary magisterium we read:

> Every believer, therefore, is required to give firm and definitive assent to these truths, based on faith in the Holy Spirit's assistance to the Church's Magisterium, and on the Catholic doctrine of the infallibility of the Magisterium in these matters. Whoever denies these truths would be in a position of *rejecting a truth of Catholic doctrine and would therefore no longer be in full communion with the Catholic Church.*[6]

Although there is no difference whatsoever in the irreformable character of both instances of infallibility, the first requires assent based directly on faith in the authority of the word of God (*doctrines de fide credenda*), while in the second, assent is based on faith in the Holy Spirit's assistance given to the magisterium, and on the Catholic doctrine of the infallibility of the magisterium (*doctrines de fide tenenda*).

Within the ordinary magisterium, there is a second level that, for us, in the context of *Amoris Laetitia*, is the heart of the matter. The Congregation of the Doctrine of Faith explains these as

> all those teachings—on faith and morals—*presented as true or at least as sure*, even if they have not been defined with a solemn judgement or proposed as definitive by the ordinary and universal Magisterium. Such teachings are, however, an authentic expression of the ordinary Magisterium of the Roman Pontiff or of the College of Bishops and therefore *require religious submission of will and intellect*. They are set forth in order to arrive at a deeper understanding of revelation, or to recall the conformity of a teaching with the truths of faith, or lastly to warn against ideas incompatible with those truths or against dangerous opinions that can lead to error.

The document continues by stressing:

> A proposition contrary to these doctrines can be qualified as erroneous or, in the case of teachings of the prudential order, as rash or dangerous and therefore *"tuto doceri non potes"*....As examples of doctrines belonging to the third paragraph [the second level of the ordinary magisterium], one can point in general to teachings set forth by the authentic ordinary Magisterium in a non-definitive way, which require degrees of adherence differentiated according to the mind and the will manifested; this is shown especially by the nature of the documents, by the frequent repetition of the same doctrine, or by the tenor of the verbal expression.[7]

It is noticeable that even within the second level of the ordinary magisterium there is absolutely no mention of possible "errors" in faith and morals.[8] So do we find confirmation of this fact within other sources?

In a series of general audiences between 1992 and 1993, St. John Paul II taught at length concerning various aspects of the papal magisterium. In one, he focused on the "ordinary" and explained how the Holy Spirit assists even in this permanent and ongoing way:

> Alongside this infallibility of *ex cathedra* definitions, there is the charism of the Holy Spirit's assistance, granted to Peter and his successors *so that they would not err in matters of faith and morals*, but rather shed great light on the Christian people. *This charism is not limited to exceptional cases*, but embraces in varying degrees the *whole exercise of the Magisterium.*[9]

In a separate address, he also quoted Pope Innocent III, who in his Letter *Apostolicae Sedis Primatus* (November 12, 1199) stated: "The Lord clearly intimates that Peter's successors will *never at any time* deviate from the Catholic faith, but will instead recall the others and strengthen the hesitant."[10] Pope Benedict XVI in a homily for the Feast of St. Peter and Paul stated: "The Petrine ministry is a guarantee of freedom in the sense of full adherence to the truth, to the authentic tradition, so that the People of God may be preserved from errors concerning faith and morals."[11]

Going further back, Pope Leo XIII, in his Encyclical *Inscrutabili Dei Consilio* strikingly stated: "Pope Pius IX (1846–78) proclaimed the dogmas of the Immaculate Conception and of the infallibility of the Popes in *all matters related to faith and morals.*"[12] This teaching was also present in the *Catechism* of St. Pius X, where question 55 reads: "Can the Pope err when teaching the Church? Answer: The Pope cannot err, that is, he is infallible, in definitions regarding faith and morals."[13] Pope Pius XI wrote in his Encyclical *Divini Illius Magistri*:

> Hence it is that in this proper object of her mission, that is, in faith and morals, God Himself has made the

143

Church sharer in the divine magisterium and, by a special privilege, *granted her immunity from error;* hence she
is the mistress of men, supreme and absolutely sure,
and she has inherent in herself an inviolable right to
freedom in teaching.[14]

In the First Vatican Council decree on papal infallibility, it is
important to note there are two distinctions being made: on the
one hand, the specific definition relating to *ex cathedra* declarations
as we have already seen, and on the other, two statements that
precede this, confirming popes are always free from error in faith
and morals no matter what level of authority a teaching is given:

Indeed, their apostolic teaching was embraced by all the
venerable fathers and reverenced and followed by all the
holy orthodox doctors, for they knew very well that this
See of St. Peter always remains unblemished by any error,
in accordance with the divine promise of our Lord and
Savior to the prince of his disciples: I have prayed for
you that your faith may not fail; and when you have
turned again, strengthen your brethren.[15]

And again:

This gift of truth and never-failing faith was therefore
divinely conferred on Peter and his successors in this
See so that they might discharge their exalted office for
the salvation of all, and so that the whole flock of Christ
might be kept away by them from the poisonous food
of error and be nourished with the sustenance of heavenly doctrine.[16]

So we see from various papal sources a constant teaching that
errors are not possible in any magisterial teaching concerning
faith and morals. That is not to say that certain disciplinary issues
cannot be changed, or doctrinal development cannot expound the
truth more clearly through time. In a simple way, we know that no
teaching deriving from the ordinary magisterium can lead us astray
from the truth of Christ. If we doubt this, we should perhaps ask

ourselves the following: Why would the Holy Spirit only give popes a certain amount of protection in faith and morals? What would be the point of knowing that artificial contraception is wrong yet euthanasia is right? Or in vitro fertilization is wrong but surrogacy right? The path to heaven, laden as it is with so many trials and tribulations requires an absolute authority that can guarantee the correct path in all instances, and that is why Jesus prayed for Peter's faith to remain firm forever.

Apart from papal teachings concerning their own magisterial authority, we also gain confirmation of this reality from a related dogma that should be known far more than it currently is: that of the indefectibility of the Church.[17] So what do we mean by this? In essence, there are three senses in which Christ's Bride is indefectible:

1. That she is indestructible; she will remain steadfast against the powers of hell until the end of the world.

2. She will always have the means of carrying out her mission to be the Sacrament of salvation for the world, through her constitution and ministerial priesthood.

3. She will never at any time betray the truth of Christ's teaching.

It is this third sense that is of utmost importance to our discussion, and that gives us confidence to remain ever faithful and obedient to the teachings of the ordinary magisterium.

The teaching on the indefectibility of the Church has very firm biblical roots; some of which we have already discovered. Other passages, notably from St. Paul, highlight the reality that the Church is the guardian of sound doctrine, "the pillar and bulwark of the truth" (1 Tim. 3:15).[18] Throughout the Patristic era and beyond, many theologians and popes sought to explain and promote this teaching. The "Formula of Pope St. Hormisdas," for instance, from the sixth century,[19] speaks of the necessity of keeping the "norm of correct faith and to deviate in no way from what the Fathers have established."[20] The holy Pope goes on to stress that in the "Apostolic See, the Catholic religion has always been preserved immaculate."[21]

145

Essentially then, we cannot separate the figure of the Roman Pontiff from the See of Rome, a point stressed by the great Jesuit theologian Francisco de Suarez: "the faith of the Roman Church is the Catholic faith, and the Roman Church has never departed from this faith nor could she ever so depart because the chair of Peter presides over her."[22]

In more recent times, the indefectibility of the Church was seen as an essential antecedent for the proclamation of the dogma of papal infallibility. The official *relatio* of the First Vatican Council recalls how one Council Father stated (during the composition of the Dogmatic Constitution *Pastor aeternus*) that he wanted the dogma to be "deduced expressly from the apostolicity and indefectibility of the Church." The suggestion was rejected by Bishop Vincent Ferrer Gasser because indefectibility was already strongly implied within the text itself.[23]

Several popes of the past century have reaffirmed the absolute importance of this dogma—especially in light of the promotion of heresies or the questioning of papal authority. Pius XII, for instance in his great Encyclical *Mystici Corporis Christi*, wrote:

> That Christ and His Vicar constitute one only Head is the solemn teaching of Our predecessor of immortal memory Boniface VIII in the Apostolic Letter *Unam Sanctam*; and his successors have never ceased to repeat the same. They, therefore, walk in the path of dangerous error who believe that they can accept Christ as the Head of the Church, *while not adhering loyally to His Vicar on earth* [author's emphasis]…for both the juridical mission of the Church, and the power to teach, govern and administer the Sacraments, derive their supernatural efficacy and force for the building up of the Body of Christ from the fact that Jesus Christ, hanging on the Cross, opened up to His Church the fountain of those divine gifts, *which prevent her from ever teaching false doctrine* [author's emphasis].[24]

Blessed Pope Paul VI similarly stated:

> When the Church received its Founder's mandate to proclaim the Gospel to every creature, it was set up as the absolutely trustworthy teacher of truth and endowed with the charism of indefectible truth, so that thus it might fulfil its mission properly. The Church is ever mindful of this fact, and it never ceases to proclaim that in the world it is the pillar and ground of truth. In accordance with Christ's divine will, however, the proximate universal norm of this indefectible truth is to be found only in the authentic magisterium of the Church.[25]

This particular text of Paul VI also brings magisterial weight to the teaching of Suarez concerning the binding of the Church of Rome and the Supreme Pontiff. If the authentic magisterium is the only place that indefectibility can be found, then the See of Rome cannot lay claim to this without Christ's Vicar. This is important for us because any suggestion from papal dissenters that an individual pope can somehow become "divorced" from the indefectibility of the See of Rome is not only without foundation, but quite possibly heresy. Indefectibility in doctrinal matters is an essential element without which it could never be Christ's rightful Bride. Its pillars could never withstand all that the world and the devil hurls at it, and it would inevitably succumb in one way or another to doctrinal corruption. Instead, Jesus is "present indefectibly as the ages run their course: through the Church which He constituted,"[26] and because of that sublime and wondrous blessing, the Bride will forever remain faithful to her Bridegroom.

Through our deliberations thus far, we have discovered the Holy Spirit's special charism of assistance is ever present in the teaching office of the pope; he resides in the heart of the Church as a most wondrous fruit of Jesus' prayer for Peter, and for that we can be truly thankful. At this point, however, it would be prudent to address the issues surrounding several supposed errors of past popes that would seem to suggest heresy is possible, and consequently a failing of the dogma of indefectibility. Unfortunately, there are Catholics who are misinformed on these cases and thus they are under the impression that if it happened in the past, then it can happen again.

Some of the great theologians through the ages have looked into the question concerning a pope teaching heresy; St. Robert

Bellarmine in his *De Romano Pontefice* ruled it out, basing his view on Jesus' prayer for Peter, just as Innocent III had done:

> Because it seems to require the sweet disposition of the providence of God. For the Pope not only should not, but cannot preach heresy, but rather should always preach the truth. He will certainly do that, since the Lord commanded him to confirm his brethren, and for that reason added: "I have prayed for thee, that thy faith shall not fail," that is, that at least the preaching of the true faith shall not fail in thy throne. How, I ask, will a heretical Pope confirm the brethren in faith and always preach the true faith? Certainly God can wrench the confession of the true faith out of the heart of a heretic just as he placed the words in the mouth of Balaam's ass. Still, this will be a great violence, and not in keeping with the providence of God that sweetly disposes all things....It is proved *ab eventu. For to this point no [Pontiff] has been a heretic, or certainly it cannot be proven that any of them were heretics; therefore it is a sign that such a thing cannot be.*[27]

Francisco de Suarez shared this same opinion, while St. Alphonus Liguori stated: "We ought rightly to presume as Cardinal Bellarmine declares, that God will never let it happen that a Roman Pontiff, even as a private person, becomes a public heretic or an occult heretic."[28]

One of the most often cited cases of a "heretical" pontiff concerns Pope Honorius (625–38). During his pontificate, he was confronted by the heresy of Monothelitism, which attributed to Christ only one will and one divine-human activity. Sergius, Patriarch of Constantinople, himself a monothelite (although seemingly unknown to Honorius) almost certainly sought to allow the heresy to grow and thus enlisted the help of the Pope. He wrote to Honorius asking if "in future that no-one be permitted to affirm the two operations in Christ Our God." Sergius' argument was that if we admit that Christ has two wills, it follows that the two wills must be opposed: a divine nature that can only do good, but a human nature that can possibly be bad. It would thus lead to the idea that the human will of the Son of God would be opposed to the will of his Father. The Pontiff replied by saying: "We confess one will of our Lord Jesus Christ, since our (human) nature was plainly assumed by the Godhead, and this being faultless, as it was before the Fall." The Pope also affirmed that in the one Person of Christ who operated in two natures, the divine nature operated divine actions, and the human nature operated human actions. For the monothelites, Pope Honorius was in agreement, but in reality, his concern was clearing up the issue of Christ's opposition to God the Father. As the Pope did not want to give a formulaic definition at the time, he allowed Sergius to remain silent on the matter.

The Council of Constantinople in 681 declared: "We define that there shall be expelled from the Holy Church of God and anathematized Honorius who was for a time the Pope of old Rome, because of what we found written by him to Sergius, that is in all respects he followed his view and confirmed his impious doctrines."[29] What is significant here is that at the time of Pope Honorius, the doctrine of the two wills of Christ had not been defined. This only occurred at the Lateran Council of 649 by Pope Martin. Blessed Cardinal Newman, writing on the issue, states that: "we may rather hope and believe that the anathema fell, not upon him, but upon his letters in their objective sense, he not intending personally what his letters legitimately expressed."[30] This interpretation was similar to Pope Leo II (682–83), who stated that Honorius was not anathematized for teaching heresy, but for his negligence in permitting "the immaculate faith to be stained." He also told the Spanish bishops it was "for not having extinguished the heretical teaching."[31]

So the truth of the matter is that Honorius was not a heretic; he was unfortunately negligent in not seeing the threat and dealing with it. Even Pope Agatho (678–81), while condemning Honorius' affirmation of Christ's one will, still felt able to say: "Resting on his protection, this Apostolic Church of his has never turned aside from the way of truth to any part of error, and her authority has always been faithfully followed and embraced as that of the Prince of the Apostles."[32]

The case of Pope John XXII is another that causes some confusion. For a time, he held the opinion that the souls of the just do

not behold the beatific vision until the last judgment. He maintained that as the doctrine had not been formulated, theologians
were free to discuss the issue. This was his own speculative theology that was based in part on the writings of some Fathers, and
Matthew 25, concerning the parable of the Last Judgment. He
preached three sermons on the issue between November 1331 and
January 1332. Eventually, after vociferous opposition from theologians in Paris, John XXII relented, and on the eve of his death—
maintaining that his was only ever a private opinion—retracted
his belief in the theory. It was his successor, Pope Benedict XII
who, on January 29, 1336, defined as a dogma of the faith that
souls receive the beatific vision immediately upon entrance into
heaven. The reason why this cannot be considered heresy is shown
in can. 751:

> Heresy is the obstinate denial or obstinate doubt after
> the reception of baptism of some truth which is to be
> believed by divine and Catholic faith; apostasy is the
> total repudiation of the Christian faith; schism is the
> refusal of submission to the Supreme Pontiff or of com-
> munion with the members of the Church subject to
> him.[33]

Even in his "private" opinion, John XXII did not qualify as
a heretic because at the time open discussion was still possible.
A reasonable comparison would be the theory of limbo. This has
never been a doctrine of the Church and thus theologians are free
to discuss it. However, at some stage in the future, a pope could
rule it out completely. At that point, if it came, the faithful would
be obliged to accept the pope's ruling.

There is one further unusual and little-known case worth
considering, concerning Pope Celestine III (1191–98). The case
involved a Catholic woman whose Catholic husband, leaving the
faith, abandoned her, and married another woman with whom
he then had children. The abandoned wife consulted her archdeacon and was given permission to enter into a second marriage—
even though the validity of her first marriage was not in question.
With her archdeacon's approval, the woman remarried and had
children with her new spouse. Matters became complicated when

her first husband returned to his faith, left the other woman, and desired to be reconciled with his wife. The case eventually reached Pope Celestine III who opined that the woman should remain in her second adulterous union, rather than returning to her true husband. Pope Celestine's error was due to a misinterpretation of the Pauline Privilege (see 1 Cor. 7:15), which permits the bond of a natural marriage—that is, a true marriage by spouses who are not baptized—to be dissolved if one of the spouses becomes a believer and is then abandoned by the unbeliever. His conviction was that heresy dissolved the first marriage. Celestine's successor, Innocent III, writing to the Bishop of Ferrara, saw things differently and suggested a situation of heresy could not dissolve a previous marriage.

St. Robert Bellarmine in *de Romano Pontefice* argued that Celestine could not be accused of heresy because "the whole matter was still being thought out."[34] Pope Celestine III had merely offered his *opinion* at a time when diverse opinions were possible. This is proved by the fact that the Pauline privilege was only formulated in the following century, and also significantly, six months after Innocent III wrote to the Bishop of Ferrara,[35] he wrote his famous Apostolic Letter *Apostolicae Sedis Primatus,* which stated: "The Lord clearly intimates that Peter's successors will never at any time deviate from the Catholic faith, but will instead recall the others and strengthen the hesitant." Thus, for Innocent III, Celestine III was innocent. As in the case of John XXII, this is a situation where doctrine had not been formulated,[36] and thus problematic situations were requiring quick judgments at a time when the magisterium had not officially spoken on the matter.

Based on the teachings of the popes themselves up until the present day, and taking into consideration these individual cases, we can affirm at no time has heresy marred the throne of St. Peter. The Lord promised the gates of the underworld would not prevail, and as the Pope stands for the Church, his faith is constantly protected for the benefit of the Church. It reminds us of St. Ambrose' famous phrase: "Where Peter is, there is the Church. Where the Church is, there is no death but life eternal."[37]

Returning to the issue of ordinary magisterial teachings, we need to look in more detail at the charism of assistance given by the Lord, as this will help us discern the direction Pope Francis took concerning the divorced and remarried. Blessed Pius IX in his

Letter *Tuas Libenter* of 1863 confirmed the importance of the ordinary magisterium in response to certain theologians who thought adherence was only necessary with truths of the faith that had solemnly been declared:

> Even when it is only a question of the submission owed to divine faith, this cannot be limited merely to points defined by the express decrees of the Ecumenical Councils, or of the Roman Pontiffs and of this Apostolic See; this submission must also be extended to all that has been handed down as divinely revealed by the ordinary teaching authority of the entire Church spread over the whole world.[38]

Three decades later, Pope Leo XIII, sensing the onset of theological dissent and modernism even within the Church stated decisively:

> "Whatsoever thou shall bind upon earth it shall be bound also in Heaven, and whatsoever thou shalt loose on earth it shall be loosed also in Heaven." This metaphorical expression of binding and loosing indicates the power of making laws, of judging and of punishing; and the power is said to be of such amplitude and force that God will ratify whatever is decreed by it. Thus it is supreme and absolutely independent, so that, having no other power on earth as its superior, it embraces the whole Church and all things committed to the Church.[39]

In more recent times, the Congregation for the Doctrine of the Faith has issued several documents that are extremely beneficial for our discussion: *Donum Veritatis*, on the ecclesial vocation of the theologian (1990) and *Considerations on the Primacy of the Successor of Peter in the Mystery of the Church* (1998). *Donum Veritatis* explains that the primary mission of the magisterium is one of service, service that does not place itself above faith, or the Word of God, but is fundamental to revealing the entire truth as salvation history proceeds. It is "an institution positively willed by Christ as a constitutive element of His Church."[40] Along these lines, the document also stresses "It is also to be borne in mind that *all acts*

of the Magisterium derive from the same source, that is, from Christ
who desires that His People walk in the entire truth. For this same
reason, *magisterial decisions in matters of discipline*, even if they are
not guaranteed by the charism of infallibility, *are not without divine
assistance* and call for the adherence of the faithful."[41]

Without doubt, this passage is of great significance vis-a-vis
the decision of Pope Francis to alter sacramental discipline for
some divorced and remarried.[42] If we are told that all acts of the
magisterium derive from Jesus himself—including disciplinary—
then we must affirm that Jesus himself inspired Pope Francis in this
matter. There is no way of avoiding this conclusion, and for those
honest Catholics who have struggled to understand this change,
being aware of the "divine assistance" given to the Holy Father
should allow them to see this act as one approved in heaven. It
is worth noting that St. John Paul II—even though he took a very
strict stance on this issue—was wise enough to recognize that different times would require different responses from whoever was
in the chair of Peter: "In its form of expression [the magisterium] it
can vary according to the person who exercises it, *his interpretation
of the needs of the time*, his style of thought and communication.
However, its relationship to the living truth, Christ, has been, is
and *will always be its vital force*."[43]

It is in the light of the Holy Spirit's charism of assistance, and
the magisterial activity deriving from Christ Jesus that we should
also accept the moral theology present in *Amoris Laetitia*. Of particular interest should be the teaching on conscience, which would
seem to be a welcome doctrinal development for those struggling
with the morality of their situation:

> Yet conscience can do more than recognize that a given
> situation does not correspond objectively to the overall
> demands of the Gospel. It can also recognize with sin-
> cerity and honesty what for now is the most generous
> response which can be given to God, and come to see
> with a certain moral security that it is what God himself
> is asking amid the concrete complexity of one's limits,
> while yet not fully the objective ideal.[44]

Taking everything we have said into consideration, it seems logical to suggest that *Amoris Laetitia* is a fruit of the era of divine mercy proclaimed by the Lord through St. Faustina Kowalska in the 1930s. Over the following decades, the Holy Spirit has inspired the popes to embrace this doctrine in a more profound way through their magisterial teachings: in the first instance through the actions of St. John Paul II, and more recently by those of Pope Francis.[45] In fact, we may recall at the opening of the Second Vatican Council, St. John XXIII spoke of the Church utilizing the "medicine of mercy": "But at the present time, the spouse of Christ prefers to use the medicine of mercy rather than the weapons of severity; and, she thinks she meets today's needs by explaining the validity of her doctrine more fully rather than by condemning."[46] In the context of the divorced and remarried, this would undoubtedly refer to the reality of subjective culpability and the acknowledgment of their sufferings as a grace for the Church. If Pope Francis was the beneficiary of "divine assistance" in writing *Amoris Laetitia*, then we know that it cannot possibly contain any errors in matters of faith and morals. That encompasses his teaching on marriage, conscience, guilt, mortal sin, Holy Communion, and Confession. If we cannot accept this premise, then we actually call into question the teachings of previous popes and Ecumenical Councils, to say nothing of the Lord's promise to St. Peter. Surely it is more pleasing to God to humbly pray: "Lord it is a mystery that I don't need to understand, but I willingly accept." In such a way can pride and arrogance be banished.

The Congregation for the Doctrine of the Faith's document on the primacy of Peter contains some important facts that support the notion that Pope Francis has not gone over and above his authority as Christ's Vicar on earth. In *Amoris Laetitia*, Pope Francis makes clear he is allowing pastoral guidelines to be written by individual bishops, or bishops conferences: "Each country or region, moreover, can seek solutions better suited to its culture and sensitive to its traditions and local needs";[47] similarly, later in the document, he says: "If we consider the immense variety of concrete situations such as those I have mentioned, it is understandable that neither the Synod nor this Exhortation could be expected to provide a new set of general rules, canonical in nature and applicable to all cases."[48] In *Considerations on the Primacy of the Successor of Peter in the Mystery of the Church*, we read:

> Together with the magisterial role of the primacy, the mission of Peter's Successor for the whole Church entails the right to perform acts of ecclesiastical governance necessary or suited to promoting and defending the unity of faith and communion…to issue laws for the whole Church, *to establish pastoral structures to serve various particular Churches*, to give binding force to the decisions of Particular Councils, to approve supradiocesan religious institutes, etc. Since the power of the primacy is supreme, there is no other authority to which the Roman Pontiff must juridically answer for his exercise of the gift he has received: *"prima sedes a nemine iudicatur."*[49]

Far from abusing papal authority, Pope Francis has actually taken the Second Vatican Council's teaching on collegiality and utilized it in a way that can allow bishops to discern the best approach for their particular circumstances. The document cited above clearly states that not only is this possible, but having full, supreme, and immediate authority to govern, the Pope does not answer to anyone on earth. Not only that. The document also states:

> For this reason too, the immutable nature of the primacy of Peter's Successor has historically been expressed in different forms of exercise appropriate to the situation of a pilgrim Church in this changing world. The concrete contents of its exercise distinguish the Petrine ministry insofar as they faithfully express the application of its ultimate purpose (the unity of the Church) to the circumstances of time and place. The greater or lesser extent of these concrete contents will depend in every age on the *necessitas Ecclesiae*. The Holy Spirit helps the Church to recognize this necessity, and *the Roman Pontiff, by listening to the Spirit's voice in the Churches, looks*

for the answer and offers it when and how he considers it appropriate.[50]

When we look at the process that led to *Amoris Laetitia*, we can see a long and careful process of discernment with divine guidance stretching back years. From the abandonment of excommunication, the acceptance of little or no guilt in some cases, to the salvific value of suffering, we see how attitudes have changed for the better. The two synods and contemporary theological reflection have also been essential means of listening to the voice of the Holy Spirit. This maturation of understanding is evident in the words Pope Francis spoke at the conclusion of the first Synod in 2014:

> And this is the Church, the vineyard of the Lord, the fertile Mother and the caring Teacher, who is not afraid to roll up her sleeves to pour oil and wine on people's wound; who doesn't see humanity as a house of glass to judge or categorize people. This is the Church, One, Holy, Catholic, Apostolic and composed of sinners, needful of God's mercy. This is the Church, the true bride of Christ, who seeks to be faithful to her spouse and to her doctrine. It is the Church that is not afraid to eat and drink with prostitutes and publicans. The Church that has the doors wide open to receive the needy, the penitent, and not only the just or those who believe they are perfect! The Church that is not ashamed of the fallen brother and pretends not to see him, but on the contrary feels involved and almost obliged to lift him up and to encourage him to take up the journey again and accompany him toward a definitive encounter with her Spouse, in the heavenly Jerusalem.[51]

In conclusion, we must affirm with Pope Pius XII: "Whatever may be the name, the face, the human origins of any Pope, it is always Peter who lives in him; it is Peter who rules and governs."[52] Peter therefore lives in Pope Francis, and it is certain, that when Jesus said to him: "I have prayed for you that your faith may not fail," he saw every Pope until the end of the world. He spoke those words to Jorge Mario Bergoglio. Because of this, we must *always* hold tight to the barque of Peter. We must be loyal to him, and support him with prayer and sacrifice so that he receives the necessary strength to courageously govern the Church. For our part, even when the temptation arises to "correct" him, we must remind ourselves that in truth—in doctrinal matters of faith and morals—he cannot be corrected. Any other conclusion is not from God, but from the evil one.

In the one-hundredth anniversary year of Fatima, when a crescendo of criticism rose against the Holy Father, I was reminded of a vision St. Jacinta Marto experienced of a Pope on his knees in a house while people threw stones and cursed him.[53] It seems as if it was addressed particularly to us in these tumultuous times, and thus invites us to look within our own consciences and to consider whether in some way we are part of that vision. Jesus demands that we as Catholics love, respect, and obey our Pope, and therefore these words of the great Pope St. Pius X seem a suitable way to conclude this discussion:

> Therefore, when we love the Pope, there are no discussions regarding what he orders or demands, or up to what point obedience must go, and in what things he is to be obeyed; when we love the Pope, we do not say that he has not spoken clearly enough, almost as if he were forced to repeat to the ear of each one the will clearly expressed so many times not only in person, but with letters and other public documents; we do not place his orders in doubt, adding the facile pretext of those unwilling to obey—that it is not the Pope who commands, but those who surround him; we do not limit the field in which he might and must exercise his authority; we do not set above the authority of the Pope that of other persons, however learned, who dissent from the Pope, who, even though learned, are not holy, because whoever is holy cannot dissent from the Pope.[54]

NOTES

1. The Old Testament contains several instances where name changes occurred, which would signify a unique mission entrusted by the Lord. Abram became Abraham in his ninety-ninth year when he was made the Father of a multitude of nations (see Gen. 17:5), and Jacob became Israel after wrestling with the Lord (see Gen. 32:28). It is significant that Jesus didn't change the names of any other apostles; thus Simon's role was to be unique.

2. First Vatican Council Session 4, July 18, 1870, *First Dogmatic Constitution of the Church of Christ*, ch. 4 (DS 3074).

3. St. John Paul II, "General Audience," March 10, 1993, www.vatican.va.

4. The ordinary, *universal* magisterium consists in the *unanimous* proclamation of the Bishops in union with the Pope. This common witness encompasses all eras, not just the present.

5. Congregation for the Doctrine of the Faith, "Doctrinal Commentary on the Concluding Formula of the *professio fidei*" June 29, 1998, www.vatican.va.

6. Ibid.

7. Ibid.

8. It seems pertinent here to recall a teaching from *Donum Veritatis: On the Ecclesial Vocation of the Theologian*. It explains (concerning interventions of the prudential order), how there may be "deficiencies" in teachings—attributed in the text to individual bishops and their advisers—who may not always "take into immediate consideration every aspect or the entire complexity of a question." Also noteworthy is the assertion that certain judgments of the magisterium may be justified in a certain era, but may change over time "because while the pronouncements contained true assertions and others which were not sure, both types were inextricably connected. Only time has permitted discernment and, after deeper study, the attainment of true doctrinal progress." See Congregation for the Doctrine of the Faith, *Donum Veritatis*, May 24, 1990, www.vatican.va. Cardinal Joseph Ratzinger explained this understanding in an essay soon after *Donum Veritatis* was published: "There are magisterial decisions which cannot be and are not intended to be the last word on the matter as such, but are a substantial anchorage in the problem and are first and foremost

an expression of pastoral prudence, a sort of provisional disposition. Their core remains valid but the individual details influenced by the circumstances at the time may need further rectification. In this regard one can refer to the statements of the Popes during the last century on religious freedom as well as the anti-modernistic decisions at the beginning of this century, especially the decisions of the Biblical Commission of that time. As a warning cry against hasty and superficial adaptations they remain fully justified; a person of the stature of Johann Baptist Metz has said, for example, that the antimodernist decisions of the Church rendered a great service in keeping her from sinking into the liberal-bourgeois world." *L'Osservatore Romano*, English ed., July 2, 1990, 5.

9. St. John Paul II, "General Audience," March 24, 1993, http://totus2us.com/vocation/jpii-catechesis-on-the-church/the-holy-spirit-assists-the-roman-pontiff/.

10. St. John Paul II, "General Audience," December 2, 1992, http://totus2us.com/vocation/jpii-catechesis-on-the-church/peter-strengthens-his-brothers-in-faith/.

11. Pope Benedict XVI, "Homily for the Feast of St. Peter and Paul," June 29, 2010, www.vatican.va.

12. Pope Leo XIII, Encyclical Letter, *Insctutabili Dei Consilio*, April 21, 1878, www.vatican.va.

13. St. Pius X, *Catechism*, Q.55, https://www.ewtn.com/library/CATECHSM/PIUSXCAT.HTM.

14. Pope Pius XI, Encyclical Letter, *Divini Illius Magistri*, December 31, 1929, www.vatican.va.

15. First Vatican Council Session 4, July 18, 1870, *First Dogmatic Constitution of the Church of Christ*, ch. 4 (DS 3070).

16. Ibid (DS 3071).

17. For a more detailed understanding of the Indefectibility of the Church, I highly recommend "The Petrine Ministry and the Indefectibility of the Church" by Dr Robert Fastiggi, published in *Called to Holiness and Communion: Vatican II and the Church*, ed. Fr. Stephen Boguslawski and Dr Robert Fastiggi (Scranton: University of Scranton Press, 2009).

18. In ch. 4 of St. Paul's Letter to the Ephesians, he reminds his readers that in order to avoid succumbing to false doctrine, it is essential to be children *within* the Mystical Body of Christ: "The gifts he gave were that some would be apostles, some prophets,

some evangelists, some pastors and teachers, to equip the saints for the work of ministry, for building up the body of Christ, until all of us come to the unity of the faith and of the knowledge of the Son of God, to maturity, to the measure of the full stature of Christ. We must no longer be children, tossed to and fro and blown about by every wind of doctrine, by people's trickery, by their craftiness in deceitful scheming" (Eph. 4:11–14).

19. This Formula was affirmed by the Fathers of the Fourth Council of Constantinople in 869 when it was incorporated into the final decree.

20. D-H, 363.

21. Ibid.

22. Francisco de Suarez, *Defensio Fidei Catholicae Adversus Anglicanae Sectae Errores*, ch. 5, no. 7; Vives ed., vol. 24, 22.

23. Official Relatio of Chapter IV of *Pastor aeternus* par. 57.

24. Pope Pius XII, Encyclical Letter, *Mystici Corporis Christi*, June 29, 1943, nos. 40–41, 31, www.vatican.va.

25. Blessed Pope Paul VI, "Theology: A Bridge between Faith and Authority," October 1, 1966. *The Pope Speaks* 11, no. 4 (1966): 348–55.

26. Pope Pius XII, Encyclical Letter, *Mediator Dei*, November 20, 1947, no. 18, www.vatican.va.

27. St. Robert Bellarmine, *De Romano Pontefice*, Bk. IV, ch. 6.

28. St. Alphonsus de Liguori, *Dogmatic Works of St. Alphonsus Maria de Liguori* (Turin, 1848), vol. VIII, 720.

29. Labbe and Cossart, *Sacrosacnta concilia ad regiam editionem exacta* (Madrid, 1729), vol. VI, col. 943.

30. Blessed Cardinal John Henry Newman, *Difficulties of Anglicans* (London: Longmans, Green & Co, 1896), 317.

31. Grisar, *Kirchenlexicon*, vol. VI, 255.

32. "Letter of Pope Agatho," *Patrologiae cursus completus* (Migne), vol. 87, 1161.

33. Code of Canon Law, can. 751, www.vatican.va.

34. St. Robert Bellarmine, *De Romano Pontefice*, Bk. IV, ch. 14.

35. Pope Innocent III, Letter to the Bishop of Ferrara "Quanto te Magi," May 1, 1199.

36. Not in the case of a true marriage, but the reasons *why* one would be considered invalid.

37. St. Ambrose, *Explanatio*, Psalm 40, 30, 5.

38. Blessed Pius IX, *Tuas Libenter*, December 21, 1863.

39. Pope Leo XIII, Encyclical Letter, *Satis Cognitum*, June 29, 1896, www.vatican.va.

40. Congregation for the Doctrine of the Faith, *Donum Veritatis*, no. 14, May 24, 1990, www.vatican.va.

41. Ibid, no. 17.

42. Some bishops, priests, and commentators have suggested that Pope Francis has not altered sacramental discipline in any way. This appears to be a deliberate strategy aimed at diverting attention away from the issue of whether he has the authority to change it. Rather than suggest error is being taught, it is more straightforward to deny the reality of what has happened. Even if we were to give credence to the idea that *Amoris Laetitia* is not explicit in this fact, two interventions of the Holy Father prove otherwise: in the press conference on the return from Lesvos, in response to the question, Has there been any alteration in sacramental discipline for the divorced and remarried? He said: "I could say yes and leave it at that. But that would be too brief a response. I recommend that all of you read the presentation made by Cardinal Schönborn."Second, in a Letter to the Bishops of Buenos Aires, Argentina (who had issued guidelines on *Amoris Laetitia* allowing Holy Communion in certain cases), Pope Francis wrote: "There are no other interpretations." This Letter (upgraded to an Apostolic Letter) and the guidelines themselves are now, significantly, part of the "authentic magisterium" and appear in the October 2016 edition of the *Acta Apostolicae Sedis*. One important question however remains: Was the "Lesvos" answer magisterial? It seems to me it was, based on St. John Paul's teaching on the ordinary magisterium. He referred to "oral and written interventions" when they "derive from an explicit or implicit intention to make pronouncements on matters of faith and morals." Pope Francis' oral intervention during the plane press conference fulfilled this requirement. See St. John Paul II, "General Audience," March 10, 1993.

43. St. John Paul II, "General Audience,"March 10, 1993, www.vatican.va.

44. Pope Francis, Apostolic Exhortation, *Amoris Laetitia*, no. 303, www.vatican.va.

45. The most impressive manifestation of this being the *Extraordinary Jubilee Year of Mercy* that ran from December 8, 2015, to November 20, 2016.

46. St. John XXIII, "Opening Speech of the Second Vatican Council," October 11, 1962, www.vatican.va.

47. Pope Francis, Apostolic Exhortation, *Amoris Laetitia*, no. 3.

48. Ibid, no. 300.

49. Congregation for the Doctrine of the Faith, *Considerations on the Primacy of the Successor of Peter in the Mystery of the Church*, *L'Osservatore Romano*, Weekly Edition in English, November 18, 1998, 5–6.

50. Ibid.

51. Pope Francis, "Address for the Conclusion of the Third Extraordinary General Assembly of the Synod of Bishops," October 18, 2014, www.vatican.va.

52. Pope Pius XII, "Address to Newlyweds," January 17, 1940, Pope Pius XII, *The Pope Speaks* (New York: Pantheon Book Inc., 1957), 215.

53. Sr. Lucia of Fatima, *Fatima in Lucia's Own Words* (Fatima, Secretariado Dos Pastorinhos, 2007), 128.

54. St. Pius X, "Allocution to Priests on the 50th anniversary of the Apostolic Union," November 18, 1912, http://w2.vatican .va/content/pius-x/it/speeches/documents/hf_p-x_spe_19121118 _unione-apostolica.html. For clarity's sake, we must state that at no stage are we advocating ultramontanism, which was rejected by the Church (see *The Primacy of the Successor of Peter in the Mystery of the Church*). The protection in faith and morals are the essential factors that have governed our discussion.

VIII THE INTERNAL FORUM: HEART SPEAKS UNTO HEART

Our deliberations thus far have allowed us reflect on the urgent issue of reintegration for the divorced and remarried from a variety of angles. We have seen the will of God expressed through the convocation of two Synods, the magisterium of Pope Francis—in particular his Apostolic Exhortation, *Amoris Laetitia*—and the gradual development of doctrine—in this case moral theology. We have explored the mysterious way grace works through the unlikeliest of people in Sacred Scripture, and we have analyzed the divine promise that protects Popes from error in faith and morals. In this way, we have the assurance that the alteration in sacramental discipline for the divorced and remarried is willed by Christ himself. This is not to say that a future Pope couldn't change it; but in the present historical circumstances, this is what the Holy Spirit is saying to the Churches (see Rev. 2:7).

So the question we need to consider at this point is how do those Catholics in irregular civil unions discern their situation? How can they best respond to the promptings of the Holy Spirit? In order to answer this question, we need to look at what provisions Canon Law provides for problematic situations that are in the interests of individuals and the ecclesiastical community.

Canon 130 is where we discover the primary source for this discussion:

> Of itself, the power of governance is exercised for the external forum; sometimes, however, it is exercised for the internal forum alone, so that the effects which its exercise is meant to have for the external forum are not

recognized there, except insofar as the law establishes it in determined cases.[1]

Essentially, the way the Church understands this is that there are two ways of governance: one, for the social relations of all the faithful—marriages, baptisms, deaths, and the like. This would be under the competence of the external forum, where public verification of ecclesiastical acts is known; and the second, for individuals, where they may discern their relationship with God. This is known as the internal forum. It may be sacramental in the sense of utilizing the Sacrament of Confession, or non-sacramental, through spiritual direction. With the sacramental form, there is the added element of the "seal" of confession, which binds the confessor to absolute secrecy. The internal forum does not concern itself so much with the legal as with the primacy of conscience, which should always search for the truth no matter what the situation.

Pope Francis refers to the internal forum in *Amoris Laetitia* no. 300:

> What we are speaking of is a process of accompaniment and discernment which "guides the faithful to an awareness of their situation before God. Conversation with the priest, in the internal forum, contributes to the formation of a correct judgment on what hinders the possibility of a fuller participation in the life of the Church and on what steps can foster it and make it grow. Given that gradualness is not in the law itself" (cf. *Familiaris Consortio*, 34), this discernment can never prescind from the Gospel demands of truth and charity, as proposed by the Church. For this discernment to happen, the following conditions must necessarily be present: humility, discretion and love for the Church and her teaching, in a sincere search for God's will and a desire to make a more perfect response to it."[2]

So we see how the internal forum cannot be seen as a Monopoly style "get out of jail free" card. It must not be abused but respected; otherwise it becomes nothing more than a sham court of disobedience where insult and contempt are directed at God himself. Due to the secretive and rather mysterious nature of this solution, we must consider certain things that the internal forum cannot do:

1. It cannot validate a new marriage if both spouses are still alive from an original valid union.
2. It does not serve judicial procedures, but rather offers pastoral solutions contingent on authentic moral/canonical principles.
3. It cannot make exceptions to moral law as if promoting them as a "good" option.
4. It cannot allow a "creative conscience" to undermine the search for truth in any situation.

Due to the pastoral rather than legalistic nature of the internal forum, it must be said that there is at times confusion as to what is allowed, especially in the serious realm of grave sin and the Sacraments. Discussions with priests in several countries on different continents have led me to understand that this is an issue that is to a certain extent unavoidable. This is due to the fact that priests are there to help form consciences, and then to respect them. And as spiritual lives are always on the move, there is a certain amount of fluidity back and forth depending on the moral situation and other factors. A moral theologian once said that if a clear definition was given as to what it is and how it works, it would at once become a mechanism of the external forum. When dealing with individual souls with unique problems, that is not possible, and that is why opponents of the Pope have such difficulty accepting it. It is seen as a secretive way of circumventing God's law by applying pastoral (i.e., liberal) remedies that do not respect Tradition. It also does not fit with a conviction that no gray areas exist and that all cases are black and white (especially in the cases that concern us).

At this point, I would like to briefly look at the recent historical usage of the internal forum in matters pertaining to the divorced and remarried.[3] Contrary to the arguments of those who claim that what Pope Francis has allowed is a rupture with the past, there is evidence that this is not the case. In 1973, Cardinal Franjo Seper, Prefect of the Congregation for the Doctrine of the

Faith, issued a letter concerning the indissolubility of marriage. In closing the document he wrote:

> Regarding the administration of the Sacraments, local Ordinaries should strive, on one hand, to encourage the observance of the discipline in force in the Church, and on the other hand, to act so that pastors of souls show particular solicitude toward those who live in an irregular union, seeking to resolve these cases through the use of the *approved practices of the Church in the internal forum*, as well as other just means.[4]

Two years later, on March 21, 1975, the Secretary of the CDF, Archbishop Jerome Hamer, upon a request for clarification from Bishops of the United States, stated that the divorced and remarried could be admitted to the Sacraments in certain cases:

> I would like to state now that this phrase must be understood in the context of traditional moral theology. These couples may be allowed to receive the sacraments on two conditions, that they try to live according to the demands of Christian moral principles and that they receive the sacraments in churches in which they are not known so that they will not create any scandal.[5]

The significance of these two interventions from the highest level reveals internal forum solutions were acceptable in the time prior to St. John Paul II's almost blanket ban. There seems to be sufficient wiggle room in the wording (*trying* to live according to Christian moral principles) that would not categorically rule out those still engaged in sexual relationships in a second civil marriage.[6] Each case would have to be discerned carefully to determine the various factors. In a July 2016 interview between Fr. Antonio Spadaro and Cardinal Christoph Schornborn, Archbishop of Vienna, the Cardinal referred to a question he asked Cardinal Ratzinger[7] in 1994 concerning the use of the internal forum for discerning the possibility of the divorced and remarried receiving the Sacraments: "Is it possible that the old praxis that was taken for granted, and that I knew before the [Second Vatican] Council, is still valid?" The

German Cardinal replied that there is no general norm that can cover all the particular cases. The general norm is very clear; and it is equally clear that it cannot cover all the cases exhaustively."[8] Again we should take note of Cardinal Schonborn's use of the phrase "the old praxis that was taken for granted." This implies that within seminary training even before the 1960s, moral theology was allied to pastoral concern in these cases.

In a 1998 Letter of the Congregation for the Doctrine of the Faith, Cardinal Ratzinger acknowledges that in the early Church, even though officially Holy Communion was not allowed for the divorced and remarried, there were certain exceptions of a pastoral nature: "It is true, however, that the Church did not always rigorously revoke concessions in certain territories, even when they were identified as not in agreement with her doctrine and discipline. It also seems true that individual Fathers, Leo the Great being among them, sought pastoral solutions for rare borderline cases."[9] Origen was another who while recognizing the clarity of Sacred Scripture, nevertheless understood a lesser evil could be tolerated in certain situations:

> But now contrary to what was written, some even of the rulers of the church have permitted a woman to marry, even when her husband was living, doing contrary to what was written, where it is said, A wife is bound for so long time as her husband lives, and so then if while her husband lives, she shall be joined to another man she shall be called an adulteress, (Rom. 7: 3) not indeed altogether without reason, for it is probable this concession was permitted in comparison with worse things, contrary to what was from the beginning ordained by law, and written.[10]

St. Basil, the great Father of the Eastern Church, taught in a similar way:

> He who abandons the wife, lawfully united to him, is subject by the sentence of the Lord to the penalty of adultery. But it has been laid down as a canon by our Fathers that such sinners should weep for a year, be hearers for two

years, in kneeling for three years, stand with the faithful in the seventh; and thus be deemed worthy of the oblation, if they have repented with tears.[11]

Returning to more recent times, Cardinal Ratzinger addressed the issue in his 1996 book-length interview, *Salt of the Earth*. He was asked: "Is discussion of this question [possible reception of Holy Communion for divorced and remarried] still open, or is it settled once and for all? The Cardinal replied: "The principles have been decided, but factual questions, individual questions, are of course always possible."[12] This is not the only intervention of Cardinal Ratzinger concerning the internal forum. As far back as 1980, in the immediate aftermath of the Synod that led to *Familiaris Consortio* as Archbishop of Munich, he wrote a pastoral letter that touched on the issue of conscience where invalidity of marriage could not be proven:

> The Synod established a special category for those who have reached the conviction in conscience that their first marriage was null, even when the juridical proof is not available: in such instances, in conformity with a judgment based on conscience, and provided that scandal be avoided, admission to the Eucharist may be authorized.[13]

By examining these facts, we are able to see that it is not correct to claim that the Church has always maintained the exact same sacramental discipline for divorced and remarried. What we can say, is that in the external forum it has remained unchanged, but that is only one arm of the power of governance entrusted to the Church by the Lord. The historical facts prove beyond any doubt that the internal forum has had at least the tacit blessing of the Church to decide on matters that cannot be adequately dealt with externally. Why is this important? Because it tells us that even if the official practice of the Church has been constant since the birth of the Church, there is more to the truth than that. This issue cannot be considered the same as a constant tradition applying to ordination for men only, or the evil of contraception.[14] It is far more nuanced when we take into account moral theology and subjective guilt as we have already seen. Even the words of Jesus on adultery (see Mk. 10:11–12) that were used by St. John Paul II as the basis for the ban in 1981 do not actually allude to Holy Communion anyway; they simply refer to the truth of marriage and the grave sin of adultery. On this basis alone, the implication cannot be correct that states two thousand years of Catholic teaching have been jettisoned.

If the internal forum is the correct meeting place between the penitent and God for situations that require delicate spiritual guidance, it begs the question: How does the process of discernment work? How does the confessor/spiritual director navigate a path that may eventually lead to the resumption of a sacramental life? It seems that first and foremost the sincerity of the penitent must be apparent; a spark of love that is reminiscent of the woman who wiped Jesus' feet with her hair (see Lk. 7:36–50). This immediately gives something for the confessor to work with; the soul is clearly open to grace. For the confessor, on the other hand, Pope Francis has some very wise words as a guiding light:

> The confessor, for example, is always in danger of being either too much of a rigorist or too lax. Neither is merciful, because neither of them really takes responsibility for the person. The rigorist washes his hands so that he leaves it to the commandment. The loose minister washes his hands by simply saying, "This is not a sin" or something like that. In pastoral ministry we must accompany people, and we must heal their wounds. How are we treating the people of God? I dream of a church that is a mother and shepherdess. The church's ministers must be merciful, take responsibility for the people and accompany them like the good Samaritan, who washes, cleans and raises up his neighbour. This is pure Gospel. God is greater than sin.[15]

This last point of the Holy Father is of paramount importance; it reminds the confessor of St. Paul's words: "But where sin increased, grace abounded all the more" (Rom. 5:20). This should give him confidence that he has divine help on his side; that his gentle coaxing of a timid repentant soul is the way of the Good

Shepherd. In fact, we may recall how Jesus would often tell St. Faustina Kowalska that she must obey her confessor because it was he who spoke through the priest.

In *Amoris Laetitia*, Pope Francis advises priests to avoid scrupulosity in demanding "a purpose of amendment so lacking in nuance that it causes mercy to be obscured by the pursuit of a supposedly pure justice."[16] He also warns that the possibility of further falls should not bring into question the true resolution of the penitent in leaving behind the way of sin; and along the same lines, one of his most striking acclamations concerns the danger of putting so many conditions on mercy that it risks losing its real meaning:

> That is the worst way of watering down the Gospel.... It is true, for example, that mercy does not exclude justice and truth, but first and foremost we have to say that mercy is the fullness of justice and the most radiant manifestation of God's truth. For this reason, we should always consider inadequate any theological conception that in the end puts in doubt the omnipotence of God and, especially, his mercy.[17]

We could read in these words a direct magisterial and theological ticking off for those whom pristine adherence to doctrine and the law are everything, while the truth of a person's predicament is considered of secondary importance.

Moving on to the actual discernment within the internal forum, Pope Francis lists several useful questions that may form the basis for a lengthy soul searching process under the spiritual direction of a priest:

1. How did the divorced and remarried act toward their children when the conjugal union entered into crisis?
2. Were there considerable attempts at reconciliation?
3. What has become of the abandoned party?
4. What consequences has the new relationship had on the rest of the family and the community of the faithful?

5. What example is being set for young people considering marriage?

The other indispensable part of any internal forum procedure must be discernment of the person's spiritual state: Is grace or mortal sin present? Even though we have stated throughout this book that mitigating factors will diminish guilt for many, it should not be assumed that this will be the case; St. John Paul II was careful to note that on several occasions.[18] Pope Pius XII, however, stated that "an act of love is sufficient for the adult to obtain sanctifying grace,"[19] and thus signs of this would be apparent in the penitent's adoration of Jesus, sorrow for sin, devotion to Mary, love for their family, and desire for sanctification. St. Thomas Aquinas in his *Summa Theologica* asks the question, can anyone know they have grace? He answers by affirming it is possible to know through either (1) a special private revelation of God or (2) through things that are known conjecturally by signs: "and thus anyone may know he has grace, when he is conscious of delighting in God, and of despising worldly things, and inasmuch as a man is not conscious of any mortal sin."[20] The great Dominican theologian also speculates as to how easy or difficult it is to commit mortal sin in his *de Veritate*:

> Even though grace is lost because of one act of mortal sin, it is still not easily lost, because for one who has grace, which confers an inclination to the contrary, it is not easy to perform that act. Thus even the Philosopher says "that it is difficult for a just man to act unjustly."[21]

These few quotes and the acts they speak of can help formulate a judgment that may bring great peace of mind to the penitent and a sense of moral security (see *Amoris Laetitia* 303). They present the image not of someone inherently corrupt or self-centered, but someone in a spiritual conflict where they have not dismissed the fundamental option of their Catholic faith, or contemptuously applied their own situation ethics, as if certain moral laws can be legitimately disregarded. On the contrary, they may manifest love, repentance, good will, and concern for others. St. Jose Maria Escriva once stated: "As long as there is struggle, ascetical struggle, there is interior life,"[22] and these wise words would seem to be a gauge for the discerning priest that mortal sin cannot be present when faced with a person displaying these virtues.[23]

It seems that the practice encouraged by Pope Francis would necessitate a lengthy process whereby over time, various hurdles would be overcome that would help the penitent understand the complexity of the issue theologically speaking, their duty to protect the ecclesiastical community from scandal, and their commitment to seek a resolution in time that would end the sinful nature of the relationship. In this way, misunderstanding could be avoided that would suggest Holy Communion is a "right" for every Catholic, or that the sanctity of marriage is something to be taken lightly. The internal forum would also be an excellent opportunity to form the penitent's conscience; kindling the fire of anamnesis and instilling hope for the future. It would also be the place for an annulment process to be discussed, and all avenues explored that could validate the relationship in question. A more lengthy process would also allow the possibility of discerning the practicality of living as brother and sister, and understanding what level of commitment there really is to embrace purity.

In chapter five, we discussed the moral theology that allows the Pope to reject claims that all people guilty of adultery will be in a state of mortal sin. We also looked carefully at the reasons why a firm purpose of amendment is not contradicted if the circumstances don't allow for sexual relations to end at that moment. It seems appropriate therefore, at this juncture to recall the fact that venial sin—which would be the level of guilt for souls we are referring to in this book—does not have to be confessed in the Sacrament of Penance at all from a purely technical point of view. These types of sins can be forgiven in a variety of ways. St. Augustine taught that beating one's breast asking for mercy, or praying the Lord's Prayer would suffice; St. Thomas Aquinas added blessing with Holy Water or an act of contrition. In essence, any act where the will is moved by love for God and sorrow for sin would remit venial sin; and as venial sin does not break filial love, or destroy charity, then sanctifying grace is ever present.

There can be no doubt that over a long period of time, the Church has come to realize that the divorced and remarried cannot all be judged equally; the circumstances surrounding each case are just too diverse and thus do not allow for a "one size fits all" approach. Thanks to the Holy Spirit's guidance, a maturation of understanding has led to significant changes in the way they are treated. Both adultery and civil remarriage for Catholics were excommunicable offenses under certain conditions,[24] and that is no longer the case. In recent times the popes have reassured them that they are full members of the Church who should attend Mass regularly and involve themselves in the life of a parish community. St. John Paul II, even while holding a rigorist position on Holy Communion was still prepared to offer words of encouragement that a blessed future could still be anticipated by these troubled souls:

> Dear brothers and sisters, my heartfelt recommendation today is to have confidence in all those who are living in such tragic and painful situations. We must not cease to hope against all hope (cf. Rom. 4:18) that even those who are living in a situation that does not conform to the Lord's will may obtain salvation from God, if they are able to persevere in prayer, penance and true love.[25]

Pope Benedict XVI went a step further. Not only did he recognize that the complexity of the issues needed further study (especially in relation to possible invalid first marriages) but he also stated that the sufferings of the divorced and remarried are beneficial to the Church: "I am convinced that their suffering, if truly accepted from within, is a gift to the Church. They need to know this, to realize that this is their way of serving the Church; that they are in the heart of the Church."[26] It is inconceivable that these words could have come from a pope in a previous era when we consider they refer to objective grave sinners, and yet, through divine inspiration, cold legalism is being replaced by the dew of mercy. Pope Francis has courageously taken this a step further despite the inevitable opposition, simply because he knows that truth must prevail in every individual situation. It is no longer acceptable to make sweeping generalizations when spiritual lives are at stake. The Lord does not see a humanity made up of billions of serial numbers; on the contrary, he has anticipated and loved each of us individually since before the foundation of the world.

One of the most pressing issues related to the divorced and remarried receiving Holy Communion concerns those people who consider their first marriage invalid but cannot prove it in a marriage tribunal. As we have already seen, Catholic teaching states that once a decision has been made, one's conscience is binding. So how can situations like this be resolved? Another problematic situation is where a person is fearful of proceeding down the annulment route when an abusive spouse may have their "interest" rekindled after a period of time away from the marital home. Research shows this is not an unheard of scenario and without doubt throws up a unique dilemma. If the abused spouse is now in a loving relationship convinced their abusive first marriage never existed but cannot bring themselves to go "public" are they condemned to be labelled an adulterer?

St. Thomas Aquinas provides an interesting test case that could provide an answer for the person convinced their second marriage is actually the valid one. His theory is based around ignorance of some circumstance that renders an act involuntary and excuses the will:

> For instance, if erring reason tell a man that he should go to another man's wife, the will that abides by that erring reason is evil; since this error arises from ignorance of the Divine Law, which he is bound to know. But if a man's reason, errs in mistaking another for his wife, and if he wish to give her her right when she asks for it, his will is excused from being evil: because this error arises from ignorance of a circumstance, which ignorance excuses, and causes the act to be involuntary.[27]

St. Thomas is teaching that a simple case of mistaken identity excludes one from any sin; it might be argued that he must be referring to a man in a state of drunkenness, high on drugs or even possessed. However, as the Irish Catholic author Greg Daly points out: "In this light, it is worth bearing in mind that one can be mistaken not merely as to the question of whether a certain person is who one thinks them to be, but also to the question of *what* one thinks them to be."[28] He continues by arguing that in the Middle Ages, the Church had to grapple with the reality of many clandestine marriages. In the early Middle Ages, there was no requirement under Church law that a couple had to express their mutual consent before a priest, thus many people would have made the vows themselves; possibly because they were poor and couldn't afford a church wedding, or in order to avoid marrying someone their parents desired. But a pastoral and theological problem began to arise as a result of this practice. Church records reveal that some men were seducing women, exchanging vows but then later denying they ever took place. In certain cases, these men were already married, thus it is not difficult to see the headache facing Church authorities: who to believe? It would be his word against hers.[29] Matters came to a head at the Council of Trent in 1563, where in the decree *Tametsi*, it required a priest and two witnesses to be present for a marriage to be considered valid.

Relating this back to Aquinas, it becomes obvious that many people would have been engaged in sexual relations with another whom they believed were their legitimate spouse and yet were not. In these cases no sin would be present. Moving forward to our own time, there will be cases when even though a marriage tribunal has rejected a plea for invalidity, the one applying is still certain in conscience that their first marriage was not valid, and their second relationship is the real one. As St. Thomas stated, they may consider that looking back, their "spouse" was not their spouse after all. At the time they may have thought so, but upon sincere reflection that could not have been the case. It is also apparent that annulment decisions are not infallible, as Cardinal Ratzinger stated in 1998: "Admittedly, it cannot be excluded that mistakes occur in marriage cases. In some parts of the Church, well-functioning marriage tribunals still do not exist. Occasionally, such cases last an excessive amount of time. Once in a while they conclude with questionable decisions."[30] If this is the case, then we must accept that in some instances, the truth is not apparent in the canonical law of the Church, yet in the eyes of God it is, and that is why it is simply not good enough to wash our hands of complex situations.

So what would be a possible scenario where this could apply? Let us consider a young unmarried couple who engage in sexual relations knowing it is wrong and at least one of them decides (interiorly) at some stage: "I must marry the other because I cannot bring myself to have intimate relations with anyone else after what I have done." That is not a reason to marry; it would in reality be nothing more than a self-inflicted punishment, and it may be the truth in their conscience, but a tribunal may see it as a flimsy excuse and reject it. There could be other similar cases that have a secretive yet truthful element to invalidate a first union. In the face of a tribunal rejecting a declaration of nullity, it may seem that all hope is lost. That however may not be the case; there may be a glimmer of light for certain people convinced their first marriage never existed but who live in a second union. This hope comes from the rarely considered concept known as *Epikeia.*

Epikeia is a virtue that can be traced all the way back to at least Aristotle, but for this discussion, we are interested in its theological rather than political relevance. It first appears in the Middle Ages with St. Albert the Great, St. Thomas Aquinas, Blessed John Duns Scotus, and then later, with Cardinal Thomas Cajetan, Francisco Suarez, and St. Alphonsus Liguori. So to what does it actually refer? It is concerned with several aspects of civil or ecclesiastical law; for some it is a correction of the law, for others an interpretation—not of the law itself—but the legislator, or even a dispensation from the law. The natural question would be to ask why the law is not always sufficient. St. Thomas Aquinas states that because human actions are contingent and diverse, the law cannot provide for every eventuality; legislation is based on the common pattern of behavior not the extreme. Cardinal Cajetan explained *epikeia* as: *directio, legis ubi deficit propter universale,* "a directing of the law where it is defective because of its universality."[31]

The virtue of *epikeia* stems from the wisdom of a man who knows not only the morality of certain behavior, but *why* that is so. In this way, he will act as the lawgiver would have acted in a particular circumstance, *if* the law was a hindrance to true equity. There will be occasions when the law itself could become harmful and thus *epikeia* seeks the higher principles of natural justice. St. Thomas Aquinas gives the example of a man who deposits a sword and then asks for its return while in a state of madness.[32] To follow the law in that case would be madness itself, considering the carnage that could result. The virtuous man knows the correct course of action to take guided by a conscience that overrides the rule of law, when it is obvious the law is defective in a certain instance.

We need to be clear that *epikeia* is not some arbitrary system of law mysteriously beyond good and evil. It cannot be applied to circumnavigating intrinsic evils such as adultery or abortion;

in fact, it cannot be used against divine law at all.[33] In truth, it is for the exceptional cases, and requires of the person executing it a great deal of prudence, wisdom, love of truth, honesty, and exceptional judgment.[34] Due to the danger of a free-for-all that could destroy a functioning legal system, St. Thomas Aquinas taught that the lawgiver should be consulted unless the situation required an immediate response. Francisco Suarez was of the opinion that *epikeia* could be utilized not only when the common good was at risk, but also for the individual; although for him, it was not a virtue as such, but an "act" of correcting a deficient law.

There is no doubt that respect for Canon Law needs to apply, as St. John Paul II stated in the strongest possible terms:

> Therefore, whenever doubts arise as to the conformity of an act—for example, in the specific case of a marriage—with the objective norm, and consequently, the lawfulness or even the validity itself of such an act is called into question, reference must be made to the judgment correctly emanating from legitimate authority (cf. CIC, c. 135, §3), and not to an alleged private judgment, and still less to the individual's arbitrary conviction. This principle, also formally safeguarded by canon law, establishes: "Even though the previous marriage is invalid or for any reason dissolved, it is not thereby lawful to contract another marriage before the nullity or the dissolution of the previous one has been established lawfully and with certainty" (CIC, c. 1085, §2). Whoever would presume to transgress the legislative provisions concerning the declaration of marital nullity would thus put himself outside, and indeed in a position antithetical to the Church's authentic magisterium and to canonical legislation itself—a unifying and in some ways irreplaceable element for the unity of the Church.[35]

This would seem to have closed the door to *epikeia* through the internal forum, but that may no longer be the case. Cardinal Ratzinger, in an essay three years later stated:

Here it seems that the application of epikeia in the internal forum is not automatically excluded from the outset. This is implied in the 1994 letter of the Congregation for the Doctrine of the Faith, in which it was stated that new canonical ways of demonstrating nullity should exclude "as far as possible" every divergence from the truth verifiable in the judicial process (cf. no. 9).[36]

The 1994 letter to which the Cardinal refers, specifically states that St. John Paul II approved of it and ordered its publication; and the context of his remark from 1998 about *epikeia* concern the reality that annulment tribunals do not always give the correct verdict—as we have already seen. So how can we see a way forward utilizing this virtue in a specific case? It seems obvious to suggest that a careful discernment should be undertaken even after a negative annulment decision has been reached; a searching of conscience to ascertain if this really is the truth of the matter as the individual sees it. If in the internal forum between priest and penitent that conviction remains, there seems to be a possible opening where a resolution could be found that would utilize the governing power of the local bishop and still respect Canon Law.

Pope Francis, I believe, may have opened the door to this possibility with his recent Apostolic Letter, *Mitis Iudex Dominus Iesus,* concerning annulment reform. In one section he states:

In order that a teaching of the Second Vatican Council regarding a certain area of great importance finally be put into practice, it has been decided to declare openly that the bishop himself, in the church over which he has been appointed shepherd and head, is by that very fact the judge of those faithful entrusted to his care. It is thus hoped that the bishop himself, be it of a large or small diocese, stand as a sign of the conversion of ecclesiastical structures, and that he does not delegate completely the duty of deciding marriage cases to the offices of his curia. This is especially true in the streamlined process for handling cases of clear nullity being established in the present document.[37]

What I am suggesting here, is that as the bishop is "the judge of those faithful entrusted to his care"[38] as Pope Francis teaches, and "the judge in first instance for cases of nullity or marriage for which the law does not expressly make an exception...who can exercise judicial power personally" (cf. can. 1673, § 1),[39] he would have the authority to "ratify" an authentic use of *epikeia* that had been brought to his attention. It would perhaps be even more beneficial if the bishop took it upon himself to discern with the person before he gave his blessing to their decision. We should note that although this would not be part of the bishop's judicial power as utilized in the annulment procedures, he would still be judging in the sense of agreeing to ratify and bless what had been decided in the internal forum. This would have the added benefit of taking the internal forum decision into the external forum and also compliance with can. 1085 §2: "Even if the prior marriage is invalid or dissolved for any reason, it is not on that account permitted to contract another before the nullity or dissolution of the prior marriage is established legitimately and certainly." This would then allow the couple to have a Catholic wedding in Church and end the secretive nature of their union.

Naturally, what I have stated here is purely *my own opinion* and suggestion as to how a legitimate use of *epikeia* could bring resolution to certain extremely difficult cases. In no way should it ever be seen as an easy alternative option to the annulment process; and as I have endeavored to show in this book, the search for truth in every situation must continue so that true justice and mercy is always manifest for the greater glory of God. We can also be thankful that Pope Francis, in that search for truth, has broadened the reasons why an annulment may be granted in his Apostolic Letter *Mitis Iudex*. This should help deal with many cases that would otherwise have been impossible to prove, leaving *epikeia* as the only option. Now that we have looked at the various issues related to the internal forum, it seems to me one final issue needs to be addressed: the questions posed by canon law and the attitude of certain canon lawyers to what Pope Francis has endorsed.

One of the most frequent criticisms that emanates from the magisterium of Pope Francis are those of legalism and rigidity. He condemns the cold, heartless attitude that places the letter of the law above the spirit of the law. In his view there are two paths: the path of hypocrisy, where one is so fixated by the law, that justice and love are forgotten; mercy is emptied of its true meaning and the law becomes a vehicle for arrogance, control, selfishness and pride. The second path is that of charity; it knows the true value of the law yet doesn't become attached to it. It places the sinner as its first priority, seeking to emulate Jesus' gestures of closeness and mercy, while discernment and love help keep a well-balanced attitude. Humility and compassion are the driving force for those on this path; while justice without mercy is a crime.

It cannot be denied that since the promulgation of *Amoris Laetitia* there has been a significantly critical stance taken by some canon lawyers. Although it has been aimed for the most part at Catholic writers who have championed Pope Francis' teaching in chapter 8 of the document, there is an element that has been directed at the Holy Father himself;[40] undoubtedly fuelled in part by the "four Cardinals' dubia."[41] The crux of the issue for them relates to the almost sacrosanct can. 915, and unfortunately the Holy Father's warnings are not being heeded: there is a pharisaical intransigence that doesn't bear any resemblance to the way the divine legislator—Jesus Christ—acted in the Gospels.

In order to understand this objection, we need to briefly study it. In the Code of Canon Law, can. 915 states: "Those who have been excommunicated or interdicted after the imposition or declaration of the penalty and others obstinately persevering in manifest grave sin are not to be admitted to holy communion."

For certain canon lawyers, this leaves no room for any divorced and remarried to receive Holy Communion unless they live as brother and sister and avoid scandal. That is no longer the case. In the first instance, can. 915 refers to those excommunicated or subject to a canonical penalty. Neither of these apply to cases we are discussing. In the following part, four conditions are laid down that must be met: (1) obstinately, (2) perseverance, (3) manifest, (4) grave sin.

Now when any discussion concerning can. 915 takes place, it is a prerequisite that several other canons are taken into consideration. Canon 18, for example which states: "Laws which prescribe a penalty, or restrict the free exercise of rights, or contain an exception to the law, are to be interpreted strictly." This means that in order for a restriction on free exercise of rights to apply (in the case of the ban on Holy Communion) the interpretation must be strict enough so that all the conditions are met. Anything less, and the restriction doesn't apply. Meanwhile, can. 912 states: "Any baptized person who is not forbidden by law may and must be admitted to holy communion." So this issue boils down to the following: Do the divorced and remarried Pope Francis refers to in *Amoris Laetitia* meet the four conditions laid out in can. 915?

If we look at these terms individually, "obstinately" suggests an attitude of stubborn refusal to follow God's law; it rebels *deliberately* against it. St. Thomas Aquinas states: "An obstinate will can never be inclined except to evil."[42] Can it thus be said that those who seek to obey God's law, yet who feel constrained by circumstances are the same as those who disregard them altogether? In terms of the Pope (who is the ultimate authoritative interpreter of can. 915) he clearly distinguishes between two groups that cannot be reconciled: "It is possible that in an objective situation of sin —which may not be subjectively culpable, or fully such—a person can be living in God's grace, can love and can also grow in the life of grace and charity, while receiving the Church's help to this end."[43] Contrast that with the following passage, and the Pope's teaching is clear: "Naturally, if someone flaunts an objective sin as if it were part of the Christian ideal, or wants to impose something other than what the Church teaches, he or she can in no way presume to teach or preach to others; this is a case of something which separates from the community (cf. Mt 18:17)."[44] Based on this teaching of the magisterium, we can affirm that sincere penitents would not be considered as being obstinate.

The second condition of "perseverance" implies an extension of being obstinate: someone who continues to flaunt their sinful state despite possible warnings to amend their behavior. The third condition of "manifest" speaks of the "public" knowledge of a sinner's behavior. It seems obvious that two things can be done to nullify this condition: (1) the person could discreetly receive Holy Communion in a different parish. (2) Perhaps more importantly, the parish community could and should where necessary be informed of the legitimate reasons why the person/couple in question have been readmitted to the Sacraments. This seems a sensible option that perhaps in a previous era would have been considered too dangerous to contemplate—with possible issues of confusion among the faithful. I would humbly suggest that the faithful are now ahead of some members of the hierarchy to a certain extent in understanding the turmoil surrounding countless lives. People live day in and day out with these problems among family members and thus there is an atmosphere of mercy that would not have been present sixty years ago. I firmly believe Pope Francis is well aware of this reality, and it quite possibly helped him decide that the time was now right to revisit this pressing question.

The final condition of "grave sin" would also be dealt with in the context of a priest educating a community on the moral theology concerning subjective culpability. This would also be an opportunity to quote from *Amoris Laetitia* where the Holy Father teaches on these matters. If the Church deems it necessary to teach on all matters pertaining to salvation, then there is absolutely no reason why a congregation cannot be informed in a general way of a discernment process that says: "There is moral certainty that grave [mortal] sin is not present in this situation."[45] It would also be opportune to quote from St. John Paul II's encyclical *Ecclesia de Eucharistia* in which he affirms, in relation to full participation in the Eucharistic Sacrifice: "The judgment of one's state of grace obviously belongs only to the person involved, since it is a question of examining one's conscience."[46] It could certainly be argued that situations such as these could serve as a useful lesson for a parish in humility; reaffirming the truth about marriage; and not judging. We should trust the Holy Spirit to lead the way.

What we have been able to show here is that the restriction from canon 915 doesn't apply, not because only one of the four conditions is not met, but rather at least three of them (sin of grave matter may still be present objectively, but presumably not in the case of one who in conscience believes their second marriage is the valid one).[47] It makes perfect sense for these conditions to fail because that indicates a soul on the path of salvation, not condemnation. It is sad that some canon lawyers are so keen to see the law enforced absolutely that they are actually dismissing traditional Catholic moral theology and, just as importantly, recent papal teaching. To enforce a law unjustly is not only counterproductive, but a sinful sign of arrogance and pride that is contrary to the way of the beatitudes. The law of God is a law of love and mercy. That must never be forgotten.

One of the most important developments in my view from the controversy over *Amoris Laetitia* is a realization that canon law cannot stand alone, separate from doctrinal teachings and disciplinary measures. It seems to me that without a correct balance between them, the application of certain laws can become a hindrance to aiding the salvation of souls; and that, after all is its primary duty of service. Time and history never stand still, and the complexities of life are always asking more questions, thus a rigidity of thought and process cannot be in the interests of the faithful. The recent popes have recognized this reality and warned canon lawyers of the dangers:

> It is therefore necessary to abrogate norms that prove antiquated; to modify those in need of correction; to interpret—in light of the Church's living Magisterium—those that are doubtful, and lastly, to fill possible *lacunae legis*. As Pope John Paul II said to the Roman Rota: "The very many expressions of that flexibility which has always marked canon law, precisely for pastoral reasons, must be kept in mind and applied" (Address to the Roman Rota, 18 January 1990, n. 4).[48]

I would draw particular attention to Pope Benedict's comment that laws need to be interpreted in the light of the *living magisterium*. For us, that is His Holiness Pope Francis, and thus his teachings in *Amoris Laetitia* should be obeyed willingly, knowing that he had the Holy Spirit's special charism of assistance to guide him. Concerning the peril of separation between canon law and magisterial teachings, St. John Paul II felt it necessary to remind canon lawyers of the inherent danger and temptation posed by such a view:

> A more dangerous reductionism is that which claims to interpret and apply the laws of the Church in a manner that is detached from the teaching of the Magisterium. According to this view, only formal legislative acts and not doctrinal pronouncements would have disciplinary value. It is obvious, that those operating from this reductionist perspective could sometimes come up with

two different solutions to the same ecclesial problem: one drawn from the texts of the Magisterium, and the other drawn from canonical texts. At the root of such a conception is an impoverished idea of canon law that identifies it only with the positive dictate of the norm. This is not right: in fact, since the juridical dimension, being theologically intrinsic to the ecclesial reality, can be the object of magisterial, even definitive, teaching.[49]

I earnestly hope that canon lawyers, who play such an essential and pivotal role in the life of the Church, will never lose touch with the eschatological backdrop of their ministry. Their work inevitably touches the lives of suffering people, and it is to be hoped that they endeavor to keep in mind Pope Francis' vision of the Church as a "field hospital"; one that binds up spiritual wounds, restores strength, and instills hope for salvation. I would therefore like to finish this chapter with a passage from St. John Paul II that I feel encapsulates everything it has been about: justice, truth, and mercy, bound together in a salvific pact:

In the Church, then, the purpose of law is the defense and promotion of the "glorious liberty of the children of God" (Rom 8:21)....Among these particularities is the pastoral character of law and of the exercise of justice in the Church. In fact, the pastoral character of canon law is the key to the correct understanding of canonical equity, that attitude of mind and spirit which tempers the rigor of the law in order to foster a higher good. In the Church, equity is an expression of charity in the truth, aiming at a higher justice which coincides with the supernatural good of the individual and of the community. Equity, then, should characterize the work of the pastor and the judge, who must continually model themselves on the Good Shepherd, "consoling those who have been struck down, guiding those who have erred, recognizing the rights of those who have been injured, calumniated or unjustly humiliated" (Paul VI, Address to the Roman Rota, February 8, 1973). Elements such as dispensation, tolerance, exempting or excusing causes, and *epikeia*, are to be understood not as diminishing the force of law but as complementing it, since they actually guarantee that the law's fundamental purpose is secured.[50]

NOTES

1. Code of Canon Law, can.130, http://www.vatican.va/archive/ENG1104/_INDEX.HTM.

2. Pope Francis, *Amoris Laetitia*, no. 300, www.vatican.va.

3. For a detailed analysis of the history of the internal forum stretching back a thousand years, see Joseph Goering, "The Internal Forum and the Literature of Penance and Confession," *Traditio* 59 (2004): 175–227.

4. Congregation for the Doctrine of the Faith, "Letter Regarding the Indissolubility of Marriage," April 11, 1973, http://www.vatican.va/roman_curia/congregations/cfaith/documents/rc_con_cfaith_doc_19730411_indissolubilitate-matrimonii_en.html.

5. Congregation for the Doctrine of the Faith, "Letter of Clarification to Archbishop Joseph Bernardin," Prot. No. 1284/66, March 21, 1975.

6. Based on our discussions in chapter 5.

7. Cardinal Seper's successor at the Congregation for the Doctrine of the Faith, appointed in 1981 by St. John Paul II.

8. See http://www.chicagocatholic.com/cnwonline/2016/news/0707b.aspx.

9. Congregation for the Doctrine of the Faith, "Concerning Some Objections to the Church's Teaching on the Reception of Holy Communion by Divorced and Remarried Members of the Faithful," *Documenti e Studi, On the Pastoral Care of the Divorced and Remarried* (Vatican City, LEV 1998), 20–29.

10. Origen, *Commentary on the Gospel of St. Matthew*, Bk. XIV, 23, www.newadvent.org.

11. St. Basil, "Letter 217," LXXVII, www.newadvent.org. It should be stated that there is some opposition to the claim that St. Basil was allowing second "penitential" marriages in a way similar to the Eastern practice of *oikonomia* that is utilized today. It has been suggested that St. Basil was merely concerned with a

reduction through penance of the canonical penalty for adultery. However, Fr. Joseph Ratzinger in his 1972 essay clearly suggests St. Basil does advocate the second-marriage scenario; the 1998 letter written by him quoted above also alludes to this fact.

12. Cardinal Joseph Ratzinger, *Salt of the Earth* (San Francisco: Ignatius, 1997), 207.

13. Cardinal Joseph Ratzinger, "Pastoral Letter for Advent 1980," *La Documentation Catholique 78* (1981): 389.

14. Even though contraception is always evil, the internal forum has been utilized in dealing with certain cases, especially for the avoidance of turning material sin into formal sin. With this in mind, St. Alphonsus Maria de Liguori taught the doctrine of "good faith": "If he is inculpably ignorant of some other matter (of which he can be ignorant)—even something of the divine law, the confessor should prudently decide whether the instruction will be profitable for the penitent. If it will not be profitable, he should not make the correction, but rather leave him in good faith. The reason is: the danger of formal sin is a much more serious thing than material sin. God punishes formal sin, for that alone is what offends Him. This I proved more sufficiently in my Moral Theology." St. Alphonsus Maria de Liguori, *Guide for Confessors*, Ed. R. Schiblin, 11–12, https://www.scribd.com/doc/235687056/St-Alphonsus-Liguori-Guide-for-Confessors. This advice for confessors was present in the 1917 Code of Canon Law: "The priest who hears confessions should be very careful not to pose curious and useless questions, especially concerning the sixth commandment, to anyone with whom he deals, and particularly not to ask younger persons about things of which they are unaware" (Can. 888). More recently, during the pontificate of St. John Paul II we discover the same recommendation: "The principle according to which it is preferable to let penitents remain in good faith in cases of error due to subjectively invincible ignorance, is certainly to be considered always valid, even in matters of conjugal chastity. And this applies whenever it is foreseen that the penitent, although oriented towards living within the bounds of a life of faith, would not be prepared to change his own conduct, but rather would begin formally to sin....Sacramental absolution is not to be denied to those who, repentant after having gravely sinned against conjugal chastity, demonstrate the desire to strive to abstain from sinning

again, notwithstanding relapses. In accordance with the approved doctrine and practice followed by the holy Doctors and confessors with regard to habitual penitents, the confessor is to avoid demonstrating lack of trust either in the grace of God or in the dispositions of the penitent, by exacting humanly impossible absolute guarantees of an irreproachable future conduct." Pontifical Council for the Family, "Vademecum for Confessors Concerning Some Aspects of the Morality of Conjugal Life," February 12, 1997, www .vatican.va.

15. Pope Francis, "Interview with Fr. Antonio Spadaro SJ," August 19, 2013, www.vatican.va.

16. Pope Francis, *Amoris Laetitia*, footnote 364, www.vatican.va.

17. Ibid, no. 311.

18. See St. John Paul II, Apostolic Exhortation, *Reconciliatio et Paenitentia*, no. 16, December 2, 1984, www.vatican.va, *Catechism of the Catholic Church*, no. 1859.

19. Pope Pius XII, "Allocution to Italian Midwives," October 29, 1951, *Acta Apostolicae Sedis* 43 (1951): 841. Although Pius XII was referring to an act of love in place of baptism, it seems equally appropriate to place it in this context also. The papal teaching also reminds us of Jesus' words to Simon the Pharisee concerning the sinful woman: "Therefore, I tell you, her sins, which were many, have been forgiven; hence she has shown great love" (Lk. 7:47).

20. St. Thomas Aquinas, *Summa Theologica*, I-II, 112.5, www .newadvent.org.

21. St. Thomas Aquinas, *Quaestiones disputatae de Veritate*, 27, 1.9, http://dhspriory.org/thomas/QDdeVer.htm.

22. St. Jose Maria Escriva, *The Way of the Cross* (London: Scepter, 1995), 39.

23. For a more detailed theological distinction between sin of grave matter and mortal sin, St. John Paul II discusses them in *Reconciliatio Paenitentia* 17, and *Veritatis Splendor* 70. Both extracts would be beneficial for discernment in the internal forum.

24. The Council of Elvira in Spain (c. AD 300) mentioned adultery as a cause for excommunication. Later, we see the same penalty in various councils from Coyac (1050), Toulouse (1056), Valencia (1388) among others. Excommunications for adultery were recorded in Chartres, France, in the medieval period. See Tyler Lange, *Excommunication for Debt in Late Medieval France: The Business*

of Salvation (Cambridge: Cambridge University Press, 2016), 114. In more recent times, in 1884, the Bishops of the United States made divorce and civil remarriage an excommunicable offense, while under the 1917 Code of Canon Law, Catholics who disregarded canonical form in attempting to marry before a non-Catholic minister were automatically excommunicated (1917 CIC 2319 § 1, 1°).

25. St. John Paul II, "Address to the Pontifical Council for the Family," January 24, 1997, www.vatican.va.

26. Pope Benedict XVI, "Address at the Evening of Witness, World Meeting of Families," June 2, 2012, www.vatican.va.

27. St. Thomas Aquinas, *Summa Theologica*, I-II, 19.6, www.newadvent.org.

28. Greg Daly, "The Church's Challenge to Reach out to Lost Sheep May Be More Logistical than Doctrinal," April 6, 2017, http://www.irishcatholic.ie/article/church%E2%80%99s-challenge-reach-out-lost-sheep-may-be-more-logistical-doctrinal.

29. See Paul B. Newman, *Growing Up in the Middle Ages* (Jefferson, NC: McFarland & Company, 2007), 271–73.

30. Congregation for the Doctrine of the Faith, "Concerning Some Objections to the Church's Teaching on the Reception of Holy Communion by Divorced and Remarried Members of the Faithful," *Documenti e Studi, On the Pastoral Care of the Divorced and Remarried* (Vatican City, LEV 1998), 20–29.

31. Cardinal Thomas Cajetan, *Commentary on the Summa Theologiae of St. Thomas Aquinas.* See Critical Ed. *Opera Omnia of St. Thomas Aquinas* (Rome, 1882–1906).

32. St. Thomas Aquinas, *Summa Theologica*, II-II, 120.1, www.newadvent.org.

33. St. Thomas Aquinas, *Summa Theologica*, I-II, 97.1, www.newadvent.org.

34. St. Thomas Aquinas has in mind each human being as having the possibility to utilize *epikeia* through the virtue of prudence. He specifically refers to *gnome* as a higher level of virtue intended for exceptional cases. See *Summa Theologica*, II-II, 48.1, www.newadvent.org.

35. St. John Paul II, "Address to the Tribunal of the Roman Rota," February 10, 1995, www.vatican.va.

36. Congregation for the Doctrine of the Faith, "Concerning Some Objections to the Church's Teaching on the Reception of Holy Communion by Divorced and Remarried Members of the Faithful," *Documenti e Studi, On the Pastoral Care of the Divorced and Remarried* (Vatican City, LEV 1998), 20–29.

37. Pope Francis, Apostolic Letter, *Mitis Iudex Dominus Iesus*, August 15, 2015, www.vatican.va.

38. Ibid.

39. Ibid.

40. Canonist Dr. Edward Peters wrote on his blog: "In administering holy Communion to a member of the faithful, Roman Catholic ministers are bound not by 'guidelines' supposedly fashioned from a *single, ambiguous, and highly controverted papal document,* but instead by the plain and dispositive text of another papal document, called the Code of Canon Law (especially Canon 915 thereof), and by the common and constant interpretation accorded such norms over the centuries." See https://canonlawblog.wordpress.com/2017/01/07/is-kellers-essay-really-the-way-amoris-should-be-read/, retrieved, May 5, 2017.

41. Two of the four cardinals died in 2017: Joachim Meisner and Carlo Caffara.

42. St. Thomas Aquinas, *Summa Theologica*, Supp. 98.1, www.newadvent.org.

43. Pope Francis, *Amoris Laetitia*, no. 305, www.vatican.va.

44. Ibid, no. 297. Cardinal Francesco Coccopalmerio, President of the *Pontifical Council for Legislative Texts*, which interprets canon laws, recently shared the same interpretation as the Pope in a March 1, 2017, interview: "To the one who says, 'I'm in grave sin, but I don't want to change' [absolution is not possible]. When someone comes to confess and says to you, 'I committed this sin. I want to change, but I know that I am not capable of changing, but I want to change,' what do you do? Do you send him away? No, you absolve him." See http://www.ncregister.com/daily-news/cardinal-coccopalmerio-explains-his-positions-on-catholics-in-irregular-uni.

45. Conversely, I see no reason why a priest couldn't warn a congregation about a couple who are obstinate in their immoral behavior; or at least make the distinction so that no possible confusion arises. The Church needs to accept that people *are* educated.

46. St. John Paul II, Encyclical Letter, *Ecclesia de Eucharistia*, no. 37, April 17, 2003, www.vatican.va.

47. Cardinal Gerhard Ludwig Muller, former Prefect of the Congregation for the Doctrine of the Faith, has recently stated that this scenario is a possibility and that in the eyes of God, the second union would be the true one. See http://www.lastampa .it/2017/12/31/vaticaninsider/eng/inquiries-and-interviews/ mller-buttigliones-book-has-dispelled-the-cardinals-dubia -qLOM0A9C6J1kJi8ohrveoL/pagina.html.

48. Pope Benedict XVI, "Address to the Members of the Tribunal of the Roman Rota," January 26, 2008, www.vatican.va.

49. St. John Paul II, "Address to the Prelate Auditors, Officials and Advocates of the Tribunal of the Roman Rota," January 30, 2003, www.vatican.va.

50. St. John Paul II, "Ad Limina Address to the Bishops of the Episcopal Conference of the United States of America (Colorado, Wyoming, Utah, Arizona and New Mexico)," October 17, 1998, www.vatican.va.

IX THE RETURN OF THE BRIDEGROOM: A MARRIAGE MADE IN HEAVEN

As our analysis of the Holy Father's decision to alter sacramental discipline draws to a close, I would like to direct our attention to a matter of supreme importance: the future hope of salvation, and the perfection of our relationships within the Communion of Saints at the end of time. It seems to me, that in the light of our discussions thus far, a reflection on the eschatological reality to come could be especially beneficial for those who have undergone the trauma of marriage break up, divorce, and civil remarriage. Certain questions will need to be addressed: Does anything of marriage remain in eternity? What about the case where a person has been legitimately married to more than one? Can the wounds of a first marriage be healed? Can the love found within an irregular union be perfected? It is my ardent desire to offer some hope to those beloved souls who feel bound by the weight of sin because of the nature of their relationships—that they too can look forward to partaking in the final victory over evil and experiencing once and for all the joy of true love. But before venturing into these questions, it is appropriate to meditate a little on the way Sacred Scripture presents the love of God toward humanity and especially the chosen people.

It is clear from the Old Testament that God acts as One who desires to take Israel as his Bride. Out of all the nations on earth, his divine love is centered in a most personal way on this seemingly small and insignificant people; and in return, He seeks Israel's faithfulness and reciprocal love. The Bible is quite clear on the extent of this relationship: it is nothing less than a betrothal. Several of the Prophets present this beautiful truth:

I passed by you again and looked on you; you were at the age for love. I spread the edge of my cloak over you, and covered your nakedness: I pledged myself to you and entered into a covenant with you, says the Lord God, and you became mine....Your fame spread among the nations on account of your beauty, for it was perfect because of my splendor that I had bestowed on you, says the Lord God. (Ez. 16:8, 14)

In Isaiah, the message is not only about marriage, but salvation: "For your Maker is your husband, the Lord of hosts is his name; the Holy One of Israel is your Redeemer, the God of the whole earth he is called" (Is. 54:5). In spite of this divine generosity, Israel continually betrayed the Lord in such a devastating way, that the Bible speaks of it as "adultery" and "prostitution." Time and again she committed apostasy and worshiped idols; she preferred the mire of sin to the majesty of being the Lord's Spouse. Yet the heart of God is such a furnace of love and mercy that he could not turn away from his Bride; his divine affection being nothing less than *eros*, a passionate love that was of unending restlessness. In reality, the divine Bridegroom was completely besotted, and always ready to forgive Israel.[1] He yearned for the most intimate union with her, and desired to shower her in might and holiness. But ultimately, his plan was about far more than earthly glory; he sought to redeem his Bride and grant her eternal life with a beauty unmatched, and without stain or wrinkle. Of course, Christian Tradition tells us that this betrothal could only take place once the Passover of the Lord Jesus had taken place, through his Death and Resurrection and the birth of the Church; and Israel's full participation in this marriage having to wait—because of their unfaithfulness—until the time of the Gentiles had been fulfilled (cf. Lk. 21:24, Rom. 11:25–26).

The New Testament reveals the full glory of this marriage between God and his Church, and various Scriptural passages reveal that Jesus *is* the divine bridegroom: St. John the Baptist refers to himself as the "best man" (Jn. 3:29); Jesus asks the question: "The wedding guests cannot fast while the bridegroom is with them, can they?" (Mk. 2:19); St. Paul says: "I feel a divine jealousy for you, for I promised you in marriage to one husband, to present you as a chaste virgin to Christ" (2 Cor. 11:2), and the holy author of Revelation describes the "holy city, the new Jerusalem, coming down out of heaven from God, prepared as a bride adorned for her husband" (Rev. 21:2). Within this context, we should also note the significance of the parable of the Wedding Feast (Matt. 22:1–14), and the Wedding of Cana (Jn. 2:1–12), in which Jesus not only reveals the importance of marriage, but also of himself as the bridegroom of the New Covenant—through his miraculous transformation of the water into wine. This stupendous event at the dawn of Jesus' ministry speaks of the newness—which in biblical language refers to the definitive action of God—of marriage, of wine, and of the love and mediation between the Bride[2] and Bridegroom. The fullness of time is thus announced in the most joyful setting of a marriage, and prefigures the salvific work that Jesus will carry out at his Crucifixion.

Everything the Lord accomplished through his Passion, Death, and Resurrection was geared to setting forth in motion the pilgrimage of his Bride, the Church toward her own Passover and Resurrection. This is because she must become one with Him; imitating selfless love, holiness, and mercy until the fruitfulness of their marriage begets all the children that are to be saved (See Rev. 7:9). Once that sanctifying process is complete at the end of the world, the Bridegroom will return in his glorious body together with his Bride to take possession of his Kingdom. The Universe will be renewed and eternity will consist of a perfect divine marriage. Revelation describes it thus:

> Then I heard what seemed to be the voice of a great multitude, like the sound of many waters and like the sound of mighty thunderpeals, crying out, "Hallelujah! For the Lord our God the Almighty reigns. Let us rejoice and exult and give him the glory, for the marriage of the Lamb has come, and his bride has made herself ready; to her it has been granted to be clothed with fine linen, bright and pure"—for the fine linen is the righteous deeds of the saints. And the angel said to me, "Write this: Blessed are those who are invited to the marriage supper of the Lamb." And he said to me, "These are true words of God." (Rev. 19:6–9)

So we see how the symbolism of marriage is at the heart of God's dealing with humanity throughout salvation history; exemplified most profoundly by the Cross. That is the great thread running through Biblical Revelation—a divine love story—and if that love applies to the Church as the Mystical Body of Christ, then no less does it apply to each of us individually. This is the most wondrous truth we must reflect on: the soul is the microcosm of the macrocosm that is the Church, and consequently, nuptial bliss is offered to both in the most indescribable way. Jesus desires to share *agape*, that divine, sacrificial, pure love with each redeemed soul as if they were the only one; and thus it cannot be seen as a love that is spread evermore thinly, or that some relationships are more important to him than others. In heaven, each soul, male or female, will feel this nuptial bliss through the prism of the beatific vision where the wellspring of God's love will be constantly overflowing; an unending source of communion, peace, and joy.

Before we turn to the eschatological questions that concern us, I would like to reflect a little on Jesus' true presence in the Holy Eucharist, because for the divorced and remarried who seek full participation in the life of the Church, the reception of this great Sacrament, as the "source and summit of the Christian life,"[3] is our primary concern.

Perhaps the most significant aspect of the Eucharist is that it is a divine presence that transcends time; for just as Jesus, when he took on human flesh at the Incarnation remained a divine Person sharing in his Father's glory, so too in His Eucharistic presence he bridges heaven and earth. In all the Tabernacles of the world it is the Risen Jesus who reigns; it is He who has burst through the old heaven and earth and instigated the new, thus allowing the waters of eternity to begin seeping through with each and every baptized person. The time of the Church is therefore marked by an eternal presence within its heart. The eschatological goal has already arrived, and this is why the Holy Sacrifice of the Mass is of utmost importance, not only because it makes present the Sacrifice of Jesus on Calvary, but also because it brings within the Christian community a foretaste of that communion and betrothal with God that will definitively come when the Bridegroom returns at the end of history. This explains why the great Russian theologian Sergei Bulgakov perceived the liturgy as heaven on earth, and why

St. Paul made the clear link between the Eucharist and the Day of Christ: "For as often as you eat this bread and drink the cup, you proclaim the Lord's death until he comes" (1 Cor. 11:26). In St. John's Gospel, Jesus makes the most startling revelation on the importance of receiving him in sacramental Communion:

> I am the living bread that came down from heaven. Whoever eats of this bread will live forever; and the bread that I will give for the life of the world is my flesh....Very truly, I tell you, unless you eat the flesh of the Son of Man and drink his blood, you have no life in you. Those who eat my flesh and drink my blood have eternal life, and I will raise them up on the last day. (Jn. 6:51, 53–54)

By stating the reality that eternal life—even while in exile on earth—consists of union with him through the Holy Eucharist, the Lord invites Catholics to see the marvelous possibilities of transformation and sanctification before their own last day arrives. In such a way can the words of St. John the Baptist be replicated in their souls: "He must increase, I must decrease" (Jn. 3:30). This essentially means that the nuptial bond of communion can be strengthened ever more; *agape* can become the visible way of life, and the soul can become *ipse Christus*—another Christ![4]

Sacramental Communion with Jesus therefore has a "horizontal" and a "vertical" dimension. If the vertical is geared more to the mystical, eschatological encounter, the horizontal is geared to fostering love and communion among the faithful, and those outside the Church; in essence all relationships that we have through our earthly pilgrimage. If on the one hand the sacramental union is a most intimate sharing of love and friendship between Creator and created, on the other hand, it is a summons to act as Jesus acted; living the two greatest commandments to the full: love God and love thy neighbor. In this way, our lives open out to embrace others; the Communion of Saints becomes ever more of a reality, and hostility and suspicion are quickly replaced by charity and mercy.

Within the Eucharist, we encounter the two types of love that enable us to simultaneously experience the horizontal and vertical sense of communion: *agape* and *eros*. *Agape* is an oblative love that seeks the happiness of others as its own source of joy, while *eros* is a covetous love that seeks the love of others; thus one is aimed solely at giving, while the other is concerned with receiving. In the Sacred Heart of Jesus, both forms of love are present and, of course, in perfect form; yet for us, *eros*, because of concupiscence and our weakened state, can become warped, leading to nothing more than self-centered lust. But through reception of the Holy Eucharist, we can learn to see *eros* in its divine form, seeking love and friendship because we desire to lead these souls to God; we can see members of the opposite sex as brothers and sisters in Christ rather than sexual objects. Without any doubt, Jesus offers us the grace to accomplish this, because he wants to prepare us for eternal life with him and his saints, therefore heaven on earth should not be restricted to Mass and Eucharistic adoration, but to the way our love is expressed to those God puts in our path.

Pope Benedict XVI taught in his beautiful Encyclical *Deus Caritas Est* how these two forms of love are interrelated:

> Yet *eros* and *agape*—ascending love and descending love—can never be completely separated. The more the two, in their different aspects, find a proper unity in the one reality of love, the more the true nature of love in general is realized. Even if *eros* is at first mainly covetous and ascending, a fascination for the great promise of happiness, in drawing near to the other, it is less and less concerned with itself, increasingly seeks the happiness of the other, is concerned more and more with the beloved, bestows itself and wants to "be there for the other." The element of *agape* thus enters into this love, for otherwise *eros* is impoverished and even loses its own nature. On the other hand, man cannot live by oblative, descending love alone. He cannot always give, he must also receive. Anyone who wishes to give love must also receive love as a gift. Certainly, as the Lord tells us, one can become a source from which rivers of living water flow (cf. Jn 7:37–38). Yet to become such a source, one must constantly drink anew from the origi-

nal source, which is Jesus Christ, from whose pierced heart flows the love of God (cf. Jn 19:34).[5]

So reception of the Holy Eucharist in a state of grace is a continual preparation for the life of the world to come. Echoing in the hearts of the faithful must be the words of the divine Bridegroom: "See, I am coming soon" (Rev. 22:12); and it is for us—as bride—to constantly repeat with the Holy Spirit the simple yet magnificent prayer "Come!" imploring the definitive marital union that will see love overwhelm all things, and as at any marriage there are plenty of gifts, in this marriage it will be no different. The supreme gift from the Father of the Bridegroom will be a glorious new creation serving as a stupendous and eternal backdrop for this eschatological bliss. The perfect harmony between Bride and Bridegroom will be replicated throughout the entire transformed Universe, as Pope Francis so beautifully describes:

> At the end, we will find ourselves face to face with the infinite beauty of God (cf. 1 Cor 13:12), and be able to read with admiration and happiness the mystery of the universe, which with us will share in unending pleni-tude. Even now we are journeying towards the sabbath of eternity, the new Jerusalem, towards our common home in heaven. Jesus says: "See, I am making all things new" (Rev 21:5). Eternal life will be a shared experience of awe, in which each creature, resplendently transfig-ured, will take its rightful place and have something to give those poor men and women who will have been liberated once and for all.[6]

Now that we have discovered at least in part, the eschatological significance of Holy Communion, we can seek answers to the questions that concern us the most: what is the effect of divinization on the various earthly unions between husband and wife, man and woman?

In the Gospels, we see that marriage in heaven was a ques-tion that perplexed the religious authorities of the time. The three Synoptic Gospels all record the discussion:[7]

Some Sadducees, those who say there is no resurrection, came to him and asked him a question, "Teacher, Moses wrote for us that if a man's brother dies, leaving a wife but no children, the man shall marry the widow and raise up children for his brother. Now there were seven brothers; the first married, and died childless; then the second and the third married her, and so in the same way all seven died childless. Finally the woman also died. In the resurrection, therefore, whose wife will the woman be? For the seven had married her." Jesus said to them, "Those who belong to this age marry and are given in marriage; but those who are considered worthy of a place in that age and in the resurrection from the dead neither marry nor are given in marriage. Indeed they cannot die anymore, because they are like angels and are children of God, being children of the resurrection. And the fact that the dead are raised Moses himself showed, in the story about the bush, where he speaks of the Lord as the God of Abraham, the God of Isaac, and the God of Jacob. Now he is God not of the dead, but of the living; for to him all of them are alive." Then some of the scribes answered, "Teacher, you have spoken well." For they no longer dared to ask him another question. (Lk. 20:27–40)

In order to interpret this passage correctly, we need to bear in mind that the Sadducees were not really interested in the answer. They didn't understand the Scriptures, or the power and wisdom of God; they also rejected the resurrection of the body. For them, they could not look past the first heaven and earth, and marriage in the context of being fruitful to fill creation (see Gen. 1:28). Jesus' reply—although clearly teaching that marriages do not exist in eternity—does not deny the prospect that these relationships are transformed; the doctrine of the Communion of Saints tells us that a bond of love even now unites the faithful of the Mystical Body of Christ on Earth, Purgatory, and Heaven. In fact, this was beautifully illustrated in a vision granted to Sr. Lucia of Fatima on October 13, 1917, when she saw Jesus, the Blessed Virgin, and

St. Joseph—the Holy Family—together blessing the crowd that had gathered in expectation of the miracle of the sun.

For Jesus, marriage in the first heaven and earth is preparation for fulfilment in the new, thus sexuality for instance, an essential element of human love, becomes perhaps the greatest prefigurement of the intensity of divine love that will permeate the entire being of man and woman in the resurrection. This explains why the Ten Commandments and Catholic teaching keeps it solely within marriage, because the sexual union of husband and wife mirrors in the closest earthly way possible, the unity of love within the Most Holy Trinity. This of course does not mean some higher form of sexual love will exist in eternal life—certainly not a physical aspect—rather the *eros* of God will become in a perfect way the *eros* of man. Thus the image and likeness of God that we have now will find its greatest expression in the manifestation of perfect love—*agape* and *eros*—and that will come about through the granting of the beatific vision in which all the redeemed will see God as he really is. The overflowing of divine love emanating from the bosom of the Triune God, will be for all, a tap that never runs dry.

At this point we can address the questions we posed at the beginning of the chapter. First, does anything of marriage remain in the never-ending age to come? It would seem the answer is a qualified yes, and this based on the fact that God never takes away the good or the love that has been produced through life. On the contrary, the process of sanctification and divinization is concerned with stripping away the evil and filth that has sullied the linen garments of the saints (see Rev. 19:8). In the case of children that have been produced for the glory of God and obedience to his divine will, we can also perceive how they will be the "glue" that ensures marital relationships on earth maintain some specific quality in heaven. It seems inconceivable that these relationships could be "reduced" in some manner to a level no different to any other, for sacramental marriage is a prophetic witness to the love of Christ for his Church, and so just as that love will be celebrated by all in one chorus of eternal praise and thanksgiving, so too will the individual marriages that helped fulfill God's mysterious salvific design. So the obvious question arises: How does this work in the case of those legitimately married to more than one person? The key to understanding this is Jesus' phrase:

"They are like angels" (see Lk. 20:36). By referring to these pure spirits at one with God, the Lord subtly tells us that the old ways of jealousy, self-love, pride, and selfishness will be destroyed forever. Instead, they will be replaced by the absolute perfection of charity, humility, and holiness; just as with the angels. In this way, these redeemed individuals will marvel at the love shared by their spouse with another; and this because they can look at it through no other way than through the eyes of God. For them, this reality will be nothing less than a triumph over evil; a wondrous testament to God's saving might.

Along these lines, we can also affirm that the wounds of a first marriage can be healed. The Book of Revelation tells us that when the New Jerusalem, the Holy City, descends at the end of the world, all aspects of it will be perfect; not the tiniest speck of dust or sin will be found: "But nothing unclean will enter it, nor anyone who practices abomination or falsehood, but only those who are written in the Lamb's book of life" (Rev. 21:27). Divine Revelation tells us quite categorically that any ill will, resentment, or anger will no longer exist and thus each and every soul taking their place at the Wedding Feast of the Kingdom will bask in the glory of divine mercy; that is, they will not for a single moment recall past sins, or reflect on events that caused sorrow and suffering. In fact, the great Italian mystic St. Catherine of Genoa informs us that once a soul has departed this life, they are no longer aware of the sins of others because they only see the goodness and mercy of God. Perfect charity does not allow it,[8] nor does the divine will.

Obviously the same situation applies to the couples we have spoken of at length in this book: those who have lived in an objective situation of grave sin from an invalid marital union. For those who sincerely strove to respond to grace in their lives, in spite of the irregularity of their situation, heaven will be the perfection of everything they had hoped for on earth: true love, true companionship, and the blessing of God, finally peace and harmony, never to be lost. But let us be clear, this cannot apply to those who on earth deliberately and selfishly abused the gift of sexuality trampling over innocent souls as if they were no more than a commodity. For them, the very real danger of hell exists, whereby spending eternity cursing their own wicked mind and heart. We cannot and must not avoid speaking of such things when Jesus himself spoke of them.

For all couples striving to live in God's grace and by the divine code of the beatitudes, Sacred Scripture presents us with a compelling reason to look forward in hope. In spite of the mystery of evil that confronts us all, and that seems to grow day by day, we already know that the final victory is on the horizon, when all things will be made new. The truth of the Lord's Resurrection is a pledge of the glorious future awaiting us. For now, we live bound to a certain extent by the limitations placed on us by Adam's fall. Our spirits succumb to various temptations, and we do not always respond to the grace Jesus offers us to avoid them. At the resurrection, life will be transformed to such an extent that the physical body will be subordinate to the spirit. It will permeate the body in such a way that the body will be totally obedient to the will of the spirit. However, it shouldn't be understood as some kind of triumph of the spiritual over the physical—bearing in mind that Genesis tells us that God saw his creation of man and saw that "it was very good" (Gen. 1:31)—rather it should be understood as the perfect realization of the unity of physical and spiritual that was willed by God in the beginning. We will then share in the transfiguration that Jesus showed Peter, James, and John on Mount Tabor; we will become like the angels; in fact, little less than gods (see Ps 8:6) and "children of God" (Lk. 20:36).

St. John Paul II explained much concerning the resurrection of the body in a series of general audiences concerning the theology of the body. In one, applicable to our discussion, he centered on the divinization on humanity:

> The conclusion can be drawn that the degree of spiritualization characteristic of eschatological man will have its source in the degree of his divinization, incomparably superior to the one that can be attained in earthly life. It must be added that here it is a question not only of a different degree, but in a way, of another kind of divinization. Participation in divine nature, participation in the interior life of God himself, penetration and permeation of what is essentially human by what is essentially divine, will then reach its peak, so that the life of the human spirit will arrive at such fullness which previously had been absolutely inaccessible to it. This

new spiritualization will therefore be the fruit of grace, that is, of the communication of God in his very divinity, not only to man's soul, but to his whole psychosomatic subjectivity. We speak here of subjectivity (and not only of "nature"), because that divinization is to be understood not only as an interior state of man (that is, of the subject) capable of seeing God face to face, but also as a new formation of the whole personal subjectivity of man in accordance with union with God in his Trinitarian mystery and of intimacy with him in the perfect communion of persons. This intimacy—with all its subjective intensity—will not absorb man's personal subjectivity, but rather will make it stand out to an incomparably greater and fuller extent.[9]

Through the Son's recapitulation of all creation at the end of time, humanity will finally achieve its purpose: to share in the life of God and in the Communion of Saints. All relationships, those familial or bound by a salvific significance—in the case of those whose prayers had contributed to the salvation of another—will have at their core the example of love and unity of the Most Holy Trinity, but even more than that they will exist *within* the Most Holy Trinity, as a consummation and transcendence of everything that had gone before. Even now we have a prophetic witness to this: the example of celibacy for the sake of the Kingdom by priests and religious. Their heroic way of life points toward the future where human love gives way to divine love and complete charity, and where sin gives way to the fullness of grace. It is my hope that a reflection on this may help some couples in irregular situations— where they acknowledge the sinfulness of their situation—to finally find the strength to live as brother and sister, seeing a future perfection of their love in the beatitude of heaven. Surely we may maintain the hope that God will bless this intention to break free from sin while maintaining the relationship if children are involved, and grant them not only the grace to avoid sin, but also the joy filled expectation that one day they will be able to express their love perfectly in complete conformity to the will of God.

Before we conclude this chapter, it seems to me essential that we honor those souls who having been abandoned in marriage, perhaps with young children to bring up and with great financial and emotional difficulties, have kept their Catholic faith to the letter and avoided entering new relationships. These souls without question live a type of martyrdom that in itself is a great witness to the sanctity and indissolubility of marriage. In their daily struggle, they mirror in a very real sense the abandonment that Jesus accepted willingly in the Garden of Gethsemane. Offering up their sufferings, they share in the work of co-redemption and participate in an extraordinary way in the salvation of souls. Can it be that their sufferings are salvific fruit for their spouses? Knowing at least a little of the mysterious way God works through salvation history, and through the intercession of the saints, we cannot rule out that possibility. In fact, we could easily see how this beautiful spiritual work would be celebrated in heaven; serving to reunite these relationships in eternity with a magnificence that can only come from God's inscrutable design.

In conclusion, therefore, let us pray that whatever state of life we find ourselves, we never turn our backs on the salvation offered to us. At times, the temptation may be to throw in the towel; yet no situation is beyond the merciful heart of God—even if Satan tells us it is. Some situations of irregular marriage are no doubt so complex that they will never fall into an easy category where they can be left. History cannot always be reversed and past mistakes cannot be rectified. What can be done for those souls in these situations is to maintain a clear intention to follow God's path, to tell the Lord frankly and with trust why things are as they are. If the Lord looks at the heart where man cannot (see Sam. 16:7), then he will take all the circumstances into account when judging. He is gentle, humble, and compassionate with those sincere in their difficulties; we have that knowledge from the Gospels. Many struggle for years with addictions or sins that they cannot fully control, but a trusting attitude and a confidence in divine help, allied to the practice of the virtues wherever possible, can give us the moral security that God will eventually ensure his will and our salvation is fulfilled. That must be our hope and our prayer. Let us look then toward the new heaven and new earth with great joy knowing that one day the Lord's final victory over evil will also be ours. It will be a marriage made in heaven.

NOTES

1. For a greater theological explanation of the various types of love, see Pope Benedict XVI, "Message for Lent 2007," in which he states: "God, however, did not give up [on Adam and Eve's rejection]. On the contrary, man's 'no' was the decisive impulse that moved him to manifest his love in all of its redeeming strength." Even more impressive is the Holy Father's Encyclical *Deus Caritas Est*, where *"Agape"* and *"eros"* are treated more expansively. See nos. 3–11, http://w2.vatican.va/content/benedict-xvi/en/encyclicals/doc uments/hf_ben-xvi_enc_20051225_deus-caritas-est.html.

2. As it was Mary, the Mother of Jesus who instigated the miracle of turning water into wine through her mediation, she stands for the perfection of the Church in its betrothal to Christ.

3. *Catechism of the Catholic Church*, no. 1324, www.vati can.va.

4. Pope Benedict XVI teaches: "Jesus gave this act of oblation an enduring presence through his institution of the Eucharist at the Last Supper. He anticipated his death and resurrection by giving his disciples, in the bread and wine, his very self, his body and blood as the new manna (cf. Jn 6:31–33). The ancient world had dimly perceived that man's real food—what truly nourishes him as man—is ultimately the Logos, eternal wisdom: this same Logos now truly becomes food for us—as love. The Eucharist draws us into Jesus' act of self-oblation. More than just statically receiving the incarnate Logos, we enter into the very dynamic of his self-giving. The imagery of marriage between God and Israel is now realized in a way previously inconceivable: it had meant standing in God's presence, but now it becomes union with God through sharing in Jesus' self-gift, sharing in his body and blood. The sacramental 'mysticism,' grounded in God's condescension towards us, operates at a radically different level and lifts us to far greater heights than anything that any human mystical elevation could ever accomplish." Pope Benedict XVI, Encyclical Letter, *Deus Caritas Est*, no. 13, December 25, 2005, www.vatican.va.

5. Ibid, no. 7.

6. Pope Francis, Encyclical Letter, *Laudato Si*, May 24, 2015, www.vatica.va.

7. Matt. 23:23–33, Mk. 12:18–27, Lk. 20:27–40.

8. Catherine of Genoa, *Purgation and Purgatory: The Spiritual Dialogue* (Mahwah, NJ: Paulist Press, 1979), 71–73.

9. St. John Paul II, "General Audience," December 9, 1981, www.totus2us.com.

APPENDIX

Dear Mr Walford,

I fondly recall you and your family's visit on 27 July last. To me it felt like a concrete expression of *Amoris Laetitia*. Thank you! I would also like to thank you for your book on the communion of saints which I have begun reading.

In the letter you left for me, you asked if I could write some thoughts about *Amoris Laetitia*, and you proposed some questions. I will happily respond but I think it would be better for me to write freely what is in my heart. I hope this will be useful to you.

The Post-Synodal Apostolic Exhortation *Amoris Laetitia* is the fruit of a long ecclesial journey which involved two Synods and a subsequent consultation with the local Churches through the bishops' conferences. Institutes of consecrated life and other institutions, such as Catholic universities and lay associations, also participated in this consultation. The entire Church prayed, reflected and, with simplicity, offered various contributions. Both Synods presented their conclusions.

One of the things that most impressed me in this whole process was the desire to seek God's will in order to better serve the Church. Seeking in order to serve. This was done through reflection, the exchange of views, prayer and discernment. There were of course temptations during this journey but the Good Spirit prevailed. Witnessing this brought spiritual joy.

The Exhortation *Amoris Laetitia* is a unified whole which means that, in order to understand its message, it must be read in its entirety and from the beginning. This is because there is a development both of theological reflection and of the way in which problems are approached. It cannot be considered a *vademecum* on different issues. If the Exhortation is not read in its entirety and in the order it is written, it will either not be understood or it will be distorted.

APPENDIX

Over the course of the Exhortation, current and concrete problems are dealt with: the family in today's world, the education of children, marriage preparation, families in difficulty, and so on; these are treated with a hermeneutic that comes from the whole document which is the magisterial hermeneutic of the Church, always in continuity (without ruptures), yet always maturing. In this regard, in your letter you mentioned Saint Vincent of Lérins, in his *Commonitorium Primum*: "*ut annis scilicet consolidetur, dilatetur tempore, sublimetur aetate*". With respect to the problems that involve ethical situations, the Exhortation follows the classical doctrine of Saint Thomas Aquinas.

I feel certain that your book on *Amoris Laetitia* will be helpful to families. I pray for this.

Please pass on my best wishes to your wife and your children. I thank them for their witness. And I ask you, please, do not forget to pray for me!

May Jesus bless you and the Blessed Virgin protect you.

Fraternally,

Francis

From the Vatican, 1 August 2017